On Post-Colonial Futures

Writing Past Colonialism

Edited by Warwick Anderson, John Cash, Phillip Darby, Jane Jacobs, Amanda Macdonald, Rob McQueen, David Martin, Anne Maxwell and Patrick Wolfe, Institute of Postcolonial Studies, Melbourne.

The leitmotiv of the series is the idea of difference – differences between culture and politics, as well as differences in ways of seeing and the sources that can be drawn upon. In this sense, it is postcolonial. Yet the space we hope to open up is one resistant to new orthodoxies, one that allows for alternative and contesting formulations. Though grounded in studies relating to the formerly colonized world, the series seeks to extend contemporary global analyses.

Books published in the series:

The Fiction of Imperialism: Reading Between International Relations and Postcolonialism, Phillip Darby

Settler Colonialism and the Transformation of Anthropology: The Politics and Poetics of an Ethnographic Event, Patrick Wolfe

ON POST-COLONIAL FUTURES

FUTURES

Transformations of Colonial Culture

Bill Ashcroft

CONTINUUM
London and New York

Continuum
The Tower Building, 11 York Road, London SE1 7NX
370 Lexington Avenue, New York, NY 10017-6503

First published 2001

British Library Cataloguing-in-Publication Data
A catalogue record for this book is available from the British Library.

ISBN 0-8264-5225-6 (hardback)
    0-8264-5226-4 (paperback)

Library of Congress Cataloging-in-Publication Data
Ashcroft, Bill, 1946–
    On post-colonial futures : transformations of colonial culture / Bill Ashcroft.
       p. cm. — (Writing past colonialism series)
    Includes bibliographical references and index.
    ISBN 0-8264-5225-6 (hardback) — ISBN 0-8264-5226-4 (pbk.)
    1. Postcolonialism. 2. Decolonization. 3. Social change. 4. Politics and culture. I. Title.
    II. Series.

    JV51 .A74 2001
    325'.3—dc21   00-047600

Typeset by Centraserve Ltd, Saffron Walden, Essex
Printed and bound in Great Britain by
Cromwell Press, Trowbridge, Wilts

Contents

Introduction

Since post-colonial studies took the academic world by storm in the late 1980s, it has proven to be one of the most diverse and contentious fields in literary and cultural studies, a field of apparently endless argument and debate. On one hand the very term 'colonialism' seems anachronistic, a fixation on a period of European imperial power that climaxed in the nineteenth century, but is now long past. On the other, post-colonial theory has been accused of being the latest master narrative, the explanation of all forms of oppression. In some ways the term 'post-colonial futures' embodies the paradox we find in this polarization of attitudes: Doesn't the very idea of the post-colonial valorize the colonial dominance of Europe in the last two centuries? Doesn't it construct the cultural productions of formerly colonized and now 'neo-colonized' states as reactive rather than proactive? Doesn't it lock the resistance of post-colonized societies into a 'prison of protest' (Dash, 1974: 58)?

The answer to these questions hinges on how we understand the term 'resistance'. If we see resistance to imperial hegemony as simply oppositional, a collection of strategies by which colonized societies have reacted to European power, then those societies cannot be extricated from a position of unalleviated subservience; but this view of resistance has been more often a function of political rhetoric than cultural practice. When we examine the responses of colonized societies to the discourses that have inscribed them and regulated their global reality, we see that their dominant mode has been *transformation*. It is transformation that gives these societies control over their future. Transformation describes the ways in which colonized societies have taken dominant discourses, transformed them and used them in the service of their own self-empowerment. More fascinating, perhaps, post-colonial transformation describes the ways in which dominated and colonized societies have transformed the very nature of the cultural power that has dominated them. This is nowhere more obvious than in literary and other representational arts, but it remains a strategic feature of all cultural practice. This is why cultural influence circulates, rather than moves in a straight line 'downward' from the dominant to the dominated.

It is the profound consequences of this process, the transformation of colonial cultures as well as the more subtle capacity to transform those discourses that seem to disempower them, that gives the concept 'post-colonial futures' its potency, for such futures are ultimately global. 'Circulation' describes not only the complex relationship between colonies and their European centres, but reveals why a phenomenon such as 'global culture' can exist at all. The strategies by which colonized societies have appropriated dominant technologies and discourses and used them in projects of self-representation is a model for the ways in which local communities everywhere engage global culture itself. This is because post-colonial transformation has involved a confrontation with the most powerful discourses of modernity. Apart from colonial languages, and the powerful discourses of history, geography and the whole range of disciplines that arose in European intellectual life in the nineteenth century, colonized people have subverted the tropes by which they have habitually been marginalized, and, ultimately, have permanently influenced even the educational disciplines by which those tropes were perpetuated.

The central strategy in transformations of colonial culture is the seizing of self-representation. Underlying all economic, political and social resistance is the struggle over representation that occurs in language, writing and other forms of cultural production. Representation can be defined as the process of giving concrete form to ideological concepts, and its importance in political projects of self-determination cannot be overestimated, because it involves the entire fabric of cultural life and the sense of identity that is inextricably woven into that fabric. This explains why so many post-colonial intellectuals have advocated a wholesale rejection of dominant discourses, languages and technologies as the only way to 'decolonise the mind' (Ngugi, 1981). However, any observation of everyday practice demonstrates that post-colonial futures lie in the adaptation of those discourses and technologies to local needs. In their endless inventiveness and adaptability, this appears to be what human communities do best. More importantly, perhaps, the post-colonial example becomes a powerful model for this process because the transformation of colonial cultures by local societies has been so dynamic.

The areas of cultural life in which transformation has had an effect are almost endlessly diverse. This book is therefore not an attempt to be comprehensive, but to indicate the range of discourses and practices in which a specifically 'post-colonial future' has meaning. The discipline of 'English', for instance, was invented as a vehicle of the civilizing mission, a repository of European, and particularly British, cultural values that could be effortlessly inculcated into colonial students. In some respects English symbolizes the hegemonic function of imperial culture, and so its transformation by post-colonial writers and critics can stand as an introductory model for the process itself. A subject that was invented to convey the cultural weight of empire has been transformed by those very societies to which it was disseminated into a forceful medium of self-expression. Because its inherent function as a cultural study has been appropriated, English will never be the same again.

The prominent function of English studies indicates the extent to which the British Empire has dominated post-colonial literary and cultural analysis over the last decade. This has led to considerable suspicion about the field from areas such as Latin America. Because the colonization of Latin America is so much more ancient, and the *mestizo* question so much more complex than issues of hybridity elsewhere, Latin American scholars have generally rejected post-colonial theory as an Anglocentric discourse, or at least treated it with great wariness. Chapter 2, 'Latin America and post-colonial transformation', demonstrates why the former Spanish Empire is not only an appropriate site for post-colonial analysis, but deepens and extends our understanding of many of the issues that traverse the field. It is precisely because issues of race, culture and politics in Latin America do not fall into neat categories that post-colonial analysis can be so fruitful. One kind of post-colonial future will be characterized by the 'inclusion of America' in the analysis of colonialism's effects.

Post-colonial scholars have regularly emphasized the significance of the 'prehistory' of nineteenth-century colonialism in the development of European culture. The emergence of modernity is itself almost indistinguishable from the extension of imperial power. When we examine the emergence of European society and culture, we see the subtle development of attitudes which were essential for the self-justificatory movement of European imperialism. One of the most interesting of these developments was the emergence of the concept of the child. Chapter 3 'Primitive and wingless: the colonial subject as child', examines how the concept of the child developed in concert with the concept of race, the two becoming virtually interchangeable in their importance for imperial discourse. Modern European culture needed to resolve one of the great contradictions of Western expansion: the contradiction between the *practice* of exploitation and abuse, and the *ideology* of nurture central to the civilizing mission. The contradictory nature of the child (particularly in the philosophy of John Locke) who was both unformed, yet 'in every way inclined to evil', established a view of the childlike primitive races which has continued to the present day.

The transformation of the trope of the child is a powerful indication of the way in which a post-colonial future can be discursively mapped. David Malouf's use of the child figure, in particular, demonstrates how a metaphor that had been utilized to convey the primitive nature of colonial subjects can be reshaped into a vision of post-colonial possibility. In some respects Malouf's view of what the child might represent is prophetic. By imagining what post-colonial society might have been, he conceives, imaginatively, what it might still be. Chapter 4, 'Childhood and possibility', demonstrates the extent to which post-colonial futures are limited only by the limits of the imagination, revealing why the imaginative arts are so formative in post-colonial projects of self-representation.

Despite the centrality of representation, however, the significance of post-colonial analysis, indeed that which distinguishes it from postmodern views of discursive change, is its insistence on the importance of the material realities of post-colonial life. The story of the extraordinary rise to prominence of tropical sugar, both in the economy and the diet of Britain and ultimately the diet of the world, is a story of economic, environmental degradation and social devastation for the Caribbean region. Chapter 5, 'Sweet futures', shows how the consequences of the sugar industry, in the cultural impact of West Indian societies upon the world, is a resonant demonstration of the link between the material and the discursive in the process of post-colonial transformation. Out of the ruins caused by that European obsession with sugar, an obsession that had extraordinarily damaging effects on tropical plantation colonies, arose a culture so dynamic that it had an unparalleled place in global culture.

One of the most exciting transformations effected by Caribbean societies has been upon the English language itself, but the capacity of the colonial subject to transform imperial discourse still remains a contentious issue. That earliest of representations of the Caribbean subject – the monster Caliban in Shakespeare's *The Tempest* – symbolizes this struggle. Caliban's retort to Prospero, 'You taught me your language and my profit on't is I know how to curse', is one of the most resonant and memorable in Shakespeare, and has become a slogan of cultural resistance. Caliban becomes, with this despairing cry, an evocative model of the post-colonial subject, but is he really imprisoned by language? Can he do no more than curse? Chapter 6, 'Caliban's language', suggests that the question of Caliban's potential use of language, of which the play makes no mention, opens up possibilities of transformation that Shakespeare could not have conceived, but which are crucial to our understanding of the importance of language to post-colonial resistance.

Since Edward Said's influential use of Foucault's notion of discourse in *Orientalism* (1978), the theory of discourse has been widely used both in colonial discourse theory and post-colonial analysis, but just as significant perhaps has been Said's subsequent reservation about the efficacy of discourse for the political programme of post-colonial resistance. Chapter 7, 'Fractured paradigms: the fragility of discourse' and Chapter 8, 'Post-colonial excess and colonial transformation', examine, in very different ways, the limits of discursive control and the agency of the post-colonial subject. 'Fractured paradigms' examines the phenomenon of the paradigm shift that occurred in science at the turn of the century with the emergence of quantum mechanics. If we see paradigms as discourses, we are struck by the fact that the revolutionary view of material existence embodied in quantum theory failed to affect scientists' everyday 'Newtonian' belief in what they were doing. This demonstrates that discourses, although comprehensive in their effects upon individual subjects, are provisional and negotiable by those same subjects. 'Post-colonial excess and colonial transformation' demonstrates a general feature of this agency: the capacity of post-colonial subjects, through the 'excess' of insistence, supplementarity and horizonality, to exceed the boundaries of a dominant, imperial discourse. The very existence of excess suggests the capacity of subjects to engage a dominant discourse in ways for which Foucault's theory fails to account.

One of the most powerful of these discourses, the one perhaps most responsible for European modernity's construction of 'world reality' is history. The story of the past is critical because it is the story of *what* is real and *how* it is real. History has effected its regulatory function in all forms of colonial control, and the post-colonial response to history remains one of the most complex projects of transformation. Whatever the particular way in which history dominates the local, it is *fictional* narrative that provides the most flexible and evocative response, principally because fiction is best able to reproduce the fundamentally allegorical nature of history itself. Using Edouard Glissant's notion of a history as a 'prophetic vision of the past', Chapter 9 demonstrates how Peter Carey's novel *Oscar and Lucinda* balances its prophetic vision on an allegorical journey which depicts the teleological, often visionary, but deeply contradictory progress of European civilization. The journey of Oscar's glass church up the Bellinger River is an allegory of imperial history itself: the classic journey of civilization into the wild on its historic mission to bring light into the darkness. By showing how this ordered movement of history is based on pure chance, the novel transforms and subverts the allegorical narrative of history itself.

The post-colonial disruption of history is much like the postmodern interrogation of its will to truth. One of the most persistent misconceptions has been that post-colonialism is a version or branch of postmodernism. The postmodern project of deconstructing the master discourses of the European Enlightenment is much like the post-colonial task of dismantling the discursive effects of European imperialism. This is nowhere more elegantly, if mistakenly, proposed than in Linda Hutcheon's suggestion that it is irony, 'the trope of our times', that unites these two discourses. Chapter 10, 'Irony, allegory and empire: J. M. Coetzee's *Waiting for the Barbarians* and *In the Heart of the Country*' analyses these powerful novels to explicate the history of attitudes to the trope of irony, and to demonstrate why the counter-discursive strategy of allegory is a better explanation of the post-colonial programme of Coetzee's work. While post-colonialism and postmodernism intersect at many points, the future of post-colonial analysis will draw further away from postmodernism.

The dominant themes of this discussion of post-colonial futures are the counter-discursive agency of post-colonial subjects and the transformative power of post-colonial discourse. The book investigates both the material and discursive dimensions of this process. Transformation is not contrary to resistance, but it reveals that the most effective strategies of post-colonial resistance have not become bogged down in simple opposition or futile binarism, but have taken the dominant discourse and transformed it for purposes of self-empowerment. This is not a doctrine so much as an observation of the practice of colonial subjects. It is in this everyday practice that post-colonial futures are created.

CHAPTER 1

The future of English

Post-colonial theory developed in response to the flourishing literatures written by colonized peoples in colonial languages. The disciplinary consequences of literary study are therefore of prime importance, and one of the most interesting post-colonial transformations is that effected on the discipline from which post-colonial literatures emerged. There is probably no discipline which shares the peculiar function of English in the promulgation of imperial culture. History and geography constituted unparalleled regulatory discourses for the European construction of world reality in the nineteenth century, but they were widely studied in all European countries. No other imperial power developed a subject quite like 'English' in its function as a vehicle of cultural hegemony, and no subject gained the prestige that English achieved in the curriculum of the British Empire. The effect of post-colonial literatures upon English, therefore, offers a significant model for post-colonial engagements with imperial power, and, consequently, for the concept of a post-colonial future.

For a subject with such a powerful function in the cultural dominance of empire, English is remarkably recent. A little over a hundred years ago a Jewish medievalist was appointed the first English lecturer at Cambridge University. Two years before, the English school had been established at Oxford, although it was not until 1917 that the first Oxford Chair of English placed the imprimatur on a discipline which had gained a strategic authority, as we shall see, in the cultural dominance of the British Empire. The discipline of English is extremely recent, but for all its centrality in the Empire's system of education, for all its rapidly developed cultural authority, it may also be relatively short-lived.

Why does a subject, which has performed such a central function in the discursive and hegemonic dominance of empire, have such an uncertain future? Why is a subject, which has inscribed not only the professional identities of generations of scholars and teachers, but the cultural identity, the cultural aspiration of a very large part of the globe, possibly doomed to extinction? The answer of course lies in its origin and the very nature of its power. The unravelling of English has been occurring for quite some time on two fronts: first, the Arnoldian idea of culture on which the discipline is based is being replaced by a broader sense of cultural textuality, a breaking down of the distinction between 'high and popular' in cultural analysis; second, the monolithic unity of aesthetic and cultural assumptions which has provided its canonical authority has been challenged by the vast array of post-colonial literatures in English that have emerged as a direct result of cultural colonization. These two developments have been firmly deployed in the last ten years or so around the discourses of cultural studies and post-colonial studies, and I want to propose that not only do the interests of post-colonialism and the emerging discipline of cultural studies converge, but they have been linked from the very beginning of the study of 'English'.

When we examine the surprisingly recent development of this field called English literature we discover how firmly it is rooted in the cultural relationships established by British imperialism. Not only is the very idea of 'culture' a result of the European political subjugation of the rest of the world, but the construction of Europe itself is inextricably bound up with the historical reality of colonialism and the almost total invisibility of the colonized peoples to European art and philosophy. Why, we might ask, did cultural studies emerge out of English departments, of all places? Quite simply, the discipline of English was conceived, initiated and implemented as a programme of cultural study. Virtually from its inception, it existed as a promotion of English national culture under the guise of the advancement of civilization. Most histories of cultural studies focus on the work of Richard Hoggart, Raymond Williams and E. P. Thompson in the 1950s and 1960s, and the establishment of the Birmingham Centre for Contemporary Cultural Studies in 1964, but, in fact, the founding document of 'cultural studies' is Lord Macaulay's Minute to Parliament in 1835.

This document, as Gauri Viswanathan explains, signified the rise to prominence of the Anglicists over the Orientalists in the British administration of India. The Charter Act of 1813, devolving responsibility for Indian education on the colonial administration, led to a struggle between the two approaches, ultimately resolved by Macaulay's Minute, in which we find not just the assumptions of the Anglicists, but the profoundly universalist assumptions of English national culture itself. 'We must educate a people who cannot at present be educated by means of their mother-tongue,' says Macaulay, with breathtaking confidence:

> The claims of our own language it is hardly necessary to recapitulate. It stands pre-eminent even among the languages of the west. It abounds with works of imagination not inferior to the noblest which Greece has bequeathed to us; with models of every species of eloquence ... with the most profound speculation on metaphysics, morals, government, jurisprudence, and trade.... Whoever knows that language has ready access to all the vast intellectual wealth which all the wisest nations of earth have created and hoarded in the course of ninety generations. (1835: 349–50)

The advancement of any colonized people could only occur, it was claimed, under the auspices of English language and culture, and it was on English literature that the burden of imparting civilized values was to rest. It worked so well as a form of cultural studies because 'the strategy of locating authority in the texts of English literature all but effaced the sordid history of colonialist expropriation, material exploitation and class and race oppression behind European world dominance' (Viswanathan, 1987: 22). English literature 'functioned as a surrogate Englishman in his highest and most perfect state' (*ibid.*: 23). One could add that without the profoundly universalist assumptions of English literature and the dissemination of these through education, colonial administrations would not have been able to invoke such widespread complicity with imperial culture (see Said, 1993).

Consequently, English literature became a prominent agent of colonial control; indeed, it can be said that English literary study really began in earnest once its function as a discipline of cultural studies had been established, and its ability to 'civilize' the lower classes had thus been triumphantly revealed. To locate the beginning of English at the moment of Macaulay's Minute is to some extent to display the provisionality of beginnings, for this beginning is preceded by a significant prehistory in the emergence of *Rhetoric and Belles Lettres* in Scotland and the teaching of literature in the dissenting academies. The explicit cultural imperialism of English is preceded by a different cultural movement issuing from the desire, in Scottish cultural life of the eighteenth century, for 'improvement', the desire for a civilizing purgation of the language and culture, a removal of barbaric Scottishisms and a cultivation of a 'British' intellectual purity (Crawford, 1992).

This movement within Scotland towards improvement and civilization which led to the birth of the subject we now call 'English' is very different from that movement initiated by Macaulay's Minute which actively propagated English throughout the Empire. However, the two movements reflect a dynamic that has continued in the post-colonial world to the present day. This Scottish movement of improvement and purification is centripetal, self-directed, focused on the centre as object; the movement initiated by Macaulay is centrifugal, outward-moving, enfolding, seeing the centre as subject.

English literature is the direct result of the historical confluence of these centripetal and centrifugal movements which resulted in the institutionalization of 'English', but the Scottish example reveals that the operation of imperial power is far more complex and circulatory than we might assume. We are used to seeing the course of empire as centrifugal, outward-moving, imposing cultural values through a domination of cultural institutions and a coercion effected through cultural discourse. However, we overlook the fact that the continual *centripetal* movement towards improvement, betterment and self-creation, towards a 'proper language', a 'global economy', 'international standards' – the cultural identification *initiated by the colonized themselves* – is a much more pervasive operation of hegemonic affiliation. The further complication is that each of these processes of cultural circulation generates its own forms of resistance, but as a focus of desire, English literature operated as a very dense and overdetermined site for both these movements of cultural identification. Scotland and India model two processes of hegemony which continue to operate in the post-colonial world to the present day, confirming English literature as the embodiment of universal, transcendent values, the site of an aesthetic prominence, and the object of cultural desire.

The ideological function of English can be seen to be repeated in all post-colonial societies, in very different pedagogic situations. Literature, by definition, excluded local writing. The matter was put succinctly by Edmund Gosse commenting on Robert Louis Stevenson's return to Samoa. 'The fact seems to be that it is very nice to *live* in Samoa, but not healthy to *write* there. Within a three-mile radius of Charing Cross is the literary atmosphere, I suspect' (Gosse, 1891: 375). George Lamming talks about the effect of this in his essay 'The occasion for speaking' in which he says that the recognition in America and the considerable financial rewards this brought his writing were of little consequence compared to the recognition by the literary establishment in London (1960: 26). The idea of literary value, so important to the ideological function of literature, involved a relentlessly centripetal cultural momentum towards the centre of empire.

The conviction of literature's efficacy in imparting culture to its readers found its most influential voice in Matthew Arnold, whose book *Culture and Anarchy* (1869) was concerned with the growth of philistine culture which appeared to be accelerating with the spread of literacy and democracy, thus eroding the separation between the 'cultured' and the masses. State sponsorship of education was to be the mechanism by which culture could be preserved and extended to resist the descent towards an increasingly mechanical and materialist civilization. The 'civilizing' function of the study of literature was now harnessed in earnest to preserve English national culture in Britain. The link between the idea of 'civilization', the ideal of a unitary English national culture, and the prestige of antiquity became focused in the discipline of English, in which an arbitrary and ostensively indicated set of cultural and aesthetic values were held to be universal.

Clearly the prestige of English goes hand in hand with a particular view of culture – a particular form of culturalism. This is one, as Raymond Williams elaborates, in which 'culture' is regarded as 'art' rather than a 'way of life'. So, as a form of cultural studies, the discipline of English, the repository of civilized and universal values, depends heavily on the interpretation of 'culture' and value which Arnold formulated. However, the force and tenacity of Arnold's influence lies in the fact that he created a *vocabulary* of criticism which entered the language and even today manages to take a firm hold of cultural discourse. This is why in Australia in the 1980s a professor of the history of ideas, Eugene Kamenka, could say, quite unselfconsciously,

> Culture rests on the motto that nothing human is alien to me; it thrives on admiration for and emulation of, the best that has been thought and said, felt and done anywhere. . . . For culture is not only firmly international in its nature and effects, it makes people and peoples 'transcend' themselves and their seemingly narrow, time and space-bound capacities. (Kamenka, 1984: 1)

It would be hard to find a more succinct recapitulation of the Arnoldian myth of culture. This essay, so resonantly couched in Arnoldian vocabulary, demonstrates, a century and a half later, the stunning success of the project of cultural studies initiated by Macaulay's Minute. Culture elevates, it is universal, trans-human, unassailable. The cultures of the Nigerian, the Sri Lankan, the Barbadian (or indeed the Canadian or Australian) are excluded by virtue of their very non-universality.

The conflation of the 'best cultural values that civilization has to offer' and English literature (i.e. the 'culture and civilization' form of culturalism) is present from Macaulay through Arnold, but it is in the Newbolt Report that it becomes an issue of national policy. From a post-World War I fear, among other things, of the power of Teutonic scholarship, and particularly of its tradition of philology, Henry Newbolt was commissioned in 1919 to conduct an enquiry into the state of English. The report, published in 1921 as *The Teaching of English in England*, became a best-seller, and established the study of English literature firmly at the centre of the English and colonial education systems. The language of the report and its pedagogic assumptions make it clear from which springs it drew ideological sustenance.

> what we are looking for now is not merely a means of education, one chamber in the structure which we are hoping to rebuild, but the true starting point and foundation from which all the rest must spring (Great Britain, 1921: 14)

> If we use English literature as a means of contact with great minds, a channel by which to draw upon their experience with profit and delight, and a bond of sympathy between the members of a human society, we shall succeed, as the best teachers of the Classics have often succeeded in their more limited field. (*ibid*.: 15)

Ian Hunter has suggested that English was not so much a means of ideological control as a moral technology (1988: 723–4), something we find emphasized in this report, but in practice the moral technology was heavily in the service of ideology. The moral dominance of English thus so powerfully confirmed in the 1920s provided a fertile ground for the influential culturalism of F. R. Leavis. If we can characterize English culturalism as an emerging struggle between two definitions of culture (which Raymond Williams terms 'art' or 'way of life'), we find it most acutely expressed in Leavis. For him, a common culture, that of the pre-industrial organic community, and its continuing echo in the legacy of the English language, becomes pitted against modern industrial civilization both in its capitalist and communist forms. In Leavis' programme the literary intelligentsia were to be mobilized against philistine modernity, calling into their service the universal cultural values embodied in English.

The 1930s and 1940s became a watershed in this struggle between high and popular culture, largely due to the increasing cultural dominance of America. It is commonplace these days to cast Leavis in the role of villain, but in terms of the cultural struggle being engaged in over English his position was extremely complex. Macaulay had already initiated the link between 'high' culture and the English tradition by grandly announcing the roots of English literature as somehow extending back to Classical times, but in Leavis the defence of the unified pre-industrial English became a defence of high culture against (largely American) popular culture. F. R. Leavis and Denys Thompson's *Culture and Environment* in 1933 and Q. D. Leavis' *Fiction and the Reading Public* in 1932 represented major assaults by the Scrutiny school. In essence Leavis voices a cultural struggle between two imperial powers, and while America gained control over popular culture (to the extent that it could be said that the mass culture of the world today is American popular culture), Europe, and in English-speaking colonies, England, maintained firm control over high culture.

In some respects Leavis' battle reflects the predicament of decolonizing countries trying to carve a cultural space for themselves against an overwhelming imperial presence. The difference was that the long history of cultural study in Britain and the shared dominance of European philosophical and cultural values meant that it operated from a position of power. The armory in the battle consisted of weapons from the Arnoldian vocabulary: mass culture versus culture, the shallow versus the deep, the popular versus the timeless, the local versus the universal. If the world could not resist the dominance of American *popular* culture, the Arnoldian view of *high* culture still holds sway at a level almost too deep to be expunged. Ironically, the manifestly culturalist operation of English studies throughout the Empire generated a sense of local writing in the colonies that was as densely culturally grounded. Indeed, this cultural localism was the repeated cause of the exclusion of local writing from English literature. Consequently, the very success of the ideological project of English literature, the success of its function as a moral technology, the success of its embodiment of the rhetoric of empire, is the source of its probable undoing.

From this watershed period the programme of English cultural studies embodied in English takes two directions: literary criticism becomes dominated by New Criticism, which, although it has its roots in Richards' practical criticism, is in fact an American-inspired interpretive method by which imperial or English national cultural values are expunged from the reading of texts. Richards' scientific and psychological reading experiments, because they failed to produce a coherent methodology or school, became marooned in English cultural history. Nevertheless, his psychologistic view of the practice of criticism became the intellectual energy behind the division of English into cultural studies and new criticism.

New Criticism, of course, builds upon Richards' scientism and Leavisite textual analysis to confirm literature as a discrete discourse devoid of even the cultural implications of traditional historical scholarship. Most curiously, it serves to confirm the imperialist notion of literature because it elides the cultural differences between texts. A form of criticism that can be said to have had a post-colonial impetus[1] ended up with a strongly canonical effect. In a sense the door clanged shut on the culturalist dimension of literary studies with the advent of this meticulous and text-absorbed methodology. Whatever our view of Leavis, there is no questioning the fact that he took the culturalist dimension of English seriously. For the Scrutiny school, what people read was intimately bound up with the rest of their cultural experience.

New Criticism did not affect canonical notions since it could simply be performed on all the usual texts, as could deconstruction which followed it in the 1970s.[2] It did in fact confirm canonical notions of value because great texts were those which offered themselves to extensive textual analysis.[3] As far as academic literary criticism was concerned, the catastrophic consequences of New Criticism, and its heir deconstruction, were that literary theory and literary criticism, as practised in the academy, 'for the most part isolated textuality from the circumstances, the events, the physical senses that made it possible and render it intelligible as the result of human work' (Said, 1983: 4). These apparently radical methodologies served increasingly to cut off the literary text from cultural considerations over the next thirty years. Their inevitable consequence has been to confirm that literature, as an example of something called 'high culture', is marginal to the everyday concerns of society.

While new criticism quickly rose to prominence in America during this time, the struggle over the interpretation of culture remained unresolved in Britain. The concept of the great tradition remained firmly entrenched alongside the upstart new criticism due mainly to the resilience of the Arnoldian critical vocabulary and the success of the Newbolt-inspired placement of English at the centre of the British and colonial education systems. It was as though the dual character of culture as it exists in culturalism became divided at this time between the culturalist contestants. While English remained the repository of high cultural values, its 'great' literature, the very embodiment of the notion of culture as art, its inability and unwillingness to account for the culture, the way of life, of the vast majority of English society, led to the emergence of British cultural studies in 1957, the founding text of which was Richard Hoggart's *The Uses of Literacy* (1957), in which we can see the interests of the 'culture and civilization' school of Leavis transforming into the interests of cultural studies.

Raymond Williams' publication of *Culture and Society* in 1958, revealing, as it does, the link between cultural products and cultural relations, probably had a more profound influence on the development of British cultural studies than any other text. Like Hoggart, Williams reveals a complicated relationship with Leavisism, since he uses literary analysis which also hinges on a nostalgic feel for the culture being analysed. However, in Williams the three fundamental questions of cultural studies come together: What is culture? What is the text? What is the relation between culture and ideology?

For the first question, Williams gives some impressive definitions:

> Culture is ordinary: that is the first fact. Every human society has its own shape, its own purposes, its own meanings. Every human society expresses these, in institutions, and in arts and learning. The making of a society is the finding of common meanings and directions, and its growth is an active debate and amendment under the pressures of experience, contact and discovery, writing themselves into the land. The growing society is there, yet it is also made and remade in every individual mind. . . . A culture has two aspects: the known meanings and directions, which its members are trained to; the new observations and meanings, which are offered and tested. . . . We use the word culture in these two senses: to mean a whole way of life – the common meanings; to mean the arts and learning – the special processes of discovery and creative effort. (1989: 311)

The analysis of culture, then, is the 'study of relationships between elements in a whole way of life', attempting to 'discover the nature of the organisation which is the complex of these relationships' (Williams, 1965: 63). The most crucial aspect of Williams' analysis, I think, is the bringing together of the two notions of culture resident in culturalism, a feature which is not entirely taken up by the developing discipline of cultural studies, where an interest in the lived cultures of particular classes was quickly overtaken by an intense interest in the mass media; but the next two questions did not become theorized until the encounter between culturalism and structuralism. Nor did this book invoke the question which has become an energetic one in recent cultural studies beyond the British model: What are the politics of cultural difference?

It is obvious then that the event which many take to be the birth of British cultural studies, the establishment of the Birmingham Centre for Contemporary Cultural Studies in 1964, had a very long gestation. Thomas Babbington Macaulay's chickens had now finally come home to roost. It is no accident that Stuart Hall, director from 1969, is West

Indian, for the liminal perspective of the colonized becomes very useful for seeing the problematic division in English culturalism and the affiliative network by which the state commands cultural production. With this in mind we might even say that British cultural studies is a major example of the process of 'transculturation' outlined by Pratt (1992), a circulation of a marginalized post-colonial perspective back into English cultural life; a recirculation of the idea of the irrelevance of a canonical English literature to cultural life in general. However, the very strong focus of cultural studies upon popular culture and the mass media reveals the way in which the binary division of English culturalism still operates implicitly in British cultural studies.

Post-colonial cultural studies

Criticism throughout the English-speaking world was affected both by the culturalist rationale of English studies, and by the rise of new criticism. However, the writing itself seemed to occupy a different site because the division between culture as art and culture as a way of life becomes immediately eroded when colonized peoples appropriate cultural discourses such as literary writing. It is eroded because in these cultures such a distinction between definitions of culture becomes a deeply ontological one. For these societies, culture as timeless, universal and authoritative is simply unattainable except by a process of the most parodic mimicry in which the imperial centre embodies all cultural aspirations. As Kamenka makes very clear, if culture is universal it must exclude your specifically regional art. The glowingly humanist credo 'nothing human is alien to me' only operates by incorporating an extensive array of quite specific exclusions; for you cannot have culture that is Ugandan, Australian or Jamaican. Post-colonial literatures, by definition, cannot be great or universal so they become much more obviously an aspect of a 'way of life'.

Post-colonial cultural discourse of all kinds problematizes the distinction between culture as 'art' and cultures as 'ways of life', and indeed problematizes the concept of culture itself. For when decolonizing countries appropriate cultural discourse, they must either appropriate the whole of its universalist ideology and become, for instance, 'more English than the English', or appropriate it in a way that confirms all intellectual and artistic discourse as aspects of the way of life, strands of the cultural texture, intimately and inextricably connected in the textual fabric of society. Curiously, their marginalization and exclusion from the canon has provided the ground for a much more heterogeneous conception of the cultural text.

Post-colonial and contemporary cultural studies share a commitment to textual materiality. Roland Barthes' view of the text as a methodological field distinct from the work which can be held in the hand is a very useful basis for the analysis of culture. The text which only exists as the movement of a discourse 'is also experienced only in an activity of production'. Barthes' metaphor of the text as a *network*, which issues from innumerable centres of culture (Barthes, 1971: 117–22), demonstrates that textuality cannot be confined to discrete cultural productions. So, in a sense, the notion of textuality as a semiotic field, a tissue of quotations, is a natural ally of the view of culture as a network of practices, a 'way of life'; but it is also an ally of that tendency Edward Said called the 'worldliness of the text' (1983: 31–53). For although the text is an infinite deferment, without source or origin, it is still the fabric of those human lives in whom the political realities of cultures are worked out. The notion of 'worldliness' is a key principle for post-colonial societies and runs counter to the 'unworldly' abstraction of much contemporary theory. Writing itself is affiliative rather than filiative with experience; it 'counters nature'. Yet in this affiliation with the social world, this production of experience, Said sees one of the most resonant confirmations of the text's worldliness.

What continues to hold concepts like 'literature' in place is a massive structure of cultural power, directed in educational, publishing and economic institutions. Post-colonial literary critics quickly come to realize that they are constantly thrown into conflict with this ideologically and institutionally buttressed category of literature because of its roots in the universalist ideology of English culturalism. Almost by definition, writing in post-colonial societies becomes inextricable from a network of cultural practices; exclusion from canonicity confirms its worldliness.

In its engagement with the culturalist myth of 'literature', then, post-colonialism brings to cultural studies its own well-established concepts of diversity, particularity and local difference. The global term 'culture' only becomes comprehensible as a conceptualization of local 'cultures'. Consequently the egregious distinction between 'high' and 'popular' culture is disrupted by the much more energetic and contested politics of cultural difference. Cultural studies, on the other hand, tends implicitly to support this distinction since it tends to funnel cultural analysis into the complex but circumscribed fields of mass media and popular culture. The issue of cultural difference, particularly as it is mediated in textuality, suggests that in most cultures there is no supportable distinction between 'high' and 'low' – culture is culture. Thus we may see more clearly that notions of high culture are the simple, and not always hidden, agents of cultural imperialism.

A very good example of this can be found in recent work on Samoan culture (Vaai, 1998). Analysis of the textual construction of culture in contemporary Samoa involves an examination of language use in law courts and village judicial meetings, written literature, music, drama, radio, television, oratory. Each one of these categories consists of both formal and informal domains, but even the most formal textual domain is intersected with hybrid cultural forms of discourse which diffuse any potential for hierarchical stratification. At no point, either in the production or consumption of culture, can a clear distinction of 'high' and 'low' be made, not only because the hybrid is so dominant but because this very hybridity makes it difficult to locate writers or readers, performers or viewers, producers or consumers in any fixed social hierarchy. The Samoan example suggests that the division of culture between 'art' and 'way of life', between 'high' and 'low', collapses in post-colonial societies because the social and institutional frameworks which buttress this distinction are less clear.

Post-colonial cultural studies tends to recognize the way in which intellectual endeavour is compromised and contained by state power as it is mediated through intellectual work. Bringing to mind Adorno's thesis of the state production of culture, Edward Said says: 'To a great extent culture, cultural formations, and intellectuals exist by virtue of a very interesting network of relationships with the State's almost absolute power' (1983: 169). This is a set of relationships about which all contemporary left criticism, according to Said, and indeed all literary study, remains stunningly silent:

> On the contrary, nearly everyone producing literary or cultural studies makes no allowance for the truth that all intellectual work occurs somewhere, at some time, on some very precisely mapped-out and permissible terrain, which is ultimately contained by the State. (*ibid.*: 169)

This is, I think, a huge and depressing claim about contemporary intellectual production, but it is something which is obscured by the disciplinary structure of knowledge and particularly the disciplinary study of literature. As Said goes on to point out, even if we want to claim that 'culture' as aesthetic production subsists on its own, according to an art-for-art's sake theory, no one is prepared to show how that independence was gained, nor, more importantly, how it was maintained.

The value of what we can call post-colonial cultural production lies not in its freedom from these conditions of production, but in the fact that its 'containment' is so glaringly obvious. No writer picking up a pen to write in a colonial language can avoid coming to terms with the irony of this practice at some stage. No post-colonial intellectual, no artist, no critic, can avoid the fact that this production is occurring in some already determined discursive space. The terrain is not just contained by the nation-state but by the continuing imperial reality of global capital. The post-colonial intellectual simply cannot avoid the fact that this work is 'occurring at some place at some time in a mapped-out and permissible terrain' because the reality of place, the reality of publishing requirements, markets, form some of the defining conditions of its production, and the ideological containment produces the tension against which it must constantly test itself. As is the theoretical ambition in cultural studies, the politics of the analysis and the politics of intellectual work are inseparable. However, in the actual practice of cultural subjects, 'containment' by the state is far from absolute, being negotiated at many levels by an access to and appropriation of global culture. The resilience of post-colonial production in its appropriation of imperial forms for local identity construction is, as we shall see, a model for the engagement with global culture.

This, then, suggests the political efficacy of the post-colonial perspective for contemporary cultural studies, a perspective somewhat sharpened by its distance from the 'centre'. The post-colonial intellectual, and by extension post-colonial horizons to cultural studies, must contend with the conditions of their own containment, must perform a self-conscious reflection upon their own conditions of production. Indeed, the ironies of post-colonial cultural production, and particularly the tensions inherent in language appropriation, make this difficult to avoid.

The function of post-colonial theory

So, with this rapid unravelling of English literature and its reconstruction as a network of local post-colonial practices, what intellectual identity is the post-colonial critic to construct for him or herself? Because the post-colonial critic, whether an academic or not, is an institutionally constructed subject, the relation of this practice to the status of the discipline is both troubling and metonymic. As Barbara Christian points out, post-colonial writers have always written theory; it just hasn't been recognized as such (Christian, 1987). However, although post-colonial theory was not an invention of the academy, it was, paradoxically, only its confirmation as an élite discourse within the academy that allowed it to achieve any sort of recognition or authority. This has had the rather ambiguous result of allowing the voice of the culturally marginalized and dispossessed to be heard, often for the first time, but often also within the frame of a theory which has leached that voice of all its materiality and political urgency. On the other hand a recurrent oppositional essentialism which would, understandably, reject Western discourse, reject English, reject literature, reject imperialism, finds itself locked into an illusory and self-congratulatory rhetoric which fails to see the protean nature of imperial power.

Interestingly, there are modes of critical practice which mirror the choices offered to any project of political decolonization, all of which have their particular value. There is a choice corresponding to what we might call colonialist discourse theory, a broadly post-structuralist analysis of colonial discourse which demonstrates the already present dynamic of resistance in such things as mimicry and hybridity; there is a choice corresponding to what might be called resistance or oppositional theory which is often essentialist in its racial and cultural assumptions. However, some of the most interesting theoretical interventions have occurred between these two poles, interventions which acknowledge the protean adaptability of imperial power in an increasingly globalized world, but which insist on the agency of the decolonizing subject.

There has rarely been a more hotly contested topic than the meaning, validity and applicability of the term 'post-colonial' in recent years. However, if we understand the post-colonial to mean the discourse of the colonized, rather than a discourse post-dating colonialism, then post-colonial analysis becomes that which examines the full range of responses to colonialism, from absolute complicity to violent rebellion and all variations in between. There is no post-colonial discourse which is not complicit in some way, and extremely little which is not oppositional, but all of it is about change in some form or other. A theory which may more faithfully engage the actual practice of post-colonial subjects in this situation is a poetics and a politics of *transformation*.

A poetics of transformation is concerned with the ways in which writers and readers contribute constitutively to meaning, the ways in which colonized societies appropriate imperial discourses, and how they interpolate their voices and concerns into dominant systems of textual production and distribution. Transformation recognizes that power is a critical part of our cultural life, and resists by adapting and redirecting discursive power, creating new forms of cultural production; but above all, a poetics of transformation recognizes the transformative way in which post-colonial texts operate, even those which pose as simply oppositional.

A politics of transformation works constantly within existing discursive and institutional formations to change them, rather than simply to attempt to end them. By taking hold of writing itself, whether as novel, history, *testimonio*, political discourse or political structures, interpolating educational discourse and institutions, transforming conceptions of place, even economics, the post-colonial subject unleashes a rapidly circulating transcultural energy. Ultimately, a poetics and politics of transformation effects a transformation of the disciplinary field. It is this transformative energy of post-colonial textuality, the appropriations and reconstructions of writers rather than the actions of academics, which are transforming cultural discourse; and the cultural location of this textuality is changing the disciplinary field of English.

The power of transformation can be seen in the engagement with language, with literary writing and the whole range of imperial cultural media. Indeed, some of the most widespread and influential examples of post-colonial transformation can be seen in the effects upon the English language, but the discipline of English itself is useful as a model of cultural engagement because it shows how a relevant oppositionality is bound to a strategy of transformation. One can either accept the orthodoxy of English literature with its huge edifice of disciplinary and cultural assumptions (as is often still the case in post-colonial societies), one can reject it and leave it altogether, or one can interpolate a local view of cultural textuality. This does not mean simply adding some different courses and different texts to the curriculum, or even changing the name of the discipline, but engaging the underlying assumptions, the ideology and the status of English as a moral technology. In a sense, canonicity and the immensely successful operation of imperial power through English literature has accelerated this process by consistently excluding post-colonial writing until the rearguard action of the Booker Prize, but it has been the processes of textual mimicry and the hybridization of writing rather than rejection that have transformed English.

An example of this was the successful advocacy in 1968 by James Ngugi, Taban Lo Liyong and Henry Owuor Anyumba of the abolition of the English Department in the University of Nairobi which was replaced with a Department of African Languages and Literature (Ngugi, 1972). This was a key moment in the transformation, not only of the institutional structure of the discipline but the nature and function of literature itself: an abrogation of the canonical notion of literary excellence buttressing the ideology of English and its replacement with a view of creative writing as a form of cultural textuality, a strand within a heterogeneous network of cultural practices. It was an act which was to be repeated in post-colonial societies throughout the world. As an act of resistance it was classically ambivalent, relying on a reconceptualizing of the purposes and activities of existing structures, on mimicking established institutional functions.

Ngugi's own major gesture of resistance – refusing to write in English in favour of his Gikuyu mother tongue – although performed as an unequivocal act of rejection, still appropriated the novel form which is alien to Gikuyu culture, still interpolated its message into world publishing by means of translations. Such gestures have been important ways of transforming the field of literary study, and whatever the rhetoric surrounding them they are never simply oppositional but profoundly transformative. The transformations of post-colonial literary study, therefore, have not been limited to the body of writing made available for study but in the ways in which they are read, the ways in which such writings are located in the network of cultural practices which constitutes the cultural text.

What, then, of the future? If we face the fact of the invention of English as the prestigious civilizing mode of cultural study, and add to that the further recognition that most of the imaginative writing in 'English' in the world occurs outside England, we are faced with the exciting prospect of this writing being a useful access point to the broad text of post-colonial cultures. My own vision for cultural studies into the twenty-first century is that it could reopen the door which clanged shut on literature in the 1950s. Culture includes *all* cultural practices and products, and the assessment of the processes of their production, consumption, the process of their representation and exchange, and the interrelationship of all of these elements. However, most significantly, post-colonial writing, because it is conceived in a dynamic of political and cultural engagement at both the discursive and institutional level, is peculiarly placed to initiate cultural transformation. Political and social change only occur because they occur in the minds of those who imagine a different kind of world.

Notes

1. New Criticism can be seen to be a product of an American attempt to establish the legitimacy of its literary canon against the dominance of the English tradition. As Kenneth Dauber asserts, the Americans, lacking a tradition, and distrusting literature as an institution, could never believe in the reality of received 'categorizations'. New Criticism methodized this disbelief, 'to force us to begin again with each work'. Kenneth Dauber, 'Criticisms of American literature', *Diacritics*, 7 (March 1977).

2. In fact we can trace Lacan's critique of Saussure to the 1950s, and locate the origins of deconstruction during a time when new criticism was dominant; but the popularity of post-structuralism in America (and the English-speaking world) can be generally dated from the 1966 symposium at Johns Hopkins University entitled 'The Languages of Criticism and the Sciences of Man' at which Derrida delivered his seminal paper, 'Structure, sign and play in the discourse of the human sciences'. Richard Macksey and Eugenio Donato (eds), *The Structuralist Controversy* (Baltimore and London: Johns Hopkins University Press, 1970).

3. New Criticism worked best with modernist poetry and thus ushered in a period in academic study when poetry, particularly modernist poetry, formed a comparatively larger part of the curriculum. Such poetry lent itself very readily, however, to an isolation of the text from its social and historical world.

CHAPTER 2

Latin America and post-colonial transformation

The flourishing local literatures throughout the British Empire were, as we have seen, a direct consequence of the strategic importance of English in the hegemony of imperial culture and its prominence in colonial education. While religious conversion came to be seen by all colonizing powers as a crucial method of 'civilizing' the primitive societies beyond Europe, only English literature, of all secular European discourses, carried the full moral weight of the civilizing mission. The study of 'English' operated as a specific site of cultural exclusion as well as cultural indoctrination, the local cultures of the colonized being excluded from participation in the master discourses of human (European) culture. For this very reason it became a site of resistance as the cultural orientation of post-colonial writing opposed, interpolated and then transformed the canon of English literature itself. The emerging post-colonial theory of the 1980s was therefore heavily oriented to literatures in English, as well as contemporary European theory, with some attention to Francophone African literatures generated by the stature of writers such as Aimé Césaire, Léopold Senghor and Frantz Fanon.

The great omission from the early development of post-colonial theory was the oldest, second largest and most complex modern European empire – that of Spain. But the prospect of 'Including America', as Peter Hulme evocatively put it (1995), into the subject matter of post-colonial study, is no simple task, for the idea of Latin American post-coloniality is still strongly resisted by South American intellectuals. This is surprising, because no region in the world has demonstrated so comprehensively, over such a long period, the transformation of colonial culture initiated by the Spanish. Yet still some nagging questions need to be answered: How and on what basis can we establish links between Latin America and other colonized regions? Can a word such as 'colonialism' really refer to the historical experience of Latin America? Marc Ferro, for instance, offers Argentina and Peru as examples of 'imperialism without colonization', where the city ruled until it surrendered dominance to the United States (Ferro, 1997: 19).

Certainly, Latin America *is* different. In particular the features of its colonization, from 1492, are different from British imperialism which extends roughly from 1757. They occurred, says Santiago Colas, 'at different historical moments, the colonizers belonged to different nations and to different classes within those nations, and the nations in turn occupied different international positions'. Moreover, the 'distant territories' were geographically distinct, the 'implantations' were accomplished through different financial and technical means, and the inhabitants had developed distinct social and cultural habits' (Colas, 1994: 383). To this we could add the radically different institutional location of literary study in English and Spanish cultures (see Baldick, 1987; Viswanathan, 1987). 'English' was not simply literary study but a site of such profound moral importance in English education that it was bound to focus the resistance of post-colonial intellectuals.

To some, Latin America is under threat from a new colonizing movement called 'colonial and postcolonial discourse', yet another subjection, it would seem, to foreign formations and epistemologies from the English-speaking centres of global power. There may be good reason for fearing the hegemonic effects of new global discourses, but if we forget for a minute that the term 'post-colonial' appears to be one more in a long line of 'posts' and attempt to understand the significance of colonization and its post-colonial engagements, we may discover that Latin America has given ample evidence of its post-coloniality long before the emergence of 'colonial and post-colonial discourse' from the metropolitan academy. Latin America, whose colonization coincides with the emergence of European modernity itself, may be the first colonized, and hence the oldest post-colonial region in the world.

The problem with the debate on post-colonialism in Latin America is that it has been skewed from the beginning by a rather eccentric view of post-colonialism, largely resting on the assumption that it emerged from post-structuralism, leading to an understandable resistance to its neo-hegemonic discursive character. A debate in the *Latin American Research Review* in 1993 illustrates both how a limited definition of post-colonial theory has been readily accepted and how questions about its validity have arisen. The use of the phrase 'colonial and post-colonial discourse' itself indicates the extent to which the historical event of colonialism, its discursive machinery, and post-colonial engagements with it have been blurred.

The 'field' or 'movement', it is assumed, emerged in the 1980s from a dissatisfaction with previous approaches to colonial analysis. Patricia Seed's review article in 1991, which stimulated this debate among Latin Americanists, sees post-colonial discourse as synonymous with the colonial discourse theory initiated by Said. In addition, she claims that the interest in the textual and discursive aspects of colonialism is a direct inheritance of post-structuralism. However, not only should Said's own work be distinguished from post-structuralism (see Said, 1983; Ashcroft, 1997; Ashcroft and Ahluwalia, 1999); this privileging of colonial discourse theory initiated by his *Orientalism* misrepresents the very complex emergence of post-colonial studies over several decades. Post-colonial analysis, even in its most overtly theoretical form, has been a function of the activity of writers and critics since the nineteenth century, burgeoning in the work of Frantz Fanon and other intellectuals writing in the wake of independence.

Hernan Vidal's stubbornly ethnocentric contention that the proliferation of literary criticism in Latin America 'saw the importation of North American New Criticism, Russian Formalism, German Phenomenology and French Structuralism' (1993: 115) demonstrates very clearly the perceived threat to Latin American intellectual integrity posed by outside critical movements. Such a fear appears, itself, to emerge from a tendency to homogenize the complex range of social experiences co-existing on the Continent. Outlining two strands of literary criticism which he calls 'technocratic criticism' and 'culturally oriented criticism' (*ibid*.: 116), Vidal sees the emergence of 'colonial and post-colonial discourse' as the creation of a category of research which attempts to endow these two approaches 'with a degree of affinity that they have not previously had' (*ibid*.).

However, this can be understood in another way. The employment of 'technocratic' criticism is a clear example of the tendency of colonized peoples to appropriate the formations, discourses and theoretical strategies of a dominant discourse in making their voice heard. Such a process of appropriation has a long history in Latin American cultural production. Contemporary post-colonial criticism is not a product of the 1980s, the decade in which it began to become more fully described, but a consequence of many decades of post-colonial writing in the former British and French colonies resulting in an uneasy and sometimes fractious alliance between such fields as Commonwealth literary studies, black studies and the emergent colonial discourse theory.

If we take the position that rather than a product of the experience of colonized peoples in the French- and English-speaking world, post-colonialism is the discourse of the colonized, that it does not mean 'after colonialism' since it is colonialism's interlocutor and antagonist from the moment of colonization, then 'post-colonial discourse' can be seen to emerge from the creative and theoretical production of colonized societies themselves. This averts the problems raised by the movement towards a new critical orthodoxy resulting from the expropriation of the field by contemporary centres of academic power. If, rather than a new hegemonic field, we see the post-colonial as a way of talking about the political and discursive strategies of colonized societies, we may more carefully view the various forms of anti-systemic operations within the global world system.

Post-colonial analysis leads to a simple realization: that the effect of the colonizing process over individuals, over culture and society throughout Europe's domain was vast, and produced consequences as complex as they are profound. Not all post-colonial discourse is anti-colonial, nor can it ever, in any of its various forms, dispense with that comparatively simple moment of history which began to churn its social consequences around the world. These consequences have long been the subject of attention by Latin American historians and critics. Walter Mignolo, ostensibly rejecting post-colonialism, cites the post-colonial critique of Edmundo O'Gorman in *The Invention of America* (1961), which demonstrated that 'language is not the neutral tool of an honest desire to tell the truth . . . but an instrumental tool for constructing history and inventing realities' (Mignolo, 1993: 122). Similarly, Mignolo cites Angel Rama's *La ciudad letrada* (1982), which offers a theory about the control, domination and power of alphabetic writing (*ibid.*). 'O'Gorman and Rama exemplify the perspective of social scientists and humanists located in and speaking from the Third World. They are in some sense contemporary examples of the "intellectual other"' (*ibid.*: 123). Mignolo's complaint is that O'Gorman did first what Said and Todorov did two decades later. O'Gorman and Rama were already, several decades ago, critiquing a key feature of colonial discourse, the power of language to construct and dominate the world of the colonized.

Mignolo is correct in suggesting that post-colonialism is not a child of post-structuralism conceived in the metropolitan academy for the benefit of an annoyingly ungrateful post-colonial world. It is born from the struggle of colonized intellectuals to appropriate the discursive tools of imperial discourse and to interpolate their own realities and cultural activities into the global arena. The examples of O'Gorman and Rama could be multiplied many times over. Post-colonial discourse is significant because it reveals the extent to which the historical condition of colonization has led to a certain political, intellectual and creative dynamic in the post-colonial societies with which it engages. Even in those élites complicit with imperial culture, the displacement of the dominant ideology – its relocation in colonial space – is a significant catalyst for its transformation. The struggle for self-representation occurs at all levels of society.

Objections to post-colonial analysis have been based on a limited and academically defensive view of the discourse. Post-colonial analyses have been a feature of Latin American intellectual life at least since the 1950s, but there remains a strong belief in the essential difference of Latin American post-coloniality even by those who favour its approach. Santiago Colas has adapted the theory of ideology developed by Slovenian theorist Slavoj Žižek to define the ideology of Latin American post-colonial culture (Colas, 1995); but how identifying, how distinct is this ideology? Is the difference of Latin America more a function of desire than reality?

Although Žižek's notion of ideology is not as different from Althusser's as he would like to believe, the explanation of the function of ideology as 'not to offer us a point of escape from our reality but to offer us the social reality itself as an escape from some traumatic real kernel' (Colas, 1995: 384), does provide a useful entry to Latin American post-colonial culture. This functions, according to Colas, 'as an ideology that converts the persistence of colonial relations and its effects ... into the precondition for the articulation of a non-metropolitan identity. The culture then represses this conversion, leaving that identity seemingly self-constituted and self-sufficient – in a word, independent' (*ibid.*). According to Colas, the production of ideology in Latin America is driven by 'the unconscious desire for the persistence of colonial relations in terms both of dependence on the former colonial or imperial power and of social inequality within the new nation' (*ibid.*: 385). In effect, Colas has provided a theory of ideology which is not limited to Latin America as he claims, but in fact astutely assesses the complex structure of colonial relations in all settler colonies. If we see that the post-colonial begins from the moment of colonization, then we understand that 'the unconscious desire for the persistence of colonial relations' and the conscious desire for separation and independence are two positions which can exist side by side in any colonized space, but, in the settler colony, may so overlap that they can become subject positions adopted by the same subject. Perhaps inadvertently, Colas has demonstrated one way in which the inclusion of Latin America can begin to transform the field of post-colonial studies. The complexity of Latin American post-colonial society, far from lending itself to the concept of some Latin American essence, provides the ground for an increasingly sophisticated understanding of post-colonial relations throughout the world.

Latin America, colonialism and modernity

The most energetic debate on the subject of Latin America and post-colonialism concerns the character and antiquity of the historical condition of colonization. This is where the inclusion of America not only widens the scope of post-colonial theory but demonstrates how deeply colonial discourse is rooted in global culture. Santiago Colas complains about the absence of any discussion of Latin American literature in *The Empire Writes Back* suggesting that a discussion of the literatures of former British colonies may be 'of interest and relevance' to the literatures of former Spanish colonies. Colas rightly points out that the developments in former Spanish colonies may be 'of interest and relevance' to the study of English post-colonial culture, and indeed, as he says, 'may fundamentally change understandings of that culture' (1995: 383). Indeed, Latin America fundamentally changes our view of the post-colonial with its demonstration of a post-colonial future. The antiquity and character of its colonization, the long-standing reality of its hybridized cultures, the 'continental' sense of difference which stems from a shared colonial language, the intermittent emergence of contestatory movements in cultural production – all radically widen the scope of post-colonial theory.

Jorge Klor de Alva asserts in 'Colonialism and postcolonialism as

(Latin) American mirages' that 'the very notions of colonialism and imperialism came from the modern experiences of non-Hispanic colonial powers and only subsequently and improperly were imposed on the Spanish American experience from the sixteenth to the eighteenth centuries' (1992: 5); but what is an 'improper' use? Does the cultural provenance of theory invalidate such categories as epistemological tools? Indeed, is there any system of analysis which does not have a valid retrospective function? Such retrospective analysis has deeply transformed discussion of the British Empire as well. After all, imperialism is a very recent concept, formulated in the 1880s scramble for Africa and consolidated in the late nineteenth-century expatriation of British capital, but there is no good reason why we cannot use the term to retrospectively describe five centuries of European expansion.

Indeed, the colonization of Latin America obliges us to address the question of post-colonialism at its roots, at the very emergence of modernity. Nineteenth- and twentieth-century British imperialism demonstrates the centrifugal movement by which the precepts of European modernity and the assumptions of the Enlightenment have been distributed hegemonically throughout the world. However, including America, as Hulme advocates, we find that imperial expansion is more than the dispersal of European cultural values and assumptions into a Eurocentrically mapped world; it also reveals itself as the enabling condition of that very process by which a modern Europe is conceived. Europe's world empire *is* modernity!

Latin America, then, the 'first-born child' of modernity, is simultaneously 'worlded' by Europe, as Spivak puts it, and relegated to the periphery of that world. Spivak uses this term to describe the way in which the colonized space is brought into the 'world', that is, made to exist as part of a world essentially constructed by Eurocentrism:

> If . . . we concentrated on documenting and theorizing the itinerary of the consolidation of Europe as sovereign subject, indeed sovereign and subject, then we would produce an alternative historical narrative of the 'worlding' of what is today called 'the Third World'. (Spivak, 1985: 128)

However, the process of European expansion, which begins in its modern form with the invasion of America, is an enabling condition of the 'worlding' of Europe itself. Imperial expansion, the engine of modernity, gave European societies a sense of their distinction from the traditional pre-modern societies they invaded, a difference which was taken to be superiority, a status which propelled the continuing discourse of empire itself. The transcultural realities of post-colonial experience are present from this moment as the embedding of global difference begins the process by which the colonized world becomes a crucial factor in the imagining of Europe.

Modernity, which usually refers to those modes of social organization that emerged in Europe from about the sixteenth century, broadly represented by the discovery of the 'new world', the Renaissance and the Reformation, does not actually emerge as a concept until the eighteenth century. The invasion of Latin America begins a process which, two centuries later, had come to constitute, as Habermas says, 'the epochal threshold between modern times and the middle ages' (1981: 5). Clearly, this is quite a different concept of modernity from the one which Colas has asserted 'is consolidated and reaches its highest expression in the 1960's' (1995: 24). The threshold of 'the modern world' is the confluence of the three great world systems – imperialism, capitalism and the Enlightenment. Modernity is fundamentally about conquest, 'the imperial regulation of land, the discipline of the soul, and the creation of truth' (Turner, 1990: 4), a discourse which enabled the large-scale regulation of human identity both within Europe and its colonies.

Thus the emergence of modernity is coterminous with the emergence of Eurocentrism and the European dominance of the world effected through imperial expansion. Europe constructed itself as 'modern' and constructed the non-European as 'traditional', 'static', 'prehistorical'. History itself became the tool by which these societies were denied any internal dynamic of capacity for development. Latin America, the first-born child of modernity, remained relegated to the status, if not the fact, of the pre-modern, because this continent represents the first instance of the 'worlding' of modern Europe. It was in the relationship with Latin America that the energetic Manichean rhetoric of European cultural expansion was first conceived, from Montaigne's essay 'On Cannibals' to Shakespeare's *Tempest* to Darwin's debasement of the Tierra del Fuegans in *The Voyage of the Beagle*. This binarism remains firmly in place today in various guises, most notably as the distinction between the 'international' and the 'parochial'.

José Rabasa, in his analysis of Mercator's *Atlas*, locates this link between the invention of America and the 'invention' of Europe a century after Columbus with the invention of the world map. 'From the invention of America', says Rabasa, 'emerges a new Europe':

> The millenarian dream whereby the Franciscans transferred the geographic realization of history to the New World now, with Mercator, returns the locus of universal history to Europe; the angelic nature of the natives is replaced with a universal subject that is indispensable to the knowing of truth and thus constitutes the apex of history. Europe, which in analogous allegories is invested with a sphere and a cross emblematic of Catholicism, assumes a secular version where science and knowledge define her supremacy and universality. The remaining parts of the world are posited outside truth, since Europe holds the secret of their being. (1993: 207)

However, it would be truer to say that Mercator's *Atlas* consolidates the spatial organization of modernity, and *establishes* rather than *invents*

modern Europe. The bipolar representation of the primitive subject –
angelic or cannibalistic – precedes Mercator, and this ambivalence is
both supervised by, and critical to, the simultaneous worlding of Latin
America and Europe.

The imperial origins of modernity give us a different perspective on
the contemporary eagerness to define Latin American cultural productions as postmodern. Rather than the period of the disappearance of
imperialism, the 'postmodern' remains the site of its ultimate diffusion
into global systems of economy and culture. There are several ways of
conceiving postmodernity. We can see it as superseding modernity, in
which case it appears to give credence to history, the discourse it claims
to have overcome. We can see it as a cultural phenomenon focused in
postmodernism, the 'aesthetic reflection on the nature of modernity'
(Giddens, 1990: 45); or we can see it as modernity's discovery of the
provisionality and circularity of its basic premise, the 'providential'
power of reason. This discovery can be exemplified in Nietzsche's
realization that the Enlightenment replaced divine providence with the
equally transcendental providence of reason (Habermas, 1987b). Divine
will was replaced by human autonomy but it was a socially and
culturally situated autonomy. In effect, providence was replaced by the
temporally and spatially empty dominance of the European subject. The
'providential' rise of reason coincided with the rise of European dominance over the rest of the world and subject-centred reason the philosophical centre of European dominance through the Enlightenment.

The postmodern hinges, then, on the provisionality at the centre of
modernity. According to this view, postmodernity is coterminous with
modernity and represents a radical phase of its development. Yet in the
same way post-colonialism is coterminous with colonization, and the
dynamic of its disruptive engagement is firmly situated in modernity.
The post-colonial begins from the moment of colonization, but it is from
that moment a recognition and contestation of the hegemonic and
regulatory dominance of the 'truth' of modern Europe.

My contention is this; that post-colonialism and postmodernism are
both discursive elaborations of postmodernity, which is itself not the
overcoming of modernity, but modernity coming to understand its own
contradictions and uncertainties. They are, however, two very different
ways in which modernity comes to understand itself. Post-colonial
theory reveals the socially transformative dimension of postmodernity
which actually becomes occluded by aesthetic postmodernism. This is
because post-colonialism refills, with its locally situated meanings, a time
and space that are 'emptied' by modernity,[1] and constructs a discourse
of the real which is based on the material effects of colonial dominance.
Post-colonialism, while transforming colonial culture, reveals a powerful
tendency to appropriate and transform various principles of modernity.

We can only understand modernity, and hence postmodernity and
globalism, if we understand the trajectory of imperial expansion.

Anthony Giddens, in talking about modernity and globalism, provides a classic example of the blind spot which occurs when we fail to take imperialism into account. Asking if modernity is a Western project, he replies that in terms of the two great modern systems – the nation-state and capitalism – the answer must be yes; but, he asks, is modernity peculiarly Western in terms of its globalizing tendencies? 'No', he says, 'It cannot be, since we are speaking here of emergent forms of world interdependence and planetary consciousness' (1990: 175). So, by this account, globalism is an emergent process which just happens to come from everywhere! This is an important endorsement of the *engagement* of the local in globalization, but clearly there would be no global modernity without the history of European expansion. The transcultural complexity of globalism certainly depends upon the transformations enacted by local uses and appropriations in various regions, but these do not take place outside a dialectical process of enculturation and contestation set up by the colonizing process. It is precisely the continuing reality of the imperial dynamic that a post-colonial reading exposes. For Latin America, the hegemonic spread of global economy and culture is a significant threat to its modes of cultural location, but, just as significantly, globalism can be seen as a direct legacy of the process of Eurocentrism begun several centuries ago.

We can view globalization as either the dynamic operation of nation-states or the operation of a single world system (or a combination of the two). Clearly, while nations are still the principal actors within the global political order, corporations are recognized as the dominant agents in the world economy. The question remains: What is the function of the local in this structure? A *testimonio* such as *Let Me Speak!* by Domatila Barrios de Chungara, provides a rich site for a post-colonial analysis, because it demonstrates the way in which individual lives are affected by a global system of capital initiated as the economy of the empire of modernity. This novel is amenable to Marxist and feminist readings, but an understanding of the colonial roots of the system which now appears worldwide helps to explain the racially based cycle of oppression and poverty which presents itself as the Bolivian economy. Common opinion, she says, is that '"Bolivia is immensely rich, but its inhabitants are just beggars." And that's the truth because Bolivia is dominated by the multinational corporations that control my country's economy' (1978: 20).

Chungara's anger is familiar, but she is the victim of a system begun four centuries ago. Immanuel Wallerstein's world system theory compellingly asserts that the capitalist system has been *the* world economic system since the sixteenth century and that one cannot talk about economies in terms of the nation-state, nor of 'society' in the abstract, nor of 'stages' of development, because each society is affected by, indeed, is a part of, the capitalist world economy (Wallerstein, 1974b:391). The proposition of one world capitalist system in operation since the sixteenth century radically affects how we view not only world economics but national politics, class, ethnicity and international relations in general. The theory has no place for local transformations or political change, but it is a useful critique of the historicist idea of a nation's economic growth, particularly in its approach to the economies of Latin America.

One traditional Marxist view of economic development sees all economies as passing through a series of stages, so it would see these economies as existing at a pre-bourgeois, pre-industrialized stage of development. However, world system theory holds that these economies are already a part of the capitalist world system; they are not an earlier stage of a transition to industrialization, but are undeveloped because they are 'peripheral, raw-material producing' areas, on the margins of, and exploited by, the industrialized world. Thus economies such as Bolivia's are undeveloped, not because they are at any early stage of industrialization, but because they are marginalized by the world system. Similarly, we can say that Latin America is not at a stage of development which has left the need for post-colonial analysis behind, but that its cultural productions are a lingering consequence of its imperial history; it still lies at the edges of the world system.

The imperialism of the capitalist system maintains its energy through the same kinds of rhetoric of exclusion that drive the imperial project. The miners, the peasants, all those struggling against capitalist exploitation, are invariably Indians. The Bolivian situation is a classic example of the centripetal and global system of capital which continues to marginalize and exploit those on the periphery, but *Let Me Speak!* reveals the limitations of Wallerstein's theory. The lives of individuals, and particularly their taking control of the discursive tools of the dominant powers, can effect a transformation in the local effects of the world system and ultimately in the world system itself. Capitalism is a radical example of the globalizing impetus in modernity – what happens in a local neighbourhood is likely to be influenced by factors operating at an indefinite distance away, but equally, the local community can take hold of the global influence and transform it to local uses.

Strategies of transformation in Latin American cultures

The key dynamic of post-colonial discourse, one which affects the survival of local communities within global culture, is that of transformation. In particular, the historical experience of colonization has resulted in the mechanics of a transformative appropriation of modernity by colonized societies. Such transformation is *transcultural*; that is, not only are local events affected by the operation of global factors, such as world money and commodity markets, but the global economy of representation is itself affected by processes of local transformation. Furthermore, this dialectic does not generally occur at the level of the nation-state, an entity which is itself firmly incorporated into global systems of power.

There are many strategies of transformation in Latin America cultures. These strategies come under the rubric of a process I call 'interpolation' (Ashcroft, 1995), in which the colonized culture interpolates the dominant discourse in order to transform it in ways that release the representation of local realities. The appropriation of language, the utilization of discursive systems of representation such as literature or history, the entering and taking over of systems such as economics or politics, are all examples of the colonized culture taking the dominant forms and making them 'bear the burden' of a different experience, as Chinua Achebe says of the English language. Post-colonial strategies focus on the political and historical reality of colonialism and are directed at transforming its discourses and institutions. Individual modes of resistance and transformation may have particular local exigencies, such as the oppression of Bolivian miners. But there is an epistemological substrate to the discursive dominance of colonialism which affects all colonized societies within the world system.

To represent modernity as a major revolution in the social life of European, and hence world society at a particular time in history, a view which only came about in the Enlightenment, is to employ the historical consciousness which is a characteristic of modernity itself. Modernity may be better represented by those discontinuities which signify the most radical divisions between the modern and the pre-modern and which had the profoundest effect on 'pre-modern' societies, namely, the separation of time and space, the loosening of social relations from the prominence of locality, and the 'reflexive ordering and re-ordering of those social relations in terms of continual inputs of knowledge' (Giddens, 1990: 17). Post-colonial transformation, which is directed at the engagement with and reorientation of colonizing discourses, is at base an engagement with the deepest reorientations of modernity, whether the colonized societies are pre-modern or not. It is not only 'traditional' societies which employ these strategies, rather it is modernity which has constructed them as sites of contention within the post-colonial world.

The sites of post-colonial engagement which appear the most contentious are those which stem from the most radical shift in modern consciousness, the shift in the consciousness of time, because this reorientation generated the most disorienting features of colonial regulatory power. These were the emptying of time and space by separating them from location, and the 'disembedding' of social relations from locality, which resulted in the 'lifting out of social relations from local contexts of interaction and their restructuring across indefinite spans of time and space' (Giddens, 1990: 21). Indeed, the global change in the concept of a world itself is related in some way to this revolution in modern thought. The most profound disruption, therefore, of pre-modern social life was not the military destruction wreaked by colonial invasion, nor the importation of disease nor the imposition of colonial language nor the depredations of colonial administrations, for all their devastating effects . . . but the invention of the mechanical clock.

This one invention and the associated Gregorian calendar embody the universal power of European expansion, the hegemony of the capitalist world system and the most powerful and regulatory discourses of imperialism. The extent of these effects upon the rest of the world has been extraordinary: the mapping of the world; the naming and regulation of distant lands and the dislocating power of colonial language this represented; the surveillance of the colonized; the development of systematic education, the erection of imperialism's cultural binarism with its invention of race, of cannibalism and primitivism, and its distinction between the spirituality and transcendence of Europe and the materiality and primitivism of the periphery. All these represent modes of imperial control which in turn have generated strategies of resistance and transformation in Latin American cultural production.

Three sites of cultural change – language, place and history – situate perhaps the most profoundly complex interchanges of cultural formation and transformation. In many respects the key to these strategies lies in the use of language. A persistent argument of ethnocentric resistance is that to speak in the colonizer's language is to remain colonized, but an equally persistent argument of post-colonial writers is that the language may be appropriated for the writer's own purposes, its rhythms and syntax changed to correspond to a local idiom. This is the position taken by Angel Rama in *Transculturacion narrativa en America Latin* (1982). In this book he adapts Cuban anthropologist Fernando Ortiz's conceptualization of local Latin American culture as a 'transculturation' or *neoculturacion* of metropolitan models to the task of generalizing the literary phenomenon of neo-regionalism, represented by authors such as Rulfo, Arguedes, Guimaraes Rosa and Marquez. *Neoculturacion* is a more global term for the operation of the post-colonial strategies of appropriation and interpolation. This happens at various levels and in virtually every form of cultural discourse, particularly literature, but nowhere more powerfully than in the medium of *testimonio*.

Latin America is not only the beginning of modern Europe's self-representation; it is also the site of the most powerful post-colonial textual production of modern times: *testimonio*. The *testimonio* of indigenous groups is a relatively uncontentious subject for a post-colonial analysis, as we have seen. But I want to suggest that the real relevance of such analysis to Latin America emerges in that engagement with modern time consciousness and its effects, which occurs in a great range of social groups – mestizo or Ladino, urban or peasant, bourgeois or working class. One example is Juan Rulfo, who is a much more contentious case for a post-colonial analysis. A canonical figure, he is legendary in Latin American literary studies, a formative figure whose brief career is credited with penetrating 'by sheer force of poiesis into the epical and even mythical unconscious of peasant Mexico' (Larsen, 1990: 51). Rulfo is often credited with modernist innovation, his *Pedro Paramo* 'a bold excursion into modern techniques of writing' (Translator's introduction, Rulfo 1967: ix), but his post-coloniality becomes apparent through the medium of Angel Rama's use of the concept of transculturation. Reading Rulfo's use of language in *Pedro Paramo* (1955) and *The Burning Plains*, Rama shows how language becomes the site of a conflict between the colonizing modernity of the language and the inflection of a localized place.

> The author has become reintegrated with the linguistic community and speaks from within it, with unimpeded use of its idiomatic resources. . . . Here we have the phenomenon of 'neoculturation,' to use Ortiz's term. If the principles of textual unification and the construction of a literary language of exclusively aesthetic invention can be seen as corresponding to the rationalizing spirit of modernity, by compensation the linguistic perspective that takes up this principle restores a regional world view and prolongs its validity in a form yet richer and more interiorized than before. It thus expands the original world view in a way that is better adapted, authentic, artistically solvent, and, in fact, modernized – but without destruction of identity. (Larsen, 1990: 56–7).

The perception of Rulfo's 'reintegration with the linguistic community', speaking 'from within it', is a metaphoric and essentialist description of language which would be better expressed metonymically. Rulfo does not so much speak from within local idioms as metonymically signify the local in his language variation. The fact that Rulfo's language does not actually correspond to the speech patterns and narrative forms of Jaliscan country folk (*ibid*.: 54) is immaterial to the metonymic operation of the language variation, which inscribes not authentic identity but metonymic difference. Rama's analysis is nevertheless very much in the nature of a post-colonial reading because the use of language by a Spanish speaker is seen to be adaptable to modes of reinscription of the local creating a metonymic gap in which the difference of the local can be imagined.

Transculturation in Rama's formulation represents the appropriation of the dominant language for the purpose of reinscribing place, which Rama refers to as the 'regional world view'. The primacy of place in pre-modern settings has been largely destroyed by the separation of time and space and the 'disembedding' of social groups from the significance of locality. The process of 're-embedding' is very clear in Native American *testimonio*, but place remains a significant site of contention in modern colonial cultures as well. Rulfo's writing demonstrates how a settler culture invents a language which re-invents place. An 'appropriation' of language such as Rulfo's metonymically links the language to place in a way which re-invents it in the process of reinscribing it. The separation of time and space which is central to modernity is redressed metonymically by the use of language in this way which reinscribes the concept of local difference. Crucially, this is not a feature of a clash between a pre-modern culture and a modern discourse. Colonialism embeds the cultural anxiety attending its emptying out of local space, and this becomes a site of contention in a range of colonized societies.

Rulfo may seem, to some, an odd representative of the post-colonial in Latin America. Yet his work reveals that the operation of the transformative strategies of post-colonial discourse, strategies which engage the deepest disruptions of modernity, are not limited to the recently colonized, nor to the pre-modern societies who are still the most marginalized victims of modernization. Post-colonial strategies are those set in motion by the huge effects, both material and discursive, of colonization, no matter how distant the event. This is because colonialism is the militant material working of European modernity, the repercussions and contradictions of which are still in evidence in the global structure of neo-colonial domination.

The future of Latin American may not be free from such neo-colonial dominance, but the USA is itself the second largest Latino nation in the world after Mexico. No other fact demonstrates so clearly the transcultural possibilities of 'post-colonial' transformation. The world does not divide simply into 'us' and 'them' as Edward Said remarks: 'The phoney idea of a paranoid frontier separating 'us' from 'them' – which is a repetition of the old sort of orientalist model' (Sprinker, 1992: 233). 'We' are in 'them' and 'they' are in 'us'. In the case of Latin America 'we' are also 'in the US'. The 'paranoid' border between the USA and Latin America, both geographical and cultural, is demonstrably one of the most porous in the world. Though the empire may have changed hands, the transcultural strategies of Latin American cultures offer a clear example of the transformative energies of post-colonial societies.

Notes

1. I refer here to Giddens' theory of the 'disembedding' of time and place advanced in *The Consequences of Modernity* (1990). The universalization of time through the inventions of the clock and the calendar 'disembedded' time from its relationship with place. Although the transformation of modernity engaged by post-colonial discourse involves an appropriation of dominant notions of time and space, it often reinstalls (by various means, such as transporting local experiences of temporality into literary and testimonial texts) the importance of the connections between time and place, thus 'refilling' space emptied by modernity.

CHAPTER 3

'Primitive and wingless'

The colonial subject as child

The central strategy in transformations of colonial culture is the seizing of self-representation. This is why post-colonial theory regards the phenomenon of culture as so important, for underlying all economic, political and social resistance is the struggle over representation which occurs in language, writing and other forms of cultural production. So powerful is the effect of colonial representation that it can become, as Said forcefully demonstrates in *Orientalism*, the way in which the colonized see themselves, and this can effect all social and political interchange. Orientalism remains the classic instance of this discursive construction. The particular 'textual attitude' of the Orientalist produces an influential version of 'knowledge' which achieves the status of truth by virtue of the cultural power of the knower. Such 'truth' becomes an infinite rehearsal of tropes such as exoticism, mystery, cunning, deviousness, which all place the Oriental as the other of Europe.

However, while it has become the classic demonstration of power/knowledge, Orientalism can be seen as a useful model for a wide range of imperial control over representation. The habitual tropes characteristic of a particular textual attitude come to stand, virtually, as received truth, as knowledge of the world. Long before the surge of Orientalist discourse in the late eighteenth century, the colonized other was represented in terms of tropes which invariably justified imperial rule, no matter how benign it saw itself to be. In this process, no trope has been more tenacious and more far-reaching than that of the child. When we examine the historical power of imperial discourse to represent the other, what strikes us is not so much the ubiquity, the totality and hegemony of that process as its astonishing capacity to mask its own contradictions. The trope of the child, both explicitly and implicitly, offered a unique tool for managing the profound ambivalence of imperialism, because it absorbed and suppressed the contradictions of imperial discourse itself.

As a child, the colonial subject is both inherently evil and potentially good, thus submerging the moral conflict of colonial occupation and locating in the child of empire a naturalization of the 'parent's' own contradictory impulses for exploitation and nurture. The child, at once both other and same, holds in balance the contradictory tendencies of imperial rhetoric: authority is held in balance with nurture; domination with enlightenment; debasement with idealization; negation with affirmation; exploitation with education; filiation with affiliation. This ability to absorb contradiction gives the binary parent/child an inordinately hegemonic potency.

The child became important to the discourse of empire because the invention of childhood *itself* in European society was coterminous with the invention of that other notion of supreme importance to imperialism: race. Jo-Ann Wallace claims that 'an idea of "the child" is a *necessary precondition* of imperialism – that is, that the West had to invent for itself "the child" before it could think a specifically colonialist imperialism' (1994: 176). But it was the cross-fertilization between the concepts of childhood and primitivism that enabled these terms to emerge as mutually important concepts in imperial discourse. The eighteenth century, which saw the emergence of the child as a philosophical concept, also saw the emergence of race as a category of physical and biological variation. Whereas 'race' could not exist without racism, that is, the need to establish a hierarchy of difference, the idea of the child dilutes the hostility inherent in that taxonomy and offers a 'natural' justification for imperial dominance over subject peoples.

In his book *The Future of Science*, written in 1848, Ernest Renan outlined the principles of the philological study which were to occupy his career. Posing six questions for the philologer – the ethnographic; chronological; geographical; physiological; psychological and historical – he includes under the psychological question the need to apprehend 'the condition of mankind and of the human intellect at the first stages of its existence' (Renan, 1891: 150). In order to understand those races of mankind at the earliest stages of development, such an investigator

> must be thoroughly versed in the experimental study of the child and the first exercise of its reason, in the experimental study of the savage, consequently he must be extensively acquainted with the literature of the great travellers, and as much as possible have travelled himself among the primitive peoples which are fast disappearing from the face of the earth. (*ibid.*)

The connection between the child and the savage in Renan's mind is focused in the common and growing assumption – soon to be cemented in nineteenth-century thinking by Darwin – that the races existed on a hierarchy of evolutionary stages. In a prophetic assertion, he says, 'I am convinced that there is a science of the origins of mankind' (*ibid.*), and in his formulation the very psychology of the child and the savage in such a 'science' is interchangeable.

When we examine the theory of the most influential Western thinkers of the post-Enlightenment revolution – Darwin, Marx and Freud – we discover the almost intransigent persistence of this link between childhood and primitivism. Marrouchi (1991: 56 *passim*) points out how childhood innocence which served as 'the prototype of primitive communism is one of Marx's main contributions to the theory of progress, which he conceptualises as a movement from prehistory to history and from infantile or low-level communism to adult communism'. Similarly, he argues that a 'less influential cultural role was played by some of Freud's early disciples who went out to "primitive" societies to pursue the homology between primitivism and infantility' (*ibid.*: 58).

One of the most influential outcomes of this link was the emergence in the late nineteenth century of the concept of 'development' by which non-European states were to be permanently constituted as lacking. While the term 'development' came into the English language in the eighteenth century with its original meaning conveying a sense of unfolding over time, development understood as a preoccupation of public and international policy to improve welfare and to produce governable subjects is of much more recent provenance (Watts, 1993). The two meanings of the term are connected by the link between primitivism and infantility and the need for 'maturation' and 'growth' in both. Development not only linked the child and the primitive but marked the transformation from colonial empire into 'developing world'. Development, a concept of the post-war (post-independence) period, manages to encapsulate the precise ambivalence which imperialism contained by means of the dualism of child and primitive. It is generally recognized that due to their deep Eurocentrism and dismissal of the colonized world as 'lacking', Western development models have all but completely collapsed.

This link between childhood and primitivism persists to the present day. In a recent introduction to language, a chapter on the origin of language, a topic which continues to fascinate linguists because it cannot be anything but pure speculation, demonstrates how the link between childhood and primitivism persists:

> The first articulate word pronounced by a child is often something like *da, ma, na, ba, ga* or *wa*. . . . When the child first attempts to copy words used by adults, he at first tends to produce words of this form, so that 'grandfather' may be rendered as *gaga*, 'thank you' as *tata*, and 'water' as *wawa*. This explains why, in so many languages, the nursery words for mother and father are *mama* or *dada* or *baba* or something similar: there is no magic inner connexion [*sic*] between the idea of parenthood and words of this form: these just happen to be the first articulated sounds that the child makes. . . . *Such words may also have been the first utterances of primitive man.* . . .
>
> The languages of primitive peoples, and the history of languages in literate times, may throw some light on the origin of language by suggesting what elements in it are the most archaic. (Barber, 1964: 25; emphasis is added)

Where did this persistent link between primitivism and infantility come from? We can see in the invention of childhood itself in post-medieval society the very factors which make it so amenable to imperial rhetoric. Childhood (that is, the idea of the child as ontologically different from an adult) only emerged in Western society after the invention of the printing press, when the subsequent spread of literacy had created a clear division between child and adult which could only be bridged by a more systematic form of education (Ariés, 1962: 47). In the same way, for imperialism, the idea of literacy and education, even where these were imposed on already literate societies, represented a defining separation between the civilized and the barbarous nations. We can see in the gap between childhood and adulthood created by the emergence of literacy in post-medieval culture a precise corollary of the gap between the imperial centre and the illiterate, barbarous, childlike races of empire. The strategies of surveillance, correction and instruction which lie at the heart of the child's education transfer effortlessly into the disciplinary enterprise of empire.

Just as 'childhood' began in European culture with the task of learning how to read, so education and literacy become crucial in the imperial expansion of Europe, establishing ideological supremacy, inculcating the values of the colonizer, and separating the 'adult' colonizing races from the 'childish' colonized. Literacy and education reinforce the existence of the very gap they are designed to close, the gap between colonizer and colonized, civilized and primitive; in short, the gap between adult and child. They do this because education is always on the terms of an adult consciousness to which the colonial subject can never aspire. Literature, for instance, the most potent and evocative representation of European values, becomes a supreme vehicle for withholding cultural adulthood at the very moment it is offered.

While childhood and primitivism developed interchangeably, the concept of the child became of great importance to the imperial enterprise because it actually embodied a contradiction which enabled it to absorb the contradictions of imperial rule. This contradiction becomes most explicit in the ideas of Locke and Rousseau. Locke's greatest influence on the theory of childhood was his idea that at birth the mind is a blank *tabula rasa*, a state of affairs which placed a heavy responsibility on parents and schoolmasters for what is eventually written on the mind (Locke, 1693), particularly because the sense inherited from the Puritans was that 'though his body be small, yet he hath a [wrongdoing] heart, and is altogether inclined to evil,' (Illick, 1974: 316–17). The concept of a *tabula rasa* has been of great significance in the imperial enterprise because the negation of colonial space was a necessary preparation for the civilizing processes of colonization. When Captain Cook declared Australia to be a *Terra Nullius*, he was making an explicit geographical use of Locke's notion of the *tabula rasa*, a use which remains important to the imperial process to the present day, because of its potential, its unformedness, its amenability to inscription, despite its inherent menace.

When H. M. Stanley looked west towards the Congo in 1877 he sent to the *New York Herald* a report which remains a consummate example of the ambivalence of imperial negation and desire: 'The largest half of Africa one wide enormous blank – a region of fable and mystery – a continent of dwarfs and cannibals and gorillas, through which the great river flowed on its unfulfilled mission to the Atlantic' (Spurr, 1994: 92). Stanley sees an absence which is also a region of imagination and desire, a *tabula rasa* on which imperialism can fulfil its mission. It is at the same time the uninscribed, a land of fabulous possibility, and a land of the barbarous and sub-human. The unformedness of colonial space is the geographic metaphor of the savage mind; both consciousness and space form the childlike innocence which is the natural surface of imperial inscription. This process of inscription is not merely metaphoric, because it is in writing itself that place is constructed out of empty space, and it is in the control of representation and the dissemination of this control in literacy and education that the colonial subject is subdued.

The polar opposite of Locke's view of the child in the eighteenth century is that of Rousseau, who saw the child as important because childhood is the stage of life when man most closely approximates the 'state of nature'. Whereas Locke sees the child as a tablet, an unwritten book, Rousseau sees it as a wild plant, and the child and primitive man are explicitly linked in his philosophy. Of course Rousseau was not the originator of the noble savage concept; Montaigne's essay 'On cannibals' written in 1580 (Florio, 1603: 217–32) suggested that the cannibals live in an Edenic state of purity and simplicity 'still governed by natural laws and very little corrupted by our own' (Cheyfitz, 1991). However it is in Rousseau's writing that the unspoiled child and the natural man come together as interchangeable and mutually supportive concepts. The innocent and unspoiled state of colonial space co-exists with its character as a *tabula rasa* in the literature of empire. In Haggard's *Allan Quartermain* the adventurers discover a people in a feudal monarchy resembling Britain's own days of infancy. They 'know nothing about steam, electricity or gun powder, and mercifully for themselves nothing about printing or the penny post' (Haggard, 1887: 177). Idealized though this state may be, it becomes the perfect surface for the inscription of imperial adventure and maturity.

The sense of childhood as a time of unformed nature and almost unlimited potential comes to characterize narrative perceptions of the empire's own project of expansion and growth. It is the idyllic and uncontaminated nature of colonial space which makes it, for Rider Haggard, the domain of *youthful* adventure. As Gail Ching-Liang Low points out, 'because childhood represents a world of innocence uncorrupted by age and civilization; the boy child is necessarily the only figure capable of inheriting or founding, this blank new (colonial) world' (Low, 1995: 45). In Haggard, there is an identification with the (boy) child which firmly privileges the innocence and potentiality of the colonial experience itself. In this Rousseauean use of the child the exploitation of imperialism is even more firmly suppressed. The adult man remembering himself as a boy engages in a narrative of enchantment which may be read forward as inheritance, or backward as memory and history. This simultaneous reading backward and forward 'both recovers childhood experiences and produces a dream which enables the boy/man and the man/boy to secure an inheritance of patriarchy and empire '(*ibid.*). The romance of youthful adventure was transformed, in the work of J. A. Froude, into a hope for racial regeneration. Overseas colonies could be the means of regenerating the English race which might 'renew its mighty youth, bring forth as many millions as it would and still have means to breed and rear them strong as the best which she had produced in her early prime' (Froude, 1886: 8–9).

The amenability of imperial adventure to a recovery of childhood was intensified by the Industrial Revolution's profound attack upon childhood itself, an attack mounted by subordinating the concept of the child as one who could be educated into adulthood, to one who could provide a source of cheap labour. Charles Dickens' reputation as an exposer of the reign of terror inflicted on the children of the poor by the Industrial Revolution is well established, but the Industrial Revolution could not destroy the concept of childhood because this was kept alive by the upper and middle classes. The concomitant growth in the Victorian idealization of the child and the brutalization of the actual children of the working class is a contradiction manifestly suppressed within the discourse of childhood. Indeed, one of the prime effects of that decay produced by the Industrial Revolution was the desire for moral, physical and racial regeneration which underlay the imperial adventures of Rider Haggard, Kipling and Stevenson.

Locke's metaphor of the child as a blank page, an unwritten book, makes the explicit connection between adulthood and print, for civilization and maturity are printed on the tablet of the child's mind. For him the child is an unformed person who, through literacy, education, reason, self-control and shame, may be made into a civilized adult. For Rousseau, the unformed child possesses capacities for candour, understanding, curiosity and spontaneity which must be preserved or rediscovered. In the tension between these two views we find encapsulated the inherent contradiction of imperial representations of the colonial subject.

Both views, however, justified the paternal actions of imperial formation, because the blank slate of colonial space, like the *tabula rasa* of the unformed child, or the innocence of nature, is an absence of meaning itself. Neither the child nor the colonial subject can have access to meaning outside the processes of civilization and education which bring them into being, even *when* that meaning is one of an idyllic pre-formed, pre-industrial innocence. Until they are 'inscribed' by being brought into inscription, introduced to literacy and education, they cannot be 'read' in any meaningful way. The child, then, signifying a blank slate, an innocent of nature, a subject of exotic possibility and moral instruction, as well as a barbarous and unsettling primitive, suggests an almost endlessly protean capacity for inscription and meaning.

The erasure of colonial space also involves a negation of pre-colonial history, as we see when Hegel notoriously employs the link between childhood and primitivism to negate the history of Africa:

> Africa proper, as far as History goes back, has remained – for all purposes of connection with the rest of the World – shut up; it is the Gold-land compressed within itself – the land of childhood, which lying beyond the day of self conscious history, is enveloped in the dark mantle of Night. (Hegel 1956: 91)

Africa, like the consciousness of the individual African, is locked in the period of childhood before the dawn of imperial discourse, its erasure a necessary preliminary for the inscription of world reality by history. Such is the power of this discourse that today, as Dipesh Chakrabarty says, all histories, whether 'Chinese' or 'Kenyan', 'tend to become variations on a master narrative that could be called "the history of Europe"' (1992: 1). Africa can only be brought out of the dark mantle of night when it is brought into the history of Europe. Childhood, then, imbues the negation of colonial history with the possibility of an adult-hood which will never come in any form other than an image of the West.

The child and imperialism

The flourishing children's literature of the Victorian period is a rich demonstration of the suppression and absorption of dominant class and race attitudes. Jo-Ann Wallace demonstrates how the 1984 Puffin Classic edition of Charles Kingsley's *The Water-Babies* 1863 not only abridges the text to remove race and class references offensive to contemporary tastes, but more importantly operates to 'de-historicize and depoliticize the figure of "the child" and to put under erasure a history of strategic colonialist investment in the figure' (Wallace, 1994: 182). Furthermore, *The Water-Babies*, like Kingsley's lectures at the time, argues for the salvation of children for the sake of colonial imperialism, but a mark of the success of imperial rhetoric is its success in universalizing the concept of the child. Childhood becomes a universal 'unmarked by class, place or history' (*ibid.*).

The effect of this is to lend a remarkably powerful ambiguity to representations of race, as the incorporation of the figure of the child became ubiquitous in Victorian representations of empire and its rela-tions with its subject peoples. These representations borrowed their imagery of subordination 'from an area in which subordination was legitimized – that of the family' (Griffiths, 1983: 173). Talk in terms of dependence, of development, of benevolent and paternal supervision and of the 'child' or 'childlike' qualities of the 'primitive' peoples, mirrored the clear and unquestioned hierarchical structure of power relations which pertained to the middle-class Victorian family.

The link between childhood and savagery is found everywhere in the post-Darwinian writings of Victorian travellers and explorers. In 1872, Richard Burton wrote that the tribesman of Eastern Africa 'seems to belong to one of those childish races which, never rising to man's estate, fall like worn-out links from the great chain of animated nature' (1872: 280). Such people were, he contended, the slaves of impulse, wilful passion and instinct. The ambiguity of the Africans' childlike primitivism was firmly located, for the Victorians, in a supposed lack of sexual restraint, which was as much a sign of a dangerous and unbridled savagery as it was that of an undisciplined, 'pre-civilized' immaturity. It was in this context, suggests Christine Bolt, that 'allegations of the childishness of African peoples were brought into play' (1971: 137). Lionel Phillips, who described the South African 'Kaffirs' as a 'complex mixture of treachery and cunning, fierceness and brutality, childlike simplicity and quick-wittedness', concluded that such people 'require a master, and respect justice, and firmness: generosity is a quality they do not understand' (cited in Bolt, 1971: 137). The geographer T. Griffith Taylor developed a slightly more complex racial typology which distinguished the 'black', 'white' and 'yellow' races in terms of maturity:

> The childlike behaviour of the Negro has often been referred to as a primitive characteristic. The white races are versatile, gay, and inventive – all attributes of youth. The yellow races are grave, meditative, and melancholic – which possibly indicates their more mature position in the evolution of races. (1919: 300)

Taylor's theory was the product of a kind of moral climatology which linked ethnic constitution and racial character to climatic circumstance. Childhood, laziness and indolence were the products of an enervating climate, while maturity, industry and drive developed from the more healthy European conditions.

Needless to say, such attitudes became strategic in the administration of colonial possessions. In his speech in support of the Glen Grey Bill in 1894, Cecil Rhodes announced to the House of Assembly in Cape Town that:

> As to the question of voting, we say that the natives are in a sense citizens, but not altogether citizens – they are still children. . . .
>
> Now I say the natives are children. They are just emerging from barbarism. . . .
>
> To us annexation was an obligation, whereas to the natives it will be a positive relief, for they will be freed from a seething cauldron of barbarian atrocities. (Rhodes 1900: 380, 383, 396)

What we may find most interesting in these unsurprising sentiments of Rhodes is the ease with which the imagery shifts from childhood to barbarity. Fatherhood and despotism were not regarded as sitting uneasily together and the ambivalent nature of the child 'altogether disposed to evil' (as Locke would have it), a subject in need of control and instruction, becomes even more firmly situated in the project of imperial control.

The connection between filiation and authority in colonial rhetoric and practice, the continual and virtually obsessive debasement of the colonized subject, arises, suggests David Spurr, 'not simply from fear and the recognition of difference but also, on another level, from a desire for and identification with the Other which must be resisted' (1994: 80). The child, then, is the image which normalizes this threatening identification with the other because its ambivalent and 'naturally' subordinate status, while serving as the pretext for imperial conquest and domination, is also that which continually mediates the tension between identity and difference: the child is both pre-formed self and repudiated other. This is precisely the dilemma Marlowe encounters when he looks into the savagery of the heart of darkness: 'what thrilled you was just the thought of their humanity – like yours – the thought of your remote kinship with this wild and passionate uproar' (Conrad, 1902: 69).

The child as colonial 'abject'

Hegel's identification of childhood within the 'dark mantle of night' rather than at the 'dawn' of civilization alerts us to the radical instability of the metaphor of childhood. In this tension between unformed self and repudiated other, the child embodies the crisis of colonial subjectivity which we can conceptualize in Kristeva's notion of the 'abject' (1982). The abject and its variants, such as filth, defilement, incest and sin, mark the boundary of the self and therefore constitute the limits of the speaking subject:

> The abject is neither the subject nor the object. . . . It represents the crisis of the subject . . . insofar as it would not yet be, or would no longer be separated from the object. Its limits would no longer be established. It would be constantly menaced by possible collapse into an object. It would lose definition. It is a question then, of a precarious state in which the subject is menaced by the possibility of collapsing into a chaos of indifference. (Kristeva, 1983: 39)

It is in its precarious existence somewhere between the subject and object of the parental gaze that the child seems to represent the crisis of abjection. Although we do not think of the child as being involved in the excessive repudiation directed at the other by imperial discourse, the image of the child in fact offers a filiative myth by which this repudiation can be justified; for it is always a repudiation of the not yet formed, the primitive but always imminently possible subject; it is a repudiation in the guise of paternity. Yet it is even more subtle than this, for the colonial child is not simply the abject, but occupies that interstitial space in which there is a constant slippage between abjection and subjectivity.

The central concept of colonial abjection is *cannibalism* – the absolute sign of the other in imperial thought. It was invented by Christopher Columbus, three centuries before the invention of race, and it is the central trope of the colonial myth of savagery. A century after Columbus, Montaigne attempted to articulate its contradictions by describing the childlike innocence of the cannibal, but it is in *Robinson Crusoe* that the slippage becomes clearer. When Crusoe saves Friday from being killed and eaten he is appalled to discover Friday's own base instincts:

> I found *Friday* had still a hankering Stomach after some of the Flesh, and was still a Cannibal in his Nature; but I discovered so much Abhorrence at the very thought of it . . . I had by some means let him know, that I would kill him if he offer'd it. (Defoe, 1719: 150)

Crusoe feels justified in killing Friday rather than allow him to indulge in an act which breaches the bounds of humanity itself. Thus at this point abjection (cannibalism) and death are contiguous in the mind of the colonist. However, Crusoe finds Friday undeserving of any suspicion and reflects:

> But I needed have none of all this Precaution; for never Man had a more faithful, loving, sincere Servant, than *Friday* was to me; without Passions, Sullenness or Designs, perfectly oblig'd and engag'd; his very Affections were ty'd to me, like those of a Child to a Father; and I dare say he would have sacrific'd his Life for the saving of mine upon any occasion whatsoever. (*ibid.*: 151)

As a child, Friday is prepared to give his life willingly. The interaction here between cannibalism, childhood and death is a complex demonstration of the ambivalence of subjectivity which childhood itself is designed to resolve. The child, like the abject, is constructed at the limits of subjectivity itself, the primitive, child of empire inhabiting the liminal space at which subjectivity and death intersect. There is a constant slippage between abjection and filiation; that is why Kipling can refer to the native in 'The White Man's Burden' as 'half devil and half child' (1899: 323). However, most importantly, this process shows that rather than a site of formation, the child is, in imperial rhetoric, already the site of *transformation* as it slips between abjection and subjectivity, and this is critical to post-colonial interventions into the trope.

An example of the tension between the child and the 'cannibal' can be found in *The Tempest* where Prospero's child, Miranda, adopts her father's revulsion towards Caliban, Prospero's slave. Here the clarity of the split between the child and the monster is complicated by the fact that Miranda herself, by virtue of her subordination to Prospero's discourse, and the commodification of her virginity by Prospero's ambition, is as much Prospero's subject as Caliban (see this volume,

Chapter 6). Furthermore, it is clear that, despite the slave's monstrosity, the relationship between Prospero and Caliban has had the seeds of filial dependence: 'When thou cam'st first,/ Thou strok'st me and made much of me' (I, ii, 333–4), says Caliban. The apparent lack of contradiction in the figures of child and primitive in this play can be seen to be a historical consequence of the uncontradictory and openly exploitative relationship between Britain and the Americas in the period of Eliza-bethan exploration, but Miranda, the child, embodies the ambivalence of the colonial relationship that will become all the more contradictory as the rhetoric of Britain's civilizing mission increases. At this formative period in Britain's imperial expansion she is already the site of an ambivalent and transformative relationship between the empire and its subjects.

In *Black Skin, White Masks*, Fanon makes the point that the treatment of the black as a child stems from the myth that the Negro is 'the link between monkey and man – meaning, of course, white man' (1952: 30). The treatment of the Negro as a child is the natural outgrowth of an assumption of black primitivism. 'A white man addressing a Negro behaves exactly like an adult with a child and starts smirking, whisper-ing, patronizing, cozening. It is not one white man I have watched but hundreds . . . [including] physicians, policemen, employers' (*ibid.*: 31). In Fanon's view it is the internalizing of this relationship which leads to the pathology of the colonial subject, in turn leading to the widespread appropriation of language and other dominant cultural forms as a form of parent identification.

The link between abjection and death is ubiquitous in imperial dis-course, for indeed such abjection is the condition which justifies various forms of genocide. This is why the image of the child becomes so powerful. For the child represses the liminal intersection of subjectivity and death and transforms the abject into a subject of change, which, in imperial rhetoric is always a sign of growth, maturity and development. This leads to a further dimension in the relationship between imperial adult and colonial child, the moral obligation expressed in the mythology of liberation.

This contiguity of filiation and abjection can be seen in a speech delivered by Teddy Roosevelt before he became President in 1901. 'The object lesson of expansion', he declared,

> is that peace must be brought about in the world's waste spaces. . . . Peace cannot be had until the civilized nations have expanded in some shape over the barbarous nations. . . . It is our duty toward the people living in barbarism to see that they are freed from their chains . . . and we can free them only by destroying barbarism itself. (Beale, 1956: 32, 34)

It is fascinating that we find in this consummate imperial exhortation the same tropes found in Stanley's description of Africa: blankness (the world's waste spaces); abjection (the barbarous nations); and exotic possibility (freed from their chains), all driven by the moral responsibility of paternity. Given its capitalist motives, the immensity of this fabrication is breathtaking, and the full force of its contradiction is invested in the sentence 'and we can free them only by destroying barbarism itself', which can only be achieved by putting them back into colonial chains.

How can imperialism manage to contain this huge and disabling contradiction? I believe it does so in the concept of paternity and the transfer of the disciplinary regime of education to the colonial subject. For dominance, adulthood, paternity is accompanied by its moral imperative, which hinges firmly on the dominance of the Anglo-Saxon race. The myth of the child therefore promises the development of the primitive unformed subject into the 'self' while at the same time maintaining that subject as the abject other, the object of imperial rule. The moral crusade of empire brings with it the critical experience of shame to the abject barbarous nations, for this is the condition which most clearly separates the childlike primitive from the adult, and manages to keep the shameful colonized subject in a position of abjection.[1] In these ways exploitation and debasement are continually suppressed and absorbed into the universal conditions of paternity and filiation.

Filiation and Affiliation have become very useful terms for describing the ways in which colonized societies are compliantly linked to imperial culture. These societies may replace filiative connections to indigenous cultural traditions with affiliations to the social, political and cultural institutions of empire. However, there is a different affiliative trajectory constantly at work in colonized societies, an implicit network of assumptions, values and expectations which continually places and replaces the colonized subject in a *filiative* relationship with the colonizer. Put simply, affiliation invokes an image of the imperial culture as a parent, linked in a filiative relationship with the colonized 'child'; empire may be the oppressor but she is still the mother. Thus, while filiation gives birth to affiliation, in colonized societies the reverse is also true. The affiliations with hegemonic culture continually reproduce the representation of the subject as the child of empire.

I mention this concept of Said's because the distinction between filiation and affiliation has often been misunderstood, with some colonies being referred to as 'filiative' and others as 'affiliative', thus forming a spurious distinction between 'inauthentic' and 'authentic' post-colonial societies; but the filiative construction of the colonized subject as a child of empire works in *all* colonies as a product of affiliation. It does this because the concept of the child is already deeply ambivalent, its exclusions no less complete for the effectiveness of its filiative metaphors. The child is primitive, pre-literate, educable, formed and forming in the image of the parent. There are no colonies which are primitive without being childlike in their amenability to instruction; there are no colonies which are sons and daughters of empire without being marginal, negated and debased to some extent. This is because the very existence of empire itself rests upon the security of its binary logic of centre and margin through which filiation and affiliation continually reproduce one another.

Post-colonial discourse and the child

What is the response of post-colonial societies to this ambivalence of abjection and filiation? This fits our broader enquiry into how post-colonial societies transform the tropes by which they are constituted as 'other' by imperial discourse. On the face of it, one would expect the reversal of the child trope and its replacement by images of adulthood, as regularly occurs in the early stages of nationalism, but this strategy is by no means the most successful form of counter-discourse. What we notice in the appropriation of the image of the child in post-colonial discourse is a familiar tension between what we might call 'nationalist' and more subtly heterogeneous responses to the 'parenthood' of empire. The post-colonial discussion of nationalism is extensive because this originary and most strategic phase of anti-colonial politics is invariably caught in the binarism of imperial control even while rejecting that control. In Derrida's terms, nationalism *reverses* the imperial binary without *erasing* it. Thus the nationalist governments of newly independent states have, time and again, simply inherited both the administrative infrastructure and the ideological dynamic of imperial control. This can often be the most damaging consequence of decolonization: sovereignty is *transferred* to the colonized without being *transformed*.

This tendency may be a key to understanding the inordinate importance of 'founding fathers' in colonial nationalisms: father figures such as Nehru, Kenyatta, Senghore, Nkrumah, Banda and Mandela (Ahluwalia, 1996: 46). The appropriation of the infrastructure, bureaucracy and class dynamic implicit in colonial administrations is accompanied by an appropriation of the mythology and representation of parenthood in the figure of the founding father. It may be the absence of such a figure in settler colonies which makes their post-colonial nationalisms so anxious, so pervasive and persistent. I will choose three examples – from Australia, Kenya and the Caribbean – to demonstrate that while they are each quite different in their cultural traditions and practices, they all share similar strategic responses to imperial interpellation, and similar problems in those responses. This is contentious because an assertion of similarity invariably draws the accusation of an eliding of cultural difference. However, post-colonial societies share strategies of resistance regardless of the radical specificity and differences between local cultures themselves.

The first scene finds Henry Lawson standing in his school yard as a boy, looking at the sun in the north in winter (1903: 16). He has discovered in a geography class that in winter the sun is supposed to be in the south. His textbook is meant for colonial Ireland, but, like the Royal Reader series, has been distributed throughout the empire. The teacher has explained the reason for the error but, to the young Lawson, it is not the geography text that is wrong but rather that *he is living in the wrong place*. Colonial space is negated in Lawson's classroom just as surely as it is in Stanley's view of Africa. Education for the settler colonial is an entry to a fractured and dissonant world, for this, the pathway from childhood to adulthood, shows that value and reality itself lie somewhere else, indeed this is the inscriptive function of colonial education. The nationalism of the 1990s in Australia is metonymized by the experience of the young Lawson; an attempt to secure his own body and the sun itself in place, to replace the alienated, abject body in real space.

This desire is itself deeply ambivalent, for as Lacan points out, the desire of the child for the mother is the desire to exist in the mother's gaze, and this is the metonym of desire itself. All desire is a metaphor for the *desire to be*. Such a desire underlies the entire principle of colonial nationalism; that which erects itself as a mode of oppositionality and resistance is in fact a construction of colonial desire. The nation desires its difference in the gaze of the *grande autre*, but that desire itself means that nationalism cannot be anything but the reproduction of empire, the reproduction of the mother. A fundamental insight of Said's *Orientalism* is that the colonized subject, whether oppositional or complicit, finds it difficult to construct its difference outside the terms of the binarism already established by imperial discourse. Such is the power of the orientalist or imperialist 'text'.

Indeed, the image of the child achieves a peculiar potency in Australia as an overt symbol of the nation, in repeated images of Australia itself as a child in the popular press, such as the little boy from Manly in the *Bulletin*. Two centuries after the first European landing, this characterization remains firm; Australia is still a 'young country'; but it is in the myth of the 'lost child' that the full weight of Australian displacement is encapsulated (see Pierce, 1999). Newspaper reports in the late nineteenth century and the novels of Henry Kingsley, Marcus Clarke, Joseph Furphy and the poetry of Henry Lawson seem obsessed by the story of the child who wanders away from the 'battlers' hut in the bush never to be found again. It is a myth which re-emerges in various forms in the twentieth century as well. This is because the child in the bush symbolizes so well the drama of colonial displacement, a sign of the vulnerability of a society dominated imaginatively, if not in reality, with the struggle for survival against the land it is trying to reinscribe with its own post-colonial reality. The child of this myth is the child of empire whether the story is appropriated by loyalists or nationalists, because its mythic drama is above all a drama of difference and possibility, a drama of emergence. The drama of the lost child narrates in mythic form the experience of Henry Lawson looking up from his textbook to the sun and feeling he is in the wrong place. Both these uses of the child find themselves locked in the subordinating gaze of empire.

The second scene finds Njoroge, the hero of Ngugi's novel *Weep Not, Child*, looking at a sign nailed to his schoolhouse wall by the Mau Mau, threatening to kill the headmaster if the school does not close. Njoroge represents Kenya itself, a child torn between empire and traditional culture, between Mau Mau resistance and colonial education. The first child of his family to go to school, Njoroge sees in the benefits of empire the very means of separation from the parent:

> Through all this, Njoroge was still sustained by his love for, and belief in education and his own role when the time came. . . . Only education could make something out of this wreckage. He became more faithful to his studies. He would one day use all his learning to fight the white man, for he would continue the work that his father had started. (Ngugi, 1964: 92–3)

Njoroge's determination to appropriate the discursive tools of empire is here motivated by his acceptance of the explicit racial binarism set up by imperialism. Behind this response is a sense of the separation of white and black which is explicated in Fanon's *Black Skin, White Masks* (1952), in JanMohamed's concept of the 'Manichean allegory' of empire (1983, 1985), or in Senghor's notion of '*Négritude*' (1966). In this sense Njoroge's opposition is much less complicated than Henry Lawson's, but using colonial education to resist colonial rule is just as problematic as using the imperial language itself; it might be seen to be an attempt to assert 'adulthood' by invoking the very binarism it is rejecting. This is the problem of *Négritude*, but it is also the problem of settler colony nationalism. Njoroge sees education as an access to liberation, which is the way it is presented by imperial discourse itself. Does this, then, implicate the post-colonial subject in imperial discourse in a way that suppresses opposition? Is Njoroge doomed to reproduce himself in the image of the empire? Does he represent the very danger Ngugi himself attempted to avoid by eventually refusing to write in English?

Ngugi might have agreed with Audre Lorde that 'the master's tools will never dismantle the master's house' (1981), or with Gayatri Spivak that 'the subaltern cannot speak' (1988); but, in fact, the activity of post-colonial intellectuals has demonstrated time and again that the most effective transformation of imperial control has been achieved by precisely that: the appropriation of the discursive tools of empire. This is where the binary logic of empire falters, for education, while it takes the child away from tradition, also gives the child the tools to reinscribe an equally ambivalent and hybrid, but assertive, post-colonial reality. Thus the child is launched into a future created by its seizing of the opportunity offered by empire.

The third scene also occurs in the classroom, when we find Jamaica Kincaid rereading Charles Kingsley's *Water-Babies*.

Once upon a time there was a little chimney sweep whose name was Tom. . . .

You, of course would have been very cold sitting there on a September night, without the least bit of clothes on your wet back; but Tom was a water-baby, and therefore felt cold no more than a fish. (1908: 20)

Here is a moment of interpellation even more powerful than Henry Lawson's geography text. Who is this 'you' called forth by the text, the young Antiguan girl who may never have seen a chimney, or the middle-class Victorian child reader? To whom are Kingsley's reformist sentiments directed? Surely not this hybrid subject who can have no part of the scheme of racial regeneration which *The Water-Babies* addresses. How evocatively this passage demonstrates the function of denying 'adulthood' at the moment it is offered.

The very exposure of this process of interpellation is a part of the counter-discursive activity of the text. Kincaid writes back to *The Water-Babies* to contest the power of that text to construct her while revealing its capacity to do so. 'I am primitive, wingless', she says, suggesting someone who is at the pupal stage of insect development and the pupil stage of education; speaking for colonial subjects all over the empire in their inscription by imperial discourse. By inserting herself into the action of the text as a reader, by articulating her childhood and potentiality, she undermines the power of empire to negate her subjectivity. Writing back to the canon, she unsettles its impervious presentation of universal humanity by exposing its contradictions. This ambivalence lying at the heart of imperial discourse and embedded in the image of the child becomes, in the post-colonial text, an empowering ambivalent (two-powered) capacity to *interpolate* subjectivity into the dominant discourse.

These three scenes, so very different culturally, are all wrestling with similar problems of imperial interpellation and discursive negation. Each focuses on the child as a sign of colonial subjectivity and its formation through education. Each uses a particular form of counter-discursive strategy; but each achieves its power by interpolating itself into the dominant discourse, with all the problems that this entails. Like most features of imperial rhetoric, the trope of the child provides a focus of resistance by intimating a different kind of cultural trajectory.

The disappearance of childhood

If child and empire are so deeply interrelated, what of the present 'post-imperial' or neo-colonial era? Is the child of empire disappearing? Neil Postman's engaging view is that childhood itself is disappearing – the invention of electricity having removed the gap between adulthood and childhood established long ago by the printing press. Television has opened all the tabooed subjects of adulthood to a child audience, and thus removed the boundary between the two states, while the power of the televised image has produced a race of 'child/adult' consumers.

Whatever the merits of this theory, it alerts us to the perception of a similar change in the nature of imperialism in this century. Colonial imperialism utilized the concept and implications of childhood to confirm a binarism between colonizer and colonized; a relationship which induced compliance to the cultural dominance of Europe. Colonizer and colonized were separated by literacy and education, the very means by which imperial discourse aimed to close the gap between them. This separation was confirmed by the existence of geographical boundaries, and eventually by nationality, which operated as clear material signifiers of an identity bestowed by the imperial process. The gap between colonizing parent and colonized child has been masked by globalization and the indiscriminate, transnational character of neo-colonialism. The neo-colonial subject cannot be situated by literacy, geography and education, for that subject is now increasingly the interpellated subject of global capitalism.

One function of post-colonial textuality today, therefore, is to expose and critique the cultural and aesthetic assumptions which underlie this global mask of imperialism, and to hold its cultural reality clearly in view. The secret of imperial hegemony has not been economics or force of arms but the control of representation. The secret of post-colonial resistance is therefore discursive reclamation. Part of this process has been the transformation of the concept of the child, because in this concept lies a vision of possibility and of identity that emerges from the space at the limits of colonial subjectivity, and keeps the reality of colonization and its continuing effects clearly in view.

Post-colonial writing in a global economy is a force of discrimination; it discriminates between the continuing reality of imperial power and subject peoples even when postmodernism, the cultural logic of late capitalism, works to obliterate cultural discrimination. Post-colonial analysis thus attempts to do what postmodernism cannot do: resist the submergence of the neo-colonial subject. Whereas globalism reduces all subjects to 'adult children', all the same because they are all consumers, post-colonial discourse works to reveal the gap between adult and child which still remains in practice: it reveals that people belong to a society as well as an economy, and that society is still controlled by a cultural hegemony which imperialism has set in place.

For David Malouf, for instance, the child is a powerful image of formation and transformation, as we shall see in the next chapter. In *12 Edmonstone Street* he shows the emerging consciousness of the child, its gradual discovery and invention of its first surroundings; the childhood home, is a model for the emergence of place and culture in a new society. In *An Imaginary Life* (Malouf, 1978) the Child becomes an embodiment, for Ovid, of an experience of life that lies beyond the reach of empire, of civilization, beyond the reach of language and even identity itself. It is this figure of the child who re-emerges as it were out of the zone beyond language and representation to reveal, in *Remembering Babylon* (1996), what might have been in an Australian society that had more effectively turned its gaze upon its own reality. For Malouf, the child in these novels is a protean force, rather than a sign of negation. Whether leading into the pre-symbolic realm of language or into the hybrid possibilities of a post-colonial future, the child is an evocative sign of transformation.

The allegory of the child becomes a potent site of counter-discursive critique because the child is so manifestly constructed as the ambivalent trope of the colonized, 'written' into existence by empire. The allegory of the child, then, enables a reading and contestation of the social text of imperialism, as the colonial subject inhabits what becomes a subversively ambivalent confluence of colonial self and other. The child, invented by imperialism to represent the colonized subject amenable to education and improvement, becomes the allegorical subject of a different traject-ory, a site of difference and anti-colonial possibility.

This allegorical appropriation is explicitly counter-discursive because it disrupts the very function of the trope; far from becoming a potential adult, formed in the image of the father, the child becomes the site of an unstable and unpredictable potentiality. From being a trope which absorbs and suppresses the paradox of imperial control, the paradox of its exploitation and nurture of the colonial subject, the child becomes in the post-colonial text the embodiment of the paradox of mimesis and alterity (Taussig, 1993). By interpolating its dissonance into textual production of various kinds, the post-colonial subject becomes the mim-icking other, the transformed and transforming subject.

Notes

1. Neil Postman's argument in *The Disappearance of Childhood* goes something like this: One might say that one of the main differences between an adult and a child is that the adult knows about certain facets of life – its mysteries, its contradictions, its violence, its tragedies – that are not considered suitable for children to know; that are, indeed, shameful to reveal to them indiscriminately. In the modern world, as children move towards adulthood, we reveal these secrets to them, in what we believe to be a psychologically assimilable way. However, such an idea is possible only in a culture in which there is a sharp distinction between the adult's world and the child's world.

CHAPTER 4

Childhood and possibility

David Malouf's *An Imaginary Life* and
Remembering Babylon

In *An Imaginary Life* (1978) and *Remembering Babylon* (1993), David
Malouf offers two examples of the post-colonial transformation of the
child, two versions of the story of the child of the wilderness breaking
into the circle of civilization. In both novels the 'lost child' moves from
the dimensionless silence beyond language into the realm of imperial
discourse. The Child in *An Imaginary Life*, a 'wolf-boy' whom Ovid
obsessively tries to introduce to civilization, manages instead to introduce the poet to a freedom beyond the conceptual boundaries of his own
humanity. Imaginatively, this child figure returns as Gemmy in *Remembering Babylon*. A London urchin raised by Aborigines, Gemmy moves
'back' across the border between 'wilderness' and imperial discourse
which Ovid had crossed, but for a quite different purpose. These figures
of the child, far from being a sign of abjection and 'primitivism', become
the agents of radically different conceptions of the world. A trope which
had helped resolve some of the immense contradictions of empire
becomes a potent sign of post-colonial conceptions of imaginative and
cultural possibility.

The novels focus on two different but connected post-colonial issues:
first, the place of language in our understanding of who we are, and
second, the problem of 'authentic' indigeneity; but, more significantly,
these wild children introduce the possibility of very different ways of
being and knowing. The child is an important trope in representations
of language and indigeneity because these are so firmly traversed by
conceptual boundaries which, in children, are yet to be fully established.
Whereas the Child in *An Imaginary Life* takes Ovid beyond the confines
of his language and civilization, Gemmy, in *Remembering Babylon*, returns
across the borders of civilization to demonstrate how post-colonial
society might be differently imagined.

The title of *An Imaginary Life*, with its suggestion of a pre-linguistic
subjectivity, an 'imaginary phase', seems to point inevitably to Lacan.[1] It
is hard to imagine a more graphic description of the cultural imperatives
of the symbolic order than that given by Ovid, or circumscribed by the
fence on which Gemmy, in *Remembering Babylon*, perches before taking
the leap into a discourse from which he has been long excluded. These
uncivilized children of the wilderness represent for us the psychic other

of the civilized ego, the union of childhood and primitivism, the formless potentialities of a pre-Oedipal, pre-imperial language. In this sense the child's life is truly the life of the Lacanian (and imperial) imaginary. In the latter novel the figure of the imaginary child breaks through into the reader's symbolic order of language and history to indicate possibilities of human adaptation to place in Australia. Gemmy is the sign of an Australia that might have been, a post-colonial imaginary. He demonstrates a potential for social change which had seemed curiously arrested at the end of *An Imaginary Life.*

However, paradoxically, one major virtue of this Lacanian terminology is that it installs boundaries between stages of subjectivity which mirror the spatial boundaries by which the empire maintains its centrality. It alerts us to the difficulty of conceiving being outside such boundaries. Psychoanalytic discourse itself may be described as a species of cultural allegory in which the child's subjectivity illuminates the possibility of a different kind of world. Childhood has an important function in these novels because the child, in whom boundaries are unformed, reveals the provisionality of those boundaries which are crucial to imperial discourse. Ovid, for instance, finds himself in the village of Tomis at the very furthest reaches of the Roman Empire, a place where, by its marginality, its placelessness, the issue of place becomes crucial: 'We are at the ends of the earth', he says, 'centuries from the notion of an orchard or a garden made simply to please' (*An Imaginary Life*, p. 15).[2] The nineteenth-century Australia of *Remembering Babylon* is also far away from such gardens. Only three years back, 'the very patch of earth you were standing on had itself been on the other side of things, part of the unknown' (*Rembering Babylon*, p. 9).[3] This is a land only just reclaimed from the 'Absolute Dark' (*RB*, pp. 2–3). Even the ground underfoot has the touch of mystery upon it.

What we immediately notice in both of these novels is that 'who you are' is '*where* you are in the process of becoming'. Ovid is exiled to the edges of the Roman Empire, and hence to the edges of imperial discourse itself, to a place where 'I am rendered dumb. . . . As if I belonged to another species' (*AIL*, p. 17). Reduced to the apparent silence of the marginalized primitive world, he understands the very provisionality of that language, and even more of the self which it had constructed. When he asks the exile's question 'Have I survived?' (*AIL*, p. 19) he asks, in effect, 'Where am I,' or more specifically, Who can I be in this place? For he has been brought to 'the very edge of things, where Nothing begins' (*AIL*, p. 27). It is now in the face of that nothingness, that horizon beyond the certainties of imperial language, where the intersection of place, language and being becomes most acutely obvious.

Although Ovid's exile acts out the incontrovertibility of imperial power, that power, particularly the capacity of imperial language to produce reality, finds its limit at the 'edge of nothing' to which he has been exiled. It is at this margin that a fracture appears through which the agency of the subject, which had seemed imprisoned by language, is released. This is the power to step outside the boundaries of imperial language, to seize control over it and remake reality. Crucially, it is the Child, the one outside these boundaries, who becomes the agent of transformation for Ovid. In going beyond the reach of the imperial language, Ovid is at the same time going 'back' beyond the symbolic order of the patriarchal reality of the Roman Empire to the imaginary phase of being in which sexuality, language, identity are in a dynamic flux of formless potentiality. It is this 'pre-Oedipal', 'pre-imperial', even 'pre-cultural' phase which Ovid quite determinedly seeks to enter by appropriating the experience of the Child through its language.

By placing Ovid at the edges of the language, imperial power has exiled the poet to the edges of human being itself (as it 'exiles' the settlers in the later novel) to an 'uncreated' place where people have not achieved the status of being Roman (or British), of being human. This is why the Child is such a poignant figure of this condition: he magnifies the ambivalence of that interface of primitivism and civilization. Significantly, the condition of 'human being' is directly connected to the naming of place. We become the place that we have made. While we may think of Italy or any place as a land given by the gods, 'It is a created place' created in our image, which is created in the image of, created by, our language. Metaphorically, this energy exists in the spirits which 'flow back and forth between us and the objects we have made, the landscape we have shaped and move in. . . . It is our self we are making out there' (*AIL*, p. 28). The settlers in *Remembering Babylon* are similarly making themselves by making the place, but, located in the ambivalent space at the edge of colonial society, they live in a landscape that is only gradually coming into being.

When Ovid discovers a poppy, the simple beauty and colour of which remind him of a whole way of life, he keeps 'saying the word over and over to myself, scarlet, as if the word, like the colour, had escaped me till now, and just saying it would keep the little windblown flower in sight' (*AIL*, p. 31). So language creates being through its creation of experience. The poet's head fills with flowers, he has only to name them and 'they burst into bud' (*AIL*, p. 32). This process by which the landscape is given life is precisely the process by which we come into being. 'So it is that the beings we are in process of becoming will be drawn out of us' (*AIL*, p. 32).

The body itself impresses this process most forcefully. As Ovid watches the Child trying to write, his tongue 'pointed at the corner of the mouth and moving with each gesture of the hand' (*AIL*, p. 81), he asks, 'Is that perhaps where speech begins? In that need of the tongue to be active in the world?' The tongue is the body's metonymic figure of language, of the agency by which both the world and the body come into being. The body then is itself the primary metonym of place, the first creation of the subject through language.

This process is one imagined by Ovid as involving the whole of humankind. There is continual reference to the project of transcendence in which the human existence is engaged. Speaking to the readers of his work located long in the future, he asks whether we are the gods into which humankind has evolved. The irony of this does not diminish the dynamic process in which we are located. 'Our bodies are not final. We are moving, all of us in our common humankind. . . . We are creating the lineaments of some final man for whose delight we have prepared a landscape and who can only be a god' (*AIL*, p. 29). This is an ironic statement about the process of hybridization and change which characterize human life. We never arrive at the 'final man'; we are constantly changing, adapting, dividing and multiplying. One's sense is that it is Ovid's exile to the edges of colonial discourse, and the consequent insistence of the post-colonial, which has made him articulate this hybrid interconnection between being and place. It is at the margin at which the Child is encountered that he sees most clearly that there is no centre.

Nevertheless, exiled to the edges of the known world, Ovid initially feels as cut off as the spiders. It is no magic that has done this: 'All that has been evoked is the power of the law' (*AIL*, p. 20). The law has confined him to that range of beings, those 'child/primitives' 'who have not yet climbed up through a hole in their head and become fully human, who have not yet entered what we call society and become Romans under the law' (*AIL*, p. 20). Language not only maintains power over place, but through place over being itself. In all colonial discourse, those who have been given the advantages of the imperial language are ascribed the condition of human being. So it is ironic that Ovid the exile, having experienced the remorselessness of this power, should become its agent, when he expresses the philanthropic desire to free the Child 'into some clearer body' (*AIL*, p. 77) to show him what human kindness, and thus humankind, might be. In a profound statement of the ontological power of imperialism he says: 'It is out of this that he must discover *what he is*' (*AIL*, p. 77; emphasis added). Even in exile, and even in his own journey of discovery, the dynamic of power works *through* Ovid. It is out of the monocentric structure of the discourse of power that humanity is conferred, but later, when lying in a fever, the Child yells out a Latin word, Ovid observes, 'At any other moment I might be overjoyed at what has occurred. The Child has spoken at last. In his delirium he has discovered human speech' (*AIL*, p. 119). However, this cry is the metonym of colonial speech itself; it is the speech of the hysteric.

Ovid is caught in a curious ambivalence, for the Child is the Other of colonial discourse, beyond inherited conceptions of humanity; that horizon towards which the post-colonial consciousness is constantly moving. Beyond the opposition of centre and margin is the horizonality which accepts the boundless mystery of the marginal, the mystery of becoming: 'What else should our lives be', asks Ovid, 'but a continual series of beginnings, of painful settings out into the unknown, pushing off from the edges of consciousness into the mystery of what we have not yet become?' (*AIL*, p. 135). However, it is in the nature of colonialism to identify the Other, to make the Other the other, to fix that continual possibility which represents loss or unformed being.

The Child focuses all the questions that come to Ovid at the margins of empire: the nature and importance of language, its function in creating place, and the confluence of both in the emergence of being. It is through the Child that he discovers that the world is not a simple binarism of centre and margin, that the 'true language' of silence can be entered by the subject. The Child is the narrator's Other whose gaze now contests the gaze of the *grande autre*, the gaze of the empire in whose language Ovid feels himself to be made despite the subversive danger of his poetry. It is this which makes the Other, in whose gaze he now exists, so liberating. 'Does the boy watch all this, I wonder?' (*AIL*, p. 51); 'Does he speak to himself, having no other creature with whom to share his mind, his tongue? Being in that like myself' (*AIL*, p. 52); but Ovid's desire is to compel his entry into the symbolic order in which the name of the father is the name Augustus.

However, because the Child represents some timeless place in the poet's own childhood, he represents that imaginary place which has not, for Ovid, yet been created. In Ovid's own childhood the boundary stones of his father's land signify the space enclosed by the language. 'I too know all the boundary stones of our land, but to me they mean something different. They are where the world begins. Beyond them lies Rome and all the known world and all that we Romans have power over. Out there, beyond the boundary stones, the mystery begins' (*AIL*, p. 87). The ambivalence of this is palpable. The circle of home is the circle of empire, but there is a sense that in the context of childhood the empire itself lies beyond the margin of his home. The marginality of the world depends upon the direction of the gaze.

In both novels, fences and boundaries are crucial. The boundary stones around Ovid's childhood farm are like the fence on which Gemmy perches. Indeed, fences assume an almost ritual power of possession in Australian settlement; the fence defines ownership, but at the same time it defines Otherness and alienness. This is why the fence on which Gemmy perches when he is discovered and 'captured' by the children of the settlement is so significant. It represents the margin of language and culture but also a way of defining the world, and it is the possible liberation from that way of defining the world which Gemmy represents. The 'indigenous hybrid' is the post-colonial revelation of all subjectivity. Gemmy embodies what Bhabha calls the 'split-space of enunciation' (1994: 38) and through it the post-colonial capacity to enter the fractures of discourse and effect change in the world. For this space opens a way beyond the exoticism of fragmentation, multiculturalism and cultural *diversity* to 'an inscription and articulation of culture's hybridity' (Bhabha, 1994: 38).

Beyond the fence of Ovid's childhood home lies his Other, the Child, in whose gaze he can himself come into being, because for the Child the co-ordinates of his being, those features which for Ovid are paramount, have no purchase:

> What is his country? What is his parentage? At what moment did he push out into the world, under what star sign, with what planet in the ascendant, in what ephemeris of the moon? And if he does not know these things can he ever know who he is or what his fate is to be?
>
> Or does not knowing make him free? (*AIL*, p. 89)

Ovid teaching the Child to speak, teaching him 'what he is', is much like Miranda teaching Caliban to 'name the bigger light and how the less' (*The Tempest*, I, ii, 337); it is to imprison him in discourse; but instead, the Child draws Ovid himself beyond this language, beyond 'knowledge' of the world, beyond the 'human'. In a similar way, this potential for a freedom outside epistemology is signified by Gemmy in *Remembering Babylon*. The trope of the child, so important in resolving the contradictions of imperial discourse, becomes the agent of post-colonial transformation and renewal. For Ovid, not knowing is not to have power, yet both Gemmy and the Child exist *outside* power, outside the need to discover their humanity.

While teaching the Child to speak, Ovid finds that, in fact, he is learning a totally different sense of what language is. The Child's language is that of the mimic, and 'in entering into the mysterious life of its language, becomes for a moment, the creature itself, so that to my eyes he seems miraculously transformed' (*AIL*, p. 90). This demonstrates something of the energy of language in an oral society, in which language does not represent reality but actually embodies its energy: 'He is being a bird. He is allowing it to speak out of him' (*AIL*, p. 92). The oral culture with which colonialism so often comes into contact is a world beyond representation, a world of *enunciation* rather than the *enunciated*, beyond the will to truth. The exiled writer poised on the very edge of language gives himself to the process of metamorphosis which the Child's language, and hence being, offers to the now post-colonial poet. This is the language which 'lets the universe in' the language of the spiders. 'Now, led by the Child, I am on my way to it. The true language, I know now, is that speech in silence in which we first communicated, the Child and I, in the forest, when I was asleep' (*AIL*, p. 97).

However, the poet 'gives himself' to this language in a way that denies its autonomous singularity, for he records the process in the language of the reader. He must speak to his readers of the world beyond the edge of speech. He must create in language that which seems to lie beyond it: the true language. The 'true language' is the language of possibility, the point at which 'true' is totally open to question, the always unenclosable horizon of language. For the post-colonial it is the sign of the radical hybridity into which speech is constantly moving. This language is also for the poet, the language which existed before speech, the language beyond the symbolic order of civilization, the language beyond the empire, beyond the gaze of the *grande autre*.

> When I think of my exile now it is from the universe. When I think of the tongue that has been taken away from me, it is some earlier and more universal language than our Latin, subtle as it undoubtedly is. Latin is a language for distinctions, every ending defines and divides. The language I am speaking of now, that I am almost speaking, is a language whose every syllable is a gesture of reconciliation. We knew that language once. I spoke it in my childhood. We must discover it again. (*AIL*, p. 98)

Ovid follows the Child into this language, 'his whole body strained toward some distance' (*AIL*, p. 149). 'His own nature as a god that which his body is straining towards' (*AIL*, p. 150). Until he arrives at that place of the true language which is, ironically, the place beyond language, beyond life itself, the undefinable real in which the Child is simply 'there': 'It is summer. It is spring. I am immeasurably, unbearably happy. I am three years old. I am sixty. I am six. I am there.' (*AIL*, p. 151)

The word 'there' is conveyed with all the ambivalence that a point of being maintains in the narrative. Each word – he, is, there – is provisional. His place is where he is and thus who he is; not fixed but carried with him in the horizon of the real. Taken by the Child beyond the boundaries of language and empire, Ovid goes beyond the power of the text to *say* – and hence the power of those boundaries by which we understand our humanity.

The 'return' of the child in the form of Gemmy, with his tentative approach to civilization, his uncertain and fearful accommodation by the settlers and his eventual escape, seems to repeat the trajectory of the Child's contact with the edges of the Roman Empire. But this time, whereas the Child had been captured and brought into the circle of imperial language, Gemmy is also brought (or returns) into history. The entry is one that has immense social and historical significance because he symbolizes all the possibilities for human development that seem to be denied by the erection of fences, the 'worlding of a world on uninscribed earth', as Gayatri Spivak puts it (Spivak, 1985: 133), the othering of those beyond the fence and the separation of the indigenous and the settler. Gemmy reintroduces the issue of 'becoming', but this time by problematizing the question of authenticity. A London urchin who falls overboard from a ship and is raised by the aborigines who discover him washed ashore, Gemmy demonstrates how the concepts 'aboriginality', 'authenticity', 'indigeneity' are more problematic than they seem.

At the same time Gemmy reverses the implications of the 'lost child' myth in Australian culture: the recurring story of the child who wanders away from home to be lost forever in the bush, the spectre of the settler society's sense of vulnerability and displacement. Gemmy is not only Ovid's child but all those lost children returning to announce the possibility of a different kind of life, a different kind of invention of Australia.

There is an immense irony in the fact that at the beginning of the novel, Lachlan Beattie, who discovers Gemmy, is playing out in his imagination a story in the fourth-grade Reader, in which he imagines himself fighting off wolves in the Russian snow, for here is a clear demonstration of the process of colonial education in consolidating that construction of reality which language initiates. In this sense Gemmy represents something literally beyond imagination because he exists beyond that reality we learn is the world as we grow up. Lachlan's initial response – 'we're being raided by blacks' – is the signal response of the settler culture. Because what is also accomplished by the 'worlding of a world' is the simple binary division of black and white, imperialism's racial binarism which relentlessly antagonizes the hybrid development of post-colonial society.

The first view of Gemmy is of a human who not only looks like a bird but in some way had been changed into a bird, coming towards them

> out of a world over there, beyond the no-man's land of the swamp, that was the abode of everything savage and fearsome, and since it lay so far beyond experience, not just their own but their parents' too, of nightmare rumours, superstitions and all that belonged to Absolute Dark. (*RB*, pp. 2–3)

The fence on which Gemmy hovers not only symbolizes the separation of the 'civilized' from the 'primitive' world, but is also a border between two incommensurable discourses, two entirely different ways of being in the world; it is these two ways of being which his very presence offers to bring together. For Gemmy is the *authentic hybrid indigene*. In this his own perception of the moment of contact is revealing:

> It was a question of covering the space between them, of recovering the connection that would put the words back in his mouth, and catch the creature, the spirit or whatever it was, that lived in the dark of him, and came up briefly to torment or tease but could be tempted, he now saw, with what these people ate and the words they used. (*RB*, p. 33)

The creature speaks up when Gemmy is confronted, with the words *'Do not shoot. I am a British object'*. The irony of this is patent, for the dredging up of the words has itself objectified him in the language of power. His own subjectivity, developed so differently within the discourse of aboriginal life, is now made to enter the ambivalent marginal state between cultures, the edges of the empire, the region in which subjectivity itself comes into question, where its potential for trans-formation is realized.

Gemmy had 'started out white. No question' (*RB*, p. 40), but the frightening question for the settlers is 'Had he remained white? Could you lose it? Not just language, but *it*. *It*' (*RB*, p. 40). In this question lies the complete uncertainty of racial purity, a concept that nevertheless becomes embedded in the discourse of race which imperialism unleashes. Inevitably this notion of 'race' is reduced to the egregious binarism of 'black' and 'white'. It is the comfortable sense of identity that rests upon the certainty of difference which becomes undermined by Gemmy, because

> you meet at last in a terrifying equality that strips the last rags from your soul and leaves you so far out on the edge of yourself that your fear now is that you may never get back.
>
> It was the mixture of monstrous strangeness and unwelcome like-ness that made Gemmy Fairley so disturbing to them, since at any moment he could show either one face or the other; as if he were always standing there at one of those meetings, but in his case willingly, and the encounter was an embrace. (*RB*, p. 43)

Can there be such a thing as a white aboriginal? The idea undermines the binary concept of race on which not only imperial control is based but also its opposition. However, this does not mean that Gemmy's hybridity is not oppositional. Its subversiveness represents the very different, *transformative* oppositionality of post-colonial discourse.

When the Aborigines pay a visit to Gemmy, the farmers' suspicion that he is a link between the 'fenced' certainties of civilized life and the savage primitive, wild unknown is intensified. Because thought operates in terms of these binaries, becoming a dominant mode of self-identification, the other cannot be viewed as anything but fearful and treacherous. It is curious that the socially marginal, the social detritus of that 'civilized' society such as Andy, the dim-witted farm worker, the ones whose need of affirmation is greatest, are the ones who are most hostile to strangers, such as Gemmy, who call the boundaries and definitions of civilization into question.

Yet it is the responses of those most sympathetic, such as Mr Frazer, the enlightened and sympathetic parson, that are the most troubling and ambiguous. For, like Ovid with the Child, the first thing Mr Frazer wants to do is to give him a sense of who he is, and the method of doing this is to record his history. The very simple, scholarly and basically philan-thropic process of reconstructing Gemmy's history is in fact a process of *bringing him into history* itself. This a process by which imperialism works through the philanthropic subject, much as it works through Ovid in his desire to teach the Child language and thus reveal his humanity. The business of piecing together Gemmy's story could stand as an allegory of the whole construction of history in Australia, or indeed, of imperial history anywhere.

> The details of his story were pieced together the following afternoon from facts that were, as he told them, all out of their proper order, and with so many gaps of memory, and so much dislocation between what he meant to convey and the few words he could recover of his original tongue, that they could never be certain, later, how much of it was real and how much they had themselves supplied from tales they already knew, since he was by no means the first white man to have turned up like this after a spell with the blacks. (*RB*, p. 16)

This is the method of imperial history because, as Paul Carter puts it, the place is simply seen as a stage upon which teleologically directed events work themselves out (Carter, 1987: xvi); but it is also the arbitrary and circumstantial narrative by which Australia itself is brought into history. What Mr Frazer gradually glimpses is that Gemmy's life is one for which the historical process is entirely inadequate, because Gemmy exists within a different kind of language.

Gemmy's relationship with language is much like the Child's in *An Imaginary Life*. Trying to get beyond the boundaries of his habits of representation, Ovid says: 'It rains and I say, *it rains.* It thunders and I say, *it thunders.* I try to think as he must: *I am raining, I am thundering*' (*AIL*, p. 96). For Gemmy also, language does not represent, but *embodies*, reality, and so when he looks at the sheets of writing on which the earnest historians have recorded his life, they appear to have absorbed his life into them, and he begins to plot how to steal his life back (*RB*, p. 20). Gemmy is more prescient than he knows, of course, because the history which appears to be such a painstaking *record* of his life is indeed a process of absorption, of bringing him into history, and thus into that field of colonial discourse symbolized by the fence on which we first see him.

But it is in what Gemmy communicates about place to Mr Frazer that we discover his transformative potential. For if Gemmy represents the 'post-colonial imaginary', the possibility of a hybrid future for Australia, this is nowhere more evident than in his revelation to Mr Frazer of a different way of knowing the place. For here, as in *An Imaginary Life*, we discover that who you are is vitally connected with where you are, and Mr Frazer is taken by Gemmy to the edges of an imperial consciousness, a place constructed in the imperial language, to a vision of what Australia might become. 'We have been wrong', he says,

> to see this continent as hostile and infelicitous, so that only by the fiercest stoicism, a supreme resolution and force of will, and by felling, clearing, sowing with seeds we have brought with us, and by importing sheep, cattle, rabbits, even the very birds of the air, can it be shaped and made habitable. It is habitable already. (*RB*, p. 129)

The long and lyrical entry in his diary from which this is taken is an account of the ecological blindness which language has produced in settler societies and against which their literature and art have been in constant struggle. His vision is that by breaking out of this language the land might reveal its secrets, 'so that what spreads in us is an intimate understanding of what it truly is, with all that is unknowable in it made familiar within' (*RB*, p. 131). The picture of Gemmy leading the parson through the bush, giving him the aboriginal names for what they discover, is a beautiful demonstration of the very different ways in which the land is conceived. Frazer desires that the spirit of the place might come into language, while Gemmy sees that Frazer's drawings do, in fact, capture the spirit of things. This new kind of understanding requires a different kind of language, a language in which the human occupants themselves might be different. However, it is also clear that the 'true' way of seeing place is not some fixed, pre-existing aboriginal conception but a hybrid encompassed by the different kind of language, a language towards which post-colonial writing works.

> There was no way of existing in this land, or of making your way through it, unless you took into yourself, discovered on your breath, the sounds that linked up all the various parts of it and made them one. Without that you were blind, you were deaf, as he had been, at first, in their world. (*RB*, p. 65)

The operative phrase here is 'took into yourself': the process of taking in to oneself is always provisional, overlapping, syncretic. Ovid's adoption of the 'true' language of the Child is one which leads him to personal exultation but leaves the imperial discourse untouched; he is 'exiled from the universe'. Yet Gemmy's encounter with Mr Frazer represents a crucial 'Adamic' moment in the development of Australian society, a moment in which the child's return in the form of Gemmy might have led to a transformation of that society's future. The impossibility of Mr Frazer ever communicating a different way of viewing the country to the absurd colonial administration (an impossibility brilliantly demonstrated in the political nuances of the Governor's dinner party) shows why the transformation could not take place.

While Mr Frazer's vision for a different country is thwarted, it is Janet who in some ways represents a more significant failure, because Janet is one whose consciousness radically changes, but still falls short of the transformation which seems to be offered by Gemmy. Janet is conscious from childhood of her own marginality as a female, and as a woman her sense of reality is at first the most vicarious.

> She was in love with this other life her parents had lived; with Scotland and a time before they came to Australia, before she was born, that was her time too, extending her life back beyond the few years she could actually recall, and giving reality to a world she had need of;

more alive and interesting, more crowded with *things*, with people too, than the one she was in. (*RB*, p. 54)

Janet, like many settlers, even the Australian born, falls into that sense of the world in which 'real life' is 'over there'. The sense of colonial displacement is one which intersects with her position as a woman to render her own experience as secondary. This is the function of colonial language and colonial history. Therefore, if anyone is in a position to take into herself the view of the world which Gemmy suggests, it is Janet. Indeed, she experiences an epiphany of the natural world when she is covered by the 'single mind' of the bee swarm in an experience which changes her forever: 'She stood still as still and did not breathe. She surrendered herself. You are our bride, her new and separate mind told her as it drummed and swayed above the earth' (*RB*, p. 142).

Janet's experience with the bees is one which seems to have all the mysterious openness to the world which Gemmy offers Mr Frazer. She is the one white person in the novel who actually manages to give herself over to a different way of being – 'She surrendered herself'. It is this capacity in Janet which introduces the feminine economy of trans-formation. It is she who most intimately and immediately demonstrates the possibility of giving oneself over to a mode of habitation that seems demanded by the place.

It is fascinating that in a novelist who has sometimes been accused of being too 'male', the most mystical (and possibly the most powerful) experience of transformation is seen to be attained by a woman. While Gemmy embodies the material ambivalence of hybridity and integration, Janet's experience with the bees, by simultaneously symbolizing the emergence of womanhood – 'They have smelled the sticky blood flow. They think it is honey' (*RB*, p. 142) – demonstrates a 'feminine' potenti-ality in Australian life which is yet to be fully realized. The bees are an introduced agricultural phenomenon which stand for an imposed change in the natural world, and the spirituality itself emerges directly from the traditions of European literature, alluding to a similar use of the image of bees by Dante in a description of the glory of the heavenly host in *Paradiso*.[4] However, Janet's capacity to relinquish the received and famil-iar experience of the natural world, that experience which, like Pros-pero's, cannot be separated from the demand for control and refashioning, and surrender herself to a different way of being, is a profound metaphor of unrealized cultural possibility.

Because the epiphany seems to lift her 'from the face of the earth' (*RB*, p. 142), there seems to be no way in which a reconnection with the earth can be made. The deep religious nature of Janet's moment of emergence into womanhood is implied later when we find her in a convent; but this retirement from the world is also meant to be seen perhaps as a confirmation of her inability to translate the potential of that experience into a form of life connected with the earth in the way Gemmy's 'other-worldliness' is seen to be connected. Thus even her most profound moments re-enact the sense of displacement which has characterized her from the beginning.

Both *An Imaginary Life* and *Remembering Babylon* end with a sense of ambivalence. For all its triumph, Ovid's union with the Child in the realm of the real takes him beyond language, beyond the book, beyond transformation, beyond life itself. The return of Gemmy across the borders of imperial discourse opens the door to a future beyond its boundaries, a future in which the hybridity of human life is fully embraced and the discourse of Australian place constructed differently. However, although the future offered by Gemmy is rejected, it represents in radical form what must take place gradually and painfully: a transformation into the hybridity of post-colonial life of which these novels are themselves both representative and formative.

Notes

1. I am not, however, interested in using these novels to explicate Lacan. The stages of human development referred to by Lacan as the imaginary, the symbolic and the real are reasonably well known. The imaginary describes that pre-linguistic, pre-Oedipal phase of development in which the image, the identity and the identification are interdependent, one which corresponds to what Lacan calls the 'mirror phase'. The symbolic describes the entry into language by the child, a stage in which the 'name of the Father' is learned, thus according the child a gendered and named world. The real is that horizon of all things which can never be enclosed or defined. A useful introduction to this may be found in the chapter on 'The imaginary, the symbolic and the real' in Sarup (1992).

2. Hereafter abbreviated to *AIL*.

3. Hereafter abbreviated to *RB*.

4. At the beginning of Canto XXXI Dante describes the presence of the heavenly host thus:

   In form then of a pure white rose the saintly host was shown to me, which with His own blood Christ made his Bride. But the other host – who, as it flies, sees and sings His glory who enamours it and the goodness which made it so great – like a swarm of bees which one moment enflower themselves, and the next return to where their work acquires savour – was descending into the great flower which is adorned with so many petals, and thence re-ascending to where its love abides forever. (Singleton, 1975: 347)

CHAPTER 5

Sweet futures

Sugar and colonialism

While transformations of those tropes, such as 'the child', employed to 'other' colonized peoples, has been a widespread function of post-colonial discourse, the interrelation between the material economies of colonialism and the transformative dynamic of that discourse has been profoundly important. Although the transformation of representation is crucial, such practices are situated in a material world with, in most cases, urgent material implications. The story of the extraordinary rise to prominence of tropical sugar, both in the economy and the diet of Britain, illuminates what post-colonial transformation actually means in the lives of colonized peoples. The sugar industry had a catastrophic effect on the Caribbean environment, culture and people. Yet out of the ruins caused by that European obsession with sugar, an obsession which had extraordinarily damaging effects on tropical plantation colonies, arose a culture so dynamic that it has acquired a peculiar place in global culture.

In 1493, Christopher Columbus, on his second voyage to the West Indies, brought cuttings of sugar cane from the Canary Islands. The Spanish colonizers who followed him brought a formidable arsenal of cultural domination, from writing to gunpowder, but this was nothing compared to the impact of sugar. These few cuttings of sugar cane were to have the most profound effect in global structures of imperial power, in the relations between vast communities of people and, ultimately, in the political shape of the world itself.

How did sugar come to have this immense impact? The key lies in the rapid rise to power of the British Empire from the seventeenth century, and the rapid increase in sugar consumption which accompanied Britain's growing influence. The interrelation of these elements – empire, industrial power and capitalism – is so intimate in the production and consumption of sugar that it is almost impossible to unravel them. While the sugar cane industry in the Caribbean was begun by Spain, it was the subsequent British development – with its exponential increase in the slave trade, its transformation of whole islands, such as Barbados, into virtual sugar factories, its subsequent impact on world capitalism and its transformation of European domestic culture – which began the political and cultural revolution of sugar.

Sugar is significant for four reasons. First, it represents an extraord-inarily overdetermined focus of imperial economic history, a fulcrum for the connection between, and the development of, capitalism, imperial-ism, plantations and slavery. Quite simply, without sugar, none of these phenomena would have had the character, extent or significance they had by the turn of the century. Second, because of the very magnitude of its economic, social and cultural effects, sugar represents an unpar-alleled metonym of imperial discourse: its circulatory relations, its dependence on a complex link of culture and economics and its continu-ing material consequences. Third, it provides a focus for an analysis of the ways in which the dynamic of imperialism generated the explosion of twentieth-century globalization. Fourth, for many of the same reasons, it focuses the transformative cultural effects of post-colonial discourse.

The historical fulcrum: sugar and British economic history

The importance of sugar in mediating historical and economic forces in Britain is unmatched by any other commodity. Without it, the relation-ship between British imperialism and British capitalism would have been radically different. Ultimately, sugar became the focus for changes in notions of race, power, cultural dominance, and the geography of the world. Sugar initiated a complex circulation of relationships between four factors: capitalism, imperialism, slavery and plantations. None of the relationships between these phenomena was either necessary or inevitable in British history, but developed from their intersection in the growing, marketing and consumption of sugar. For instance, neither plantations, imperialism nor capitalism *require* slavery to produce profit. The spread of slavery to plantation systems throughout the world was a result of the exponential growth of slavery in sugar plantations in the Caribbean. Similarly, capitalism requires neither plantations nor slavery; indeed, these would seem peripheral to an increasingly industrialized Europe, but sugar cemented the importance of these to British capitalism through the high percentage of sugar in British imports. Nor does imperialism require plantations or slavery. The peculiar character of British imperialism as it emerged before the nineteenth century was deeply influenced by the importance of the commodity to growing British power. The link between capitalism and imperialism is more complex, but in Britain's case it is also mediated by the importance of the American sugar trade to the British economy. In every case these four monumental phenomena in Britain's economic history would either not exist, or would exist in very different form, if it were not for sugar.

Of all these relationships, the link between British capitalism and British imperialism is the most contentious. Wallerstein's view that capitalism has been the world system since the sixteenth century (1974a: 387–415; 1974b),[1] is persuasive, but depends, for the elegance of its structure, upon the exclusion of a number of other factors. The argument against this totalizing view is that capitalism is but one mode of the hugely overdetermined phenomenon of European modernity: the monumental project of Europe's self-realization (see Chapter 2). Arguably, capitalism itself, with its driving forces of profit and exchange, its dependence upon commodification and its isolation of the means of production, has a cultural basis in that same process by which modern Europe began to conceive itself through its 'othering' of the non-European world. Thus, of all these factors, imperialism, in its most general sense, was *the* key discourse by which Europe established a sense of self, by inventing its others, racially, culturally, geographically, and ultimately, economically. British imperialism, which may be characterized as everything from the general habit of sailing round the world and planting the flag, to establishing huge and complex colonial administrations, was an inextricable feature of its evolving capitalism. In both its pre-industrial and industrial stages, sugar constitutes a major proportion of British imports and exports.

The sugar plantation

The key to the impact of sugar on colonial society is the plantation, and we might ask: Why does the sugar plantation have such a profound and disruptive effect regardless of location? Is there something about the sugar plantation itself which confirms the violent hierarchy of colonialism? The basic elements of sugar production are well known: sucrose content diminishes rapidly after cutting and the sugar extracted is a tiny proportion of the raw cane, so factories must be located near the point of harvest, but this itself does not exclude the possibility of smallholders processing their cane through a central co-operatively-run factory. The development of the sugar plantation as a monocultural and socially dominant hegemony is linked to the relentless invention and promotion of its consumption as a staple. In this monocultural occupation of land, the link between colonial and capitalist expansion becomes most intense. Understanding the plantation, and by that I mean understanding its cultural as well as economic implications, is a door to understanding the processes of imperial expansion.

A model for this process can be seen in the history of Barbados (Sheridan, 1974). Discovered in 1625, Barbados had 1,400 English settlers by 1628, a number which grew to 37,000 in 1643. This was a vibrant society of planters and former indentured servants growing tobacco, cotton, indigo, pepper, citrus fruits, cattle, pigs and poultry and other consumer goods, but the planting of sugar cane in 1640 rapidly changed this situation. From an island dominated by a prosperous farming class which provided healthy domestic markets, by 1685 it became, through the massive importation of slave labour, and the development of sugar latifundia, little more than a sugar factory, owned by a few capitalists who lived abroad, and worked by a mass of alien labourers. This literally devastated the ecology, the economy and the society of Barbados as people fled to escape hunger and look for jobs which had disappeared from the island.

The plantation system focuses the enormous impact and the interrelationship of British imperialism, capitalism and slavery. It is salutary to ask whether the lasting disruptions of slavery, colonial occupation or ecological devastation would have occurred without sugar. What if Britain had, for some reason, developed beet sugar production centuries before Napoleon?[2] Would slavery have become such an essential feature of other plantation crops such as tobacco, tea or cotton if sugar plantations had not established the pattern? Would the enormous and tragic consequences of tropical plantations have occurred? What would have happened to the diet of the British working class? How rapidly would capital have been accumulated by industrial England? Looking at it this way, it is difficult to imagine how the forces of industrial capitalism might have coincided with Britain's imperial dominance without the extraordinary catalyst of cane sugar.

Slavery

Perhaps the most significant consequence of sugar was the exponential increase in slavery. Under the impetus of an exploding European consumption in the eighteenth century, a 'triangular trade' developed in which European goods were sold to Africa, and African slaves were carried to the New World, from whence tropical commodities, especially sugar, were transported to Europe.[3] In this sense, the extreme commodification and adoption of new business techniques which underpinned the sugar production process meant that slavery also became the dark underside of the European passion for progress and scientism – the hallmarks of the project of modernity. It is estimated that between 1500 and 1870, more than 12 million African captives were forcibly removed and taken to the New World. More than 1.5 million captives never reached their destination, but died under the most horrific conditions during the passage. The new business techniques which underpinned the commercialization of sugar necessitated that human labour itself was denigrated to the level of an essential but renewable resource, an indispensable commodity in sugar production.

The inequitable fact of slavery, the horrendous conditions which African slaves endured, as well as the modes of power which defined relations between slaves and their owners, necessitated some form of justificatory system to rationalize its contradictory position in modern principles of political and human rights. In this way, the concept of race already evident within Western epistemology took on a poignant significance. Central to such a system was the idea of 'white' superiority and 'black' inferiority. Wherever the system was challenged, religious sanctions were often deployed to justify a racial hierarchy and hence slavery.

The designation of black races as the 'sons of Ham' doomed by Noah to be 'hewers of wood and drawers of water' continued in South Africa into the twentieth century. More commonly, during the nineteenth century as abolitionism grew in strength, ethnological and physiognomic myths were employed to justify European domination. As the plantation system developed, these justifications became important mechanisms of control 'which both protected fellow Europeans from the rigours of full slavery and designated Africans or blacks as its proper victims' (Blackburn, 1997: 12). The key to this, of course, is that, if slavery had a radical effect on the development of racial myths to justify British imperialism, the sugar trade, which initiated and developed the exploitation of slaves, was the direct agent in this profound cultural transformation.

Slavery has been a persistently contradictory aspect of modernity. The most attractive aspect of the Enlightenment, with its confirmation of human individuality, was the promise of a greater personal freedom. In general terms, the rise both of empire and race thinking were linked by the need to marginalize and denigrate those African races who were being enslaved. Modernity was always European modernity, and its spread was the spread of empire, but the fuel of this advance was the contradiction of a form of servitude employed in the colonies which was detested at home. Europeans 'saw in slavery a notion of intense and comprehensive domination that was the antithesis of citizenship and self respect' (Blackburn, 1997: 18). Its employment as a moral and economic technology of colonial subjection was all the more telling.

Slavery exposed the duplicity at the heart of European modernity: 'the subscription to the ideals of universal humanity and democracy on the one hand, and the imperial and colonial subjugation of non-European peoples and racism on the other' (Eze, 1997: 12). However, as Eze suggests, rather than slavery being a contradiction between the ideals of the Enlightenment and the sordid reality, the establishment of European cultural and philosophical supremacy required the dialectical negation of Africa where slavery was a key feature: 'By dialectically negating Africa, Europe was able to posit and represent itself and its contingent historicity as the ideal culture, the ideal humanity, and ideal history' (ibid.: 13). This negation has a direct material effect in the commodification of Africans as slaves, commodified first as a debased cargo for sale, and second as an inhumanly exploited labour force for the improvement of sugar profits.

African slaves were hardly the passive and benign recipients of their fate as expendable plantation labour, and increasing rebellion was matched by increasing violence from plantation owners; but also, from the beginning, it was impossible to keep the races completely separate. Over time, as the plantation system developed, a new 'Creole' culture emerged which was a mixture of European, African, South Asian and Amerindian peoples. This Creole culture was the realization of a 'new synthesis or mixture, arrived at through the struggles within and between the various components of the colonial population'. It was these African slaves and their descendants who 'paid with their blood and sweat and incarceration for the phenomenal expansion of human pos- sibilities in the Atlantic world' (Blackburn, 1997: 22). While the immedi- ate costs of the slave trade were manifest in the large number of slaves who perished in the voyage to the New World, and malnutrition, brutality, disease and overwork took a further toll, they nevertheless prevailed to evolve a vibrant Creole culture (Brathwaite, 1971). This new form of diasporic culture was a further and much more complex conse- quence of Caribbean sugar production, one which continues to have its effects in the world today.

Sugar as a metonym of imperial discourse

Apart from its extraordinary function in British economic history, sugar – by which I mean the production, marketing and consumption of tropical sugar cane – is an unparalleled metonym of imperial relations. To the question: 'Why should sugar be such a powerful model of the dynamic of empire?' one answer must be that commodity is a phenom- enon of extremes. In the growth of sugar consumption, in economic expansion, in the disruption of entire regions, and the transportation of millions of slaves, sugar has been the cause of extraordinary change and dislocation. The extremity of its consequences and its importance as an economic fulcrum make it an unparalleled demonstration of the cultural and political dynamic of colonialism. It demonstrates the circulatory and transcultural dynamic of colonial contact; it focuses the nature of the relationship between class and race, and of the important place of class hegemony in imperial expansion; it exposes the extent to which British culture was built on slavery; it demonstrates the persistent material and economic effects of colonization, and it demonstrates the perpetuation of the link between class and race in contemporary globalization. Sugar focuses as no other commodity has done, the extent to which imperial class and race relations are intertwined.

Circulation

The phenomenon of 'transculturation', a term coined by Fernando Ortiz and developed by Mary Louise Pratt (1992), describes an important feature of the transformative consequences of post-colonial cultures. The effects of colonization do not go only one way, from the centre to the margins, but circulate, the imperial societies being changed as much as the colonized in the interactive relationship of imperial contact and colonial control. This cultural phenomenon is modelled in striking clarity in the circulatory nature of the sugar economy. The rapid rise in consump- tion of this luxury quickly established it as a necessity, the production, manufacture and trade in which had almost incalculable effects on British economy and society itself. Although the impact of sugar on the Caribbean was catastrophic, it was balanced by profound consequences in imperial society as well. The impact of the 'white and deadly' imperial culture upon the Caribbean was matched, in different ways, by the impact of the 'white and deadly' substance on Britain (Ahluwalia *et al.*, 1999). In fact it was not simply a *matching* of effects, but the effects of consumption at the centre and production in the colonies were absolutely interdependent. Slave economies were not simply adjuncts to, but vital parts of the European economies.

This two-way, interactive and circulatory economic effect is an enormous material demonstration of transculturation. The devastations of slavery, the plantation economy, global displacement, all caused in very large part by the production of sugar, generated dynamic and hybrid cultures which came to spread their effects throughout the world. Although it is too reductive to limit sugar to the plantation and the Atlantic, it is nevertheless true that the appalling social consequences of Caribbean sugar production initiated cultural transformations which have affected the world and are affecting it still. Because sugar is the reason for the most traumatized and disrupted colonial populations, it is also the focus of the most revolutionary cultural developments.

Class, consumption and empire

Sugar transformed British eating habits more comprehensively than those of any other European nation. Not only did it ensure the rapid increase in consumption of coffee, tea and chocolate, but by the end of the nineteenth century, sugar constituted up to 25 per cent of the working-class diet in Britain.[4] Its consumption shows the most exponential increase of any commodity in history. Able to deliver high caloric content quickly and easily to factory workers in beverages, it became, in its various forms, equal to bread in its delivery of carbohydrates to the British poor. Consequently, the replacement of beer by highly sweetened tea contributed greatly to the reduction in the nutrition of the working class by the end of the nineteenth century. If we take into account the fact that the majority of protein coming into the family went to the male bread-winner, the effects upon women and children must have been enormous (Mintz, 1985: 145).

Although sugar was initially a luxury commodity, affordable only by the aristocracy, the economies of scale which resulted from the development of the plantation industry meant that sugar usage spread into all layers and classes of society. There is a badly under-theorized assumption by historians such as Walvin (1997) that the adoption of sugar simply filtered down from the upper classes by way of their servants, who emulated them. But this movement down the scale was *demanded* by the need to provide a quick and convenient source of high energy and high caloric foods for the labouring classes who were driving Britain's rapid industrialization. It also met a demand from the other direction: a need for increased consumption to balance imports of tropical sugar against the exports of manufactured goods. Once plantations were established in the early seventeenth century they began to drive consumption.

It is no accident that per capita sugar consumption in Britain reached four times that of any other European country by the end of the nineteenth century, and was the first commodity to be protected during the war (Lewis, 1970: 19; Albert and Graves, 1988: 4). This had a huge impact on the distinction of British cuisine (such as it was) from those of other European countries. However, in broader terms, the interrelationship between the commodification of labour – both wage labour in Britain and slave labour on the plantations, the stimulation of consumption and the consequent maximization of profits – led to a surfeit of capital which Hobson claims was the driving force of late nineteenth-century imperial expansion (Hobson, 1902). Sugar was centrally implicated in this spiral of capital. Curiously (a point which undermines Hobson's argument somewhat), this capital was not repatriated back into colonial sugar, so at the end of the nineteenth century, we are faced with the paradox, of a combination of a stagnating fund of British capital and a rapidly stagnating sugar cane industry.

Culture and coercion

More than any other investment, sugar funded the leisure, and hence the *culture*, of the English landowning gentry. The surplus drain from sugar-producing countries to the imperial centre, sometimes to buy peerages and consolidate status, often to diversify into industrial ventures, was a constant and profoundly debilitating aspect of the colonial relationship (Dunn, 1973); but, while impoverishing the colonial economy and enriching the metropolis, sugar had a profound effect on the cultures of both. Arguably, its effects on metropolitan culture were invisible, as the sordid reality of plantation exploitation was submerged beneath a growing English gentility. This is the feature of English life revealed by what Said calls a contrapuntal reading of Jane Austen's *Mansfield Park*.

In this novel, Sir Thomas Bertram's absence from Mansfield Park, tending to his Antiguan plantations, leads to a process of genteel but worrying dissolution amongst the young people left in the inadequate care of Lady Bertram and Mrs Norris. A gradual sense of freedom and lawlessness is about to result in the performance of a play called *Lovers' Vows* when Sir Thomas returns and methodically puts things to rights, like 'Crusoe setting things in order', or 'an early Protestant eliminating all traces of frivolous behaviour' (Said, 1993: 104). Said's contrapuntal reading brings the reality of Antigua to the fore in this process. Sir Thomas, we assume, does exactly the same things on his Antiguan plantations, methodically and purposefully maintaining control over his colonial domain with an unimpeachable sense of his own authority:

More clearly than anywhere else in her fiction, Austen here synchron-
ises domestic with international authority, making it plain that the
values associated with such higher things as ordination, law, and
propriety must be grounded firmly in actual rule over and possession
of territory. She sees that to hold and rule Mansfield Park is to hold
and rule an imperial estate in close, not to say inevitable association
with it. What assures the domestic tranquillity and attractive harmony
of one is the productivity and regulated discipline of the other. (Said,
1993: 104)

Mansfield Park itself exists as both metaphor and metonymy of the
colonial domain of Sir Thomas, without whose overseas properties the
ordered life of the Park could not function. Such a contrapuntal reading
can be extended to the extensive vista of imperial culture in its various
manifestations. For what funded the universalist notions of value, moral-
ity and worth, which became the very basis of Britain's civilizing
mission, were based on an exploitation of the uncivilized colonial world.

Colonialism and its material consequences

The effects of the plantation economy continue to the present day and
represent the lingering material effects of colonization, effects which
continue to contribute to post-colonial futures. There is something about
the sugar plantation and its importance to structures of imperial power
that has led to continual disruption, and social and economic exploitation. In every analysis of the contemporary sugar industry in particular
locations, such as Brazil, Guyana or the Philippines, the present situation is recognized as a consequence of the colonial relationship, and
its social and economic effects. The 'high degree of centralisation of
political authority associated with colonial rule was mirrored in the
political power of the planter class' (Thomas, 1984: 13). In places such
as Guyana, there was a direct relation between sugar power and political power, as the plantocracy exercised a virtual monopoly over the
state machinery.

Sugar-producing societies have become economically lopsided,
depressed and artificially dependent on a single commodity. Plantations
have impeded the development of domestic food production, concen-
trated income in a small group of landowners, and subjugated the rural
population to the landed élite. Since slaves were not active consumers,
domestic markets remained small; and the slave's presence depressed
wages, and in most cases inhibited the development of a free rural
proletariat (Eisenberg, 1974: 7). Thus the sugar plantation, with its
occupation of large tracts of land and its resistance to diversification,
completely dominates those small economies in which sugar is grown,
and not only in the well-documented Caribbean. Planters pursued sugar
to the virtual exclusion of all other productive activity. By its very

nature, the sugar plantation, even after the abolition of slavery, was socially, materially, economically and ecologically totalitarian.

Unquestionably, one of the most lasting impacts of the sugar plantation is the mode of labour relations it developed over three centuries. The sugar plantation is labour intensive, the employment of cheap labour excludes any need to modernize the harvesting process, and it institutionalizes a violent and repressive relationship with the workforce. In turn, the labour force itself becomes highly stratified, so that a 'system of sharp and rigid class differentiation' becomes woven into a 'system of sharp and rigid racial differentiation' (Thomas, 1984: 14). After emancipation, the addition of other ethnic groups led to a similarly sharp differentiation between the two. 'To this day', says Thomas, the social relations built up by the plantation system pose 'insuperable obstacles to the transformation of rural life in Guyana' (1984: 14).

For instance, Roger Plant's *Sugar and Modern Slavery* (1987) discusses how the culture of slavery has continued in the island of Hispaniola, with Haiti co-opting its citizens and selling them to the Dominican Republic where they are used as virtual slaves. One reviewer could not see why 'he should be so concerned about the conditions under which one state transfers a relatively small number of workers to the other' and saw it as running the risk of 'diverting attention from the greater cause of frustrated aspirations' (Cameron, 1987). Such responses suggest that, unless we understand the perpetuation of inequality in labour relations as a consequence of the mode of labour relations central to the colonial process, we run the risk of seeing phenomena such as that of modern slavery in Hispaniola as a peripheral aberration. In Hispaniola, we see a stark example of the perpetuation of relations of power that colonialism established.

Sugar workers throughout the world still bear the brunt of the industry's endemic structural weaknesses and fluctuations in the market. In the Philippines, says Shoesmith, 'there are between four and five hundred thousand sugar workers with some three million dependants who live under conditions not so far removed from those in the slave plantations of the West Indies and North America in the early 1800s' (Shoesmith, 1977: 9). The corruption of President Marcos, who pocketed hundreds of millions of dollars from the US-protected industry, was only possible because the sugar industry 'has long supported an oligarchy which must take a great deal of responsibility for the way in which Spaniards, Americans, Japanese and fellow Filipinos have been able to enrich themselves while impoverishing the Philippines and the great majority of Filipinos' (ibid.: 9).

The link between sugar and colonialism needs to be stressed because it is relatively easy to see the social and economic effects of sugar purely in terms of emergent capitalism. Significantly, the abolition of slavery in the 1830s coincided with the end of the mercantilist era: the Sugar Duties Act, passed in 1846, equalized import duties on all sugars after 1851 (later postponed to 1854). Free trade was then, as it is now, the preference of the powerful, since it operated in the best interests of the large economies which could undersell competitors and which needed large supplies of cheap (untariffed) resources. However, it was disastrous for small sugar economies and led to the development of an absentee landowner class as a precursor to the development of the limited liability company. British capitalism was always mediated by its imperialism, so that the sugar economy became integrated into its capitalism as a natural extension of colonial power.

Globalization

This chronic depression of sugar-producing economies leads directly to my consideration of sugar and globalization. A survey of sugar sites on the internet will quickly reveal two things: the huge consumption of sugar in the USA and the totalitarian way in which world prices are kept low.[5] This would tempt one into a top-down view of globalization, of global capital exploiting the poor Southern hemisphere and tropical nations on behalf of the rich North. Such a view is radically destabilized by the example of post-colonial transformation, but even more interesting is that moment, as we saw in chapter 4, when America began to take charge of imperial rhetoric, a moment we can virtually date from Teddy Roosevelt's speech on the eve of his election in 1901 (see Chaper 3). Remarkably, at the exact moment when the British Empire was at its peak, America was already taking over moral responsibility for the civilizing mission. Even more interestingly, by this time, America had already exceeded Britain in total sugar consumption and was soon to outstrip it in per capita consumption. Considering how much sugar Britain consumed by the turn of the century, this is astonishing. Whether or not America drives the global economy today – and this depends upon how you view globalization – it is clear that America initiated it by inventing the three major modes of globalization: mass production, mass consumption and mass communication.

In two of these modes – production and consumption – sugar continues to have an inordinate function. Why? Because it is a drug food and an unparalleled promoter of bodily desire. Adam Smith is perhaps the first globalist, and his view of the role of commodities in distinguishing the civilized from the barbarous is deeply embedded in the ideology of empire. For him the social body is a body composed of things, a web of commodities circulating in an exchange that connects people who do not see or know each other. These things make it a 'civilized' body. Having an abundance of 'objects of comfort' is the litmus test that distinguishes 'civilized and thriving nations' from 'savage' ones, 'so miserably poor' that they are reduced to 'mere want' (Smith, 1776: lx). It is a trade that has caused certain parts of the world to progress, leaving others (such as Africa) in a 'barbarous and uncivilized state'.

Smith was the first to recognize the crucial function of desire. 'I come to desire the pleasure of desire itself. In fact it could not be otherwise. If desire *were* satiated, if it were *not* deflected onto a demand for commodities . . . then not only would the growth of wealth come to a halt but the whole social nexus of civilization would fall apart' (Buck-Morss, 1995: 452). So, as capitalism is central to civilization, desire is central to capitalism, and becomes its most resilient and captivating export. When thinking of desire, we are invariably drawn towards sexuality, and there is no doubt that the commodification of sexuality is a great driver of consumption; but the most pervasive object of bodily desire is food. When that food is a drug food, and when desire is stimulated by its presence in almost every other processed food, its function in value-adding and profit-taking becomes immense. Sugar is obviously not the only focus of bodily desire, but it comprehensively demonstrates how the operations of classical imperialism can transform effortlessly into global circulations of production and consumption by means of the potency of desire.

This element of desire is crucial to the modern consumption of processed foods. In this respect we might say that the purest metonym of desire lies in physical taste itself, for this is the key to an apparently uncontainable increase in consumption based on pleasure rather than need. The three key elements of processed food consumption are fat, salt and sugar. Two of these, fat and salt, are necessary in small quantities and play a huge part in the facilitation of smell and taste: as Adam Smith says, 'I come to desire the pleasure of desire itself'; but where the use of fat and salt has finite limits in food processing, the totally unnecessary food – the drug food, sugar – is the one most amenable to exponential increases as a food additive. For the metonym of desire – physical taste – is the key to driving the body to consume what it neither wants nor needs.

At this point, the spiral which links class and race in imperial discourse is continued in global sugar consumption. Sugar is still the food of the poor, and the poor are to a significant extent the non-white populations of the world.[6] Where sugar-producing countries continue to show the effects of the exploitative nature of sugar production, the link between sugar and desire is almost universal. One example may be found in the supply of rations to Australian aborigines: flour, tea, sugar, salt and small amounts of meat. It has been suggested that the contemporary Aboriginal body, with its excessive rates of heart dysfunction, diabetes and obesity (as well as lung cancer and alcoholism), is a direct product of those introduced foods and drugs which came to be accepted as normal.

The Caribbean: sugar and cultural transformation

The economic and political effects of sugar in colonial societies are clear consequences of the sugar plantation mode of production. The violent and exploitative mode of labour relations; the movement of millions of people, through slavery and indenture, from one part of the world to another; the totalitarian occupation of space; the excessive dependence on a single crop which went close to converting a whole region into a giant sugar factory; the consequent distortion and ruin of local economies; and the institutionalizing of poverty, have all had incalculable consequences on contemporary societies. The abolition of slavery, independence, and nationalization have done little to ameliorate the totalitarian, hegemonic and inequitable system of sugar production.

So when we talk about the Caribbean, in particular, we talk about a history of social and political decay, exploitation, disruption and ruin. The post-colonial question is: 'How did these displaced, traumatized and diasporic cultures break down the brutal binaries of the colonial plantation society to produce one of the most vibrant cultures in the world today?' The answer may be found back on the sugar plantation itself. These societies transformed themselves by utilizing the heterogeneous range of cultural backgrounds and influences which constituted them, employing many of the social strategies of resistance built up through centuries of plantation slavery. Sugar workers, under conditions of extreme exploitation, poverty, hardship and dislocation, developed forms of cultural resistance which came to characterize the vitality of the Caribbean. Ultimately, the transformative effects of these cultures circulated into the imperial and global centres. It is because of the model of post-colonial transformation that we can understand how complex and circulatory globalization is – as complex and circulatory as classical imperialism.

In sugar we find an extreme display of the transformative development of post-colonial futures. As an overwhelmingly colonial product, a product consumed everywhere, a commodity whose production devastated environments, displaced huge populations of diasporic peoples, revolutionized patterns of consumption, it is an unparalleled linchpin of economic history. Because of the extremity of its effects, it is a powerful metonym of imperial discourse; because of the pervasiveness and power of the desire it evokes, it demonstrates the effortless way in which a product of the British Empire can become a driving force of global capital. When we search for a key to the energy driving the transformations effected by the peoples whose lives were radically changed by colonialism, we can find no better location for it than the Caribbean sugar plantation. Sugar focuses the dynamic reality of post-colonial strategies as no other single product has ever done.

Notes

1. Although Wallerstein's view problematized an older historical Marxist position, with a theory of the structure of domination, it has come to underpin various versions of dependency theory, which have the effect of accepting a structure of unequal power relations as inevitable.

2. Napoleon sponsored the development of beet sugar after his defeat at the battle of Trafalgar had severely diminished his capacity to conduct overseas trade. Beet sugar, discovered by the German chemist Marggraf in 1747, became the main form of sugar consumed in continental Europe after Napoleon's intervention, and by the end of the nineteenth century Germany was the largest exporter of sugar (beet sugar) in the world.

3. The 'triangular trade' is a fairly recent conception of the shape of Atlantic commerce. Clearly, not many ships actually took cargo to Africa, filled up with slaves and transported them to America and then took sugar on to England, but as a geometrical concept of the commodity relationship which existed in the Atlantic it has proven to be extremely evocative. The most significant legacy has been the development of myths surrounding the 'Middle Passage' when slaves were brought across the Atlantic to work the burgeoning sugar plantations.

4. This is an estimate based on figures for the whole British population for whom, by 1900, 17.5 per cent of total caloric content was provided by sugar. If that figure 'could be revised to account for class, age and intrafamily differentials, the percentage for working class women and children would be astounding' (Mintz, 1985: 49).

5. For a bland but revealing statistical account see Brent Borrell, Robert Sturgiss and Gordon Wong, *Global Effects of the US Sugar Policy* (Bureau of Agriculture Economic Discussion Paper 87.3). Canberra: AGPS, 1987.

6. Mintz goes so far as to link the exponential increase in sugar to malnutrition in pre-school children which is '*de facto* the most widely used method of population control. The Reagan administration's attempt to define sucrose-rich catsup as a "vegetable" in federally supported school lunch programs is a recent demonstration' (Mintz, 1985: 149).

CHAPTER 6

Caliban's language

It is perhaps no accident, given the cultural consequences of the Caribbean sugar industry, that Caribbean novelists and poets have been among the most energetic transformers of colonial language. Already competent in moving through various registers of English, within what Bickerton calls the 'creole continuum' (1973), their inventiveness with language is virtually unparalleled in the post-colonial world. The Caribbean has also been a productive site for the rereading and rewriting of the canonical texts of English literature. Barbadian George Lamming, for instance, although not the first to recognize the colonial implications of Shakespeare's final play, *The Tempest*, is the writer who most influenced contemporary post-colonial readings. This reminds us of the importance of creative writing and the reading of canonical literature in the process of cultural transformation.

When we examine these canonical works, they often show themselves to be consummate reconstructions of the dynamic of imperial power. In analysing them we discover why they have been so attractive to rewritings. *The Tempest* has been read for nearly half a century as a powerful and remarkably comprehensive allegory of colonization. First used, somewhat eccentrically, by Octave Mannoni to demonstrate the 'dependency' complex of the colonized in 1950 (Mannoni, 1950), *The Tempest* has become, since George Lamming's reading in *The Pleasures of Exile*, a major allegory of the colonial experience, written back to, rewritten and alluded to by one post-colonial writer after another.[1]

Lamming dismantles the view of Caliban as a creature outside civilization 'on whose nature/Nurture can never stick' (IV, i, 188–9), showing him to be a human being (specifically a West Indian), whose human status has been denied by the European claims to an exclusive human condition.[2] In the relationship between Prospero, Miranda, Ariel and Caliban we find demonstrated in dramatic form some of the most fundamental features of the colonial enterprise: the consummate binary set up between colonizer and colonized; the nature of the power relationship which this binary facilitates; the hegemony of imperial notions of order and good government; the profound link between such ideas and the technology of the colonizing power (which in Prospero is symbolized by his magic art); the racial debasement and demonization of the colonized (articulated by Prospero's, and the play's, attitude to Caliban); and the belief that goals of 'improvement', of the civilizing mission, are a justification for subjugation.

Because such texts allegorize so well the dynamics of imperial power, they offer a rich site for the consideration of post-colonial issues, and one of these is the future of Caliban's language. While *The Tempest* has been a classic subject of rereadings and rewritings, it is in Caliban's encounter with Prospero's language that some of the most interesting questions of post-colonial transformation emerge. The play provides one of the most confronting demonstrations of the importance of language in the colonial encounter, but it does not share our interest in Caliban, who disappears without trace leaving us ignorant of the possibilities of his use of Prospero's speech. *The Tempest* is fascinating because, while it liberally displays the power of Prospero's language, it offers no view of Caliban's response, other than his resonant 'You taught me your language, and my profit on't is I know how to curse'. Famous though this response has become, it fails to conceive any possibility of Caliban's power to transform language. Caliban remains an evocative and controversial symbol of the post-colonial response: while many would hold that colonial language has no other function than oppression, good for nothing but cursing, writers throughout the colonized world have continued to transform it, and turn it into a vehicle that works for them.

Caliban therefore becomes a peerless figure of colonial ambivalence and the main reason for the many counter-discursive renditions of the play. Caliban is important for our purposes because he has no future; that is, Shakespeare is incapable of conceiving any future for him. Thus, to see Caliban's cursing as the only response the colonized subject might have to the colonial language is to accept Caliban as the play presents him: a vanquished and marginalized miscegenator with no hope and no future. Once we locate the colonial significance of the play, some very different possibilities open up. Because Caliban is so manifestly the cannibal/primitive, the abject other of European civilization in the play, he has become a symbol for representations of subaltern exploitation and resistance. His disappearance from the action invites us to extend the allegory and consider the trajectory of his future, specifically the future of his speaking, his use of the colonial language.

Caliban's virtual relegation to the status of cursing savage is curiously echoed in the writings of Roberto Fernández Retamar, whose Spanish essays on Caliban – 'Caliban' written in 1971, 'Caliban revisited' written in 1986 (both translated in Retamar, 1989), and 'Caliban speaks five hundred years later' written in 1992 (McClintock *et al.*, 1997) – raised the character to almost iconic status in Latin America. Retamar's essays are a trenchant attack on the huge and flimsy edifice of European imperialism. Yet in launching the attack they have as little to say about Caliban's future as *The Tempest*. Caliban appears to be unable to do anything but curse in the dominant language. This strangely futureless positioning of

Caliban's voice reaches a peak in Retamar's final essay, 'Caliban speaks five hundred years later', a long diatribe against Europe and its historic imperialist evils, in which the author adopts Caliban's identity to, in a sense, 'curse' the effects of 500 years of domination. For all its political energy, it becomes an interesting demonstration of the inability of some resistance rhetoric to take into account the kinds of transformations that have actually occurred in colonized societies. The paradoxical effect of this is to lock Caliban into the position of anti-European 'natural man'.

Clearly, Shakespeare endorses Prospero's project to civilize the 'natural man'. Prospero is also a model for the playwright himself, a creative authority at the height of his powers who looks back in the play upon the capacity of creative art to change nature. However, perhaps for this reason, the contest between Nature and Art in the play is by no means a foregone conclusion: in a significant intervention into this argument, the kindly Gonzalo proposes that in a Kingdom ruled by him, 'All things in common Nature should produce/Without sweat or endeavour' (II,i, 155–6). Furthermore, Caliban, so comprehensively demonized, is nevertheless given some of the most beautiful and powerful lines in the play. While the conflict between Prospero's Art and Caliban's natural man remains central, Caliban becomes, in a post-colonial reading, the lens through which the political issues of colonial subjection are focused. Caliban is the key to the transformation of this allegory in such a reading, for he is not only colonized by Prospero, but, in a sense, also by the assumptions on which the play is based.

Caliban, as the marginalized indigene, is the antithesis of culture. He is ignorant of gentleness and humanity, he is a savage and capable of all ill; he is born to slavery, not to freedom, of a vile rather than a noble union, and whose parents represent an evil natural magic which is the antithesis of Prospero's art. More importantly, his nature is one on which nurture, the benefits of imperial culture 'will not stick'. Thus in every respect he embodies the primitive colonized savage and indicates the comprehensiveness with which his depiction by an invading and hegemonic power justifies his subjugation. (The way in which Caliban is understood and the terms by which he is described justify the colonizing process which subjugates him, so in this way the language and the assumptions underlying its use both marginalize Caliban and justify his colonization.) Prospero's Art, on the other hand, is seen to represent civilized man's power over the world and himself, a power over Nature divorced from grace, of the mind over the senses.

The naming and depiction of Caliban (Carib – Canibal – Caliban) is a clear demonstration of the attempt by the text to refute the view of Nature as that which man corrupts, and of Montaigne's view that the natural man enjoyed a naturally virtuous life uncorrupted by civilization (Florio, 1603). Caliban's origins and character are 'natural' in the sense that they do not partake of grace, civility or art. Clearly Shakespeare's text resists the ambivalence that enters into the argument between Locke and Rousseau about the 'natural' state of the child (see Chapter 3). Caliban is ugly in body, associated with an evil 'natural' magic, and unqualified for rule or nurture. He is in every way offered as an example of the baseness of the life yet unordered by method, society, civilization or good government. The play categorically contests the assumptions of Montaigne or Rousseau that nature is that which human society corrupts (Rousseau, 1755). Culture is that which necessarily turns the savage into a human being and it is the colonizing culture that provides the model *par excellence* of this process; above all, it is language that performs this civilizing and humanizing function.

Caliban is the prototype of the colonized subject, whose baseness, as constructed by the colonizer, is the justifying prerequisite of colonization. This is why Caliban has been so consistently fascinating to writers trying to understand their own colonial condition. Edouard Glissant says:

> This is the problem of Caliban, that island creature whom a prince from the continent wished to civilize. The theme of Caliban has touched Caribbean intellectuals in a surprising way: Fanon, Lamming, Césaire, Fernández Retamar. The fact is that Caliban, as the locus of encounters and conflicts, has become a symbol. Above and beyond Shakespeare's savage cannibal, a real dynamic is at play – not only in the Caribbean but in many places in the Third World – a dynamic constituted by encounters among these three necessities: the class struggle, the emergence or the construction of the nation, the quest for collective identity. The facts of social and cultural life are only rarely combined and reinforced in harmony. It is claimed in Panama that the negritude movement promoted by Panamanians of Caribbean origin is in opposition to the will to reinforce the Panamanian nation. It is asserted in Trinidad that the resolution of political or economic problems is achieved or not achieved (depending on the ideology of the speaker) by the aggressive affirmation of either Indian or African identity. It is argued in Cuba that the solution to problems of social inequality will mean the simultaneous removal of racism. All of that is the true Caribbean problematic. It is why Caliban deserves such a passionate scrutiny. (1989: 118–19)

It is not the simplicity of Caliban's rebellion and striving for identity which makes him so relevant to post-colonial experience, but its complexity. For every discourse of resistance there are several others vying for authority. The centre of this complexity, of the contending issues of class, race, nation, is the language he speaks. For in this language freedom resides, if only he can find the discourse which will liberate it.

Language, learning and colonial power

The domination of Prospero's Art over Nature and the colonized world is above all the domination of his language and books. Indeed it is, curiously, the reason for his overthrow and exile to the island.

> And Prospero the prime Duke being so reputed
> In dignity, and for the liberal Arts
> Without a parallel; those being all my study,
> The government I cast upon my brother
> And to my state grew stranger, being transported
> And rapt in secret studies. (I, ii, 72–7)

Prospero is no cynical politician; indeed, by presenting him as deceived by his brother and naive about the politics of Milan, the play suggests that his culture dwells in a rarefied dimension far beyond the hurly-burly of ordinary political intrigue. Dedicated to 'closeness and the bettering of my mind' (I, ii, 90), he embodies the highest ideals of his culture which exist in the space of the 'timeless' and 'universal'. This, indeed, is precisely the way in which European culture maintains a hegemony of ideas and values which outlasts colonial domination itself.

There can be no doubt that the key to the moral superiority manifested in Prospero's art is the language with which he names and controls the island. His function as an educator nurtures the prototypical settler colonial – his daughter Miranda – but it has a very different effect on Caliban. In a scene between Prospero, Caliban and Miranda in Act I Scene ii (on which this chapter will principally focus), we discover how crucial language becomes in the process of colonial control.

> *Caliban:* As wicked dew as e'er my mother brush'd
> With raven's feather from unwholesome fen
> Drop on you both! a south-west blow on ye
> And blister you all o'er!

> *Prospero:* For this, be sure, tonight thou shalt have cramps,
> Side-stitches that shall pen thy breath up; urchins
> Shall, for that vast of night that they may work,
> All exercise on thee; thou shalt be pinch'd
> As thick as honeycomb, each pinch more stinging
> Than bees made 'em.

> *Caliban:*   I must eat my dinner.
> This island's mine, by Sycorax my mother,
> Which thou tak'st from me. When thou cam'st first,
> Thou strok'st me, and made much of me; wouldst give me
> Water with berries in't; and teach me how
> To name the bigger light, and how the less,
> That burn by day and night: and then I love'd thee,
> And show'd thee all the qualities o' th' isle,
> The fresh springs, brine-pits, barren place and fertile:
> Curs'd be I that did so! All the charms
> Of Sycorax, toads, beetles, bats, light on you!
> For I am all the subjects that you have,
> Which first was mine own King: and here you sty me

In this hard rock, whilst you do keep from me
The rest o' the island.

Prospero: Thou most lying slave,
Whom stripes may move, not kindness! I have us'd thee,
Filth as thou art, with human care; and lodg'd thee
In mine own cell, till thou didst seek to violate
The honour of my child.

Caliban: O ho, O ho! would't had been done!
Thou didst prevent me; I had peopled else
This isle with Calibans.

Miranda: Abhorred slave,
Which any print of goodness wilt not take,
Being capable of all ill! I pitied thee,
Took pains to make thee speak, taught thee each hour
One thing or other: when thou didst not, savage,
Know thine own meaning, but wouldst gabble like
A thing most brutish, I endow'd thy purposes
With words that made them know. But thy vile race,
Though thou didst learn, had that in't which good natures
Could not abide to be with; therefore wast thou
Deservedly confin'd into this rock,
Who hadst deserved more than a prison.

Caliban: You taught me language; and my profit on't
Is, I know how to curse. The red plague rid you
For learning me your language. (I, ii, 332–67)

This scene plays out many of the major linguistic, racial and cultural issues that emerge from the historical trauma of colonialism. Caliban's famous reply is a tortured and resonant confirmation of the various processes of colonial domination that have been articulated in the previous exchange. Language is not one aspect of a broad range of colonizing strategies, it is the very mode of cultural control, the vehicle in which those strategies are effected; but what are these processes of domination? When we examine the scene closely we will see that it rehearses several of the most profound and troubling aspects of linguistic colonization: the issue of place and the power of imperial technology; the power of naming; the relationship between language and power itself; the connection between language and race; and the constitutive and therefore putatively ontological power of a dominant language.

Language, place and imperial technology

The scene opens with a violent exchange between Caliban and Prospero in which the threats they throw at each other seem to be equally malicious. Yet there is a very subtle difference in their nature. Caliban calls upon a 'wicked dew' from 'unwholesome fen' (I, ii, 324) to drop on them both; for a 'south west blow on ye and blister ye all over' (I, ii, 325–6). Caliban's resource is the place itself, the conditions of that island which he takes for granted as his home. Prospero's threats are more sinister and painful, for they are directed at Caliban's body. 'Tonight thou shalt have cramps', he says, 'Side stitches that shall pen thy breath up'. Urchins and bees will do their work on Caliban's body at Prospero's behest.

Although Caliban belongs to the place and can call upon the natural resources of the island, Prospero's Art intervenes in nature, for this intervention is the very function of culture. Prospero's Art, therefore, that benign and unworldly profession which immerses itself in study, in books and in language, becomes directly responsible for Caliban's physical pain. That separation between the base materiality of colonial subjection and the erudite power of imperial learning is completely dissolved the moment the colonized subject offers resistance. The link between Prospero's superior technology and the intention to torture Caliban's debased body is a profound metaphor of the actual material consequences of an eloquent and 'civilizing' imperial culture.

It is clear that there is a distinct difference in the play between the ways in which Prospero and Caliban relate to place. Prospero's primary modality is mastery, effected through his 'Art' and represented in his language. Caliban's ability to experience the island 'instinctively', beyond the domination of Prospero's Art or language, is elaborated later when Trinculo and Stephano hear Ariel's music:

> Be not afeard; the isle is full of noises,
> Sounds and sweet airs, that give delight, and hurt not.
> Sometimes a thousand twangling instruments
> Will hum about mine ears; and sometimes voices,
> That, if I then had wak'd after long sleep,
> Will make me sleep again; and then, in dreaming,
> The clouds methought would open, and show riches
> Ready to drop upon me; that, when I wak'd,
> I cried to dream again. (III, ii, 132–41)

Whereas Prospero uses music to charm, punish and generally consolidate his power, music provokes in Caliban an enjoyment of the dreamlike riches of the island. In one view this is a moment of excess that exists beyond the restricting language of the colonizer. 'Caliban's production of the island as a pastoral space, separated from the world of power, takes *literally* what the discourse in the hands of a Prospero can only mean *metaphorically*' (Brown, 1985, in Bloom, 1988: 149). In this reading, Caliban desires to escape reality and return to dream as the only way to evade the control of Prospero's language, yet it is in this very language that Caliban reveals the delights of the island to the drunkards. Even in this eloquent description of the dream-like qualities of the island (or perhaps *particularly* in this description), Caliban engages the language which 'interpellates' him in a way that sets his experience of the island apart.

The colonized do not speak (even in the evocation of dream) from a space unaffected by the dominant language and culture, not even the reassuring space of one's pre-colonial mother tongue. It is this one fact which most clearly politicizes post-colonial speakers either consciously or unconsciously. In particular, the power of language to construct the physical environment is one with which they must always contend. Whatever the sense of inherent or cultural 'belonging' to place which Caliban may have, it is clear that place may be 'controlled' by being familiarized and domesticated through language. The most obvious ploy in colonial discourse in general is to name particular sites, towns, headlands, mountains and rivers with the names of imperial politicians and monarchs. There is no doubt a cynical element of repayment for patronage and expectation of advancement by the explorers, carto- graphers and pioneers who do the naming, but at a more profound level the place may be incorporated into imperial discourse by a naming of its climatic, geological, topographical and geographical features which locate the place into a modern, universal system of reference. The Mercator projection Atlas is perhaps the most comprehensive and signi- ficant example of this process, but it occurs continually and at many levels. For instance, the contestation of English names in various colonies becomes a strategic aspect of the reclamation of place.

Language and naming

The example of Prospero alerts us to the ways in which this apparently benign discourse of imperial naming may have actual, harmful effects on the lives and bodies of the colonized. In reply to Prospero's threat of torture, Caliban launches into a famous speech which confirms his own indigenous possession of the land, the power of Prospero's language and the ultimate hollowness of colonial control.

> This island's mine, by Sycorax my mother,
> Which thou tak'st from me. When thou cam'st first,
> Thou strok'st me, and made much of me; wouldst give me
> Water with berries in't; and teach me how
> To name the bigger light, and how the less,
> That burn by day and night: and then I love'd thee,
> And show'd thee all the qualities o' th' isle,
> The fresh springs, brine-pits, barren place and fertile:
> Curs'd be I that did so! (I, ii, 332–40)

Caliban's ownership of the island is based on prior occupation, which is the only practical measure of indigeneity, even though his mother

Sycorax had migrated there. However, the moral force of prior occupation pales into insignificance alongside the linguistic force of Prospero's power to name place; that is, to establish *his* names as the authoritative ones. The power to name place, by locating the speaker within a world that is recognizable through a particular language, bestows the more far-reaching capacity to construct human identity. This is because those names represent not just a language but an entire edifice of cultural assumptions: attitudes about time and space, about the relation between language and place, and even about the operation of thought itself. In European colonization names become, in effect, metonymic of modernity, in terms of which the rights to dominance are assumed.

This assumption of dominance requires that the indigenous subjects be, in effect, dehumanized, their own capacity for naming erased. In Ernest Renan's play *Caliban*, the opening scene sees Caliban and Ariel discussing the issues which arise in Act I Scene ii of *The Tempest*. Here Ariel echoes the formative and strategic assertion of colonial occupation:

> Thou sayest without cessation that the island belonged to thee. In truth, it did belong to thee, just as the desert belongs to the gazelle, the jungle to the tiger, and no more. Thou knewest the name of nothing there. Thou wast a stranger to reason and thy inarticulate language resembled the bellowing of an angry camel more than any human speech. (Renan, 1896: 17)

The pronouncement of the inarticulacy of the indigenous occupants is an important erasure, a constitution of empty space on which 'place' can then be inscribed by the various processes of colonial discourse. One of these processes involves endowing or denying human identity to the indigenous inhabitants, a role in which Miranda functions by providing the terms by which Caliban may know himself. It was she who, teaching Caliban language, taught him to 'know thine own meaning' (I, ii, 358).

Language and power

The naming and renaming of place is a potent demonstration of the ways in which the power of a discourse may operate. Renaming operates as if it were the original and authoritative naming of the place, or any other concept, and it is this authority to describe the world that Prospero's language acquires. Fundamental to this naming process is the discursive act of wiping the slate clean, of assuming that no prior naming system exists. In Renan's play *Caliban*, when Ariel replies to Caliban that 'Thou knewest the name of nothing there. Thou wast a stranger to reason' (Renan, 1986: 17) he is, in effect, articulating the doctrine of '*Terra Nullius*' which is an essential feature of the claims of a colonial language. It is this command of the naming of 'the bigger light and the lesser' which indicates the command of the colonizing culture, for to name reality is in some mysterious way to assume control of it, by fitting it into a scheme in which all things have their relation because they are related in language. These lines are deeply resonant of the power of language within colonialism, for the energy of any monologic discourse is directed towards certainty, identification, discrimination. This drive towards a unitary discourse requires that it clearly and unproblematically discriminates self from other, and in the colonial situation it radically differentiates the identities of colonizer and colonized.

The proposition that power is mediated in language is by no means universally accepted, but it is important to recognize that power does not operate in a simple top-down way, percolating through a hierarchy of institutions, exerting and distributing itself among strata of dominated subjects. 'Power must be analysed as something which circulates', says Foucault. 'Power is employed and exercised through a net-like organisation. And not only do individuals circulate between its threads; they are always in the position of simultaneously undergoing and exercising this power' (1976: 99). Imperial power, for instance, is *transcultural* (Pratt, 1992); it circulates (through subjects as well as on them), and when it operates in language, such transculturality is demonstrated by the capacity of speakers to transform the language by interpolating their own styles of usage into its wider circulation.

The key to the engagement of post-colonial discourse with power is that language does not only repress Caliban, it produces him. It produces him in very material ways, for not only does it produce his self-representation, but what he can say, where he can say it and when are all constrained by other dominant participants. In 'discourse analysis' (that is, the analysis of language as a social practice), power is all about 'powerful participants *controlling and constraining the contributions of non-powerful participants*' (Fairclough, 1989: 46; emphasis in original). How Caliban engages language will be vitally linked to how he engages powerful participants, and will hence be a key to how he transforms power to work for him.

George Lamming detects the productive nature of this power, although he expresses it as imprisonment: the issue for Caliban is one which goes deeper than a particular language, for 'There is no escape from the prison of Prospero's gift':

> Prospero has given Caliban Language; and with it an unstated history of consequences, an unknown history of future intentions. This gift of Language meant not English, in particular, but speech and concept as a way, a method, a necessary avenue towards areas of the self which could not be reached in any other way. (Lammings, 1960: 109)

Prospero's gift is the gift of method; but to interpret the productive power of imperial representation as imprisonment is to ignore the transformative agency of those produced in this discourse. Does language provide an avenue towards areas of the self that are unreachable in any other way, or does it provide the names by which those areas come into being? Prospero's names metonymize the power he has over Caliban's world, here and now, but not necessarily for all time. Caliban is not imprisoned in Prospero's language incontrovertibly because it is by *using* Prospero's language (or any other) that Caliban can actualize his own *possibility for being*. This power is the key to the transformative dynamic of post-colonial writing and cultural production. Such a dynamic emerges in Caliban's determination to answer back to one who has such manifest power over him.

> All the charms
> Of Sycorax, toads, beetles, bats, light on you!
> For I am all the subjects that you have,
> Which first was mine own King: and here you sty me
> In this hard rock, whilst you do keep from me
> The rest o' the island. (I, ii, 346–51)

This speech by Caliban goes right to the heart of post-colonial subjectivity, and specifically articulates the agency of the interpellated colonial subject to engage that power which produces him as subject. For, given the power of Prospero's language to interpellate Caliban, the discursive power that produces his subjectivity is neither absolute nor hierarchically fixed in those institutions – such as education, literature, government – through which it is perpetuated. Clearly Prospero's power over Caliban is tangibly oppressive; he commands the means of physical torture and incarceration (not to mention the emotionally disabling impact of his personal treachery to one who loved him and showed him 'all the qualities o' th' isle' (I, ii, 339)), but there is a place where the power of his language cannot reach. For Prospero's language can only have power over Caliban to the extent that it has power to cement his perception of himself, if Caliban comes to internalize the way in which he is situated in that language, accepting it as a true indication of his status and being.

Although such internalization may occur (and does occur often in the colonial experience), it is by no means inevitable or complete. Caliban's reaction demonstrates the limits of Prospero's power. For although his language assumes the status of an authoritative instrument for, in effect, bringing the world into being, it cannot obliterate Caliban's belief that he is the deposed king of the island, and that Prospero's dominion is in essence pathetic, since Caliban is his one and only subject. Imperial power as *either* repressive force *or* productive energy is not absolute or static but transformable. Although it has the power to 'produce' Caliban, it cannot prevent him from 'entering' power and reproducing himself in the language.

Language and race

Prospero's response to Caliban demonstrates the ways in which names exert power over the very being of the colonized. The 'gift' of language inscribes a power relationship, since the monster is interpellated as a linguistic subject of the master language. The question of Caliban's resistance therefore hinges at precisely this point, for the power of demonization lies in the capacity to make names stick, to make them the frame of one's self-representation. The colonized being whom Prospero at first stroked and 'made much of' is now constructed as a 'lying slave', 'filth', 'hag-seed', while to Miranda he is an 'abhorred slave', 'savage', 'brutish', of a 'vile race'. What motivates this change? Nothing less than the horror of miscegenation.

> Thou most lying slave,
> Whom stripes may move, not kindness! I have us'd thee,
> Filth as thou art, with human care; and lodg'd thee
> In mine own cell, till thou seek'st to violate
> The honour of my child.

To which Caliban replies

> O ho, O ho! would't had been done!
> Thou didst prevent me; I had peopled else
> This isle with Calibans.

This passage radically skews the play against Caliban, undermining his protestations of hospitality to the father and daughter (I, ii, 333–46). The effect of this charge is to show that he is incapable of recognizing proper civil boundaries and, by implication, of understanding the boundaries of place, thus abrogating any rights to the island which he occupies. This failure to recognize proper boundaries is a sign of primitiveness which is embedded in the discourse of race. The attempted rape threatens to introduce a race of hybrid post-colonial subjects, a threat of an almost dehumanizing racial pollution.

The issue of population is one which lies squarely at the intersection of race and colonialism, for 'to govern is to populate', as the South American Alberdi says. Roberto Fernández Retamar, in his essay 'Caliban', quotes Sarmiento's discussion of this slogan: 'Many difficulties will be presented by the occupation of so extensive a country; but there will be no advantage comparable to that gained by the extinction of savage tribes.' 'That is to say', says Retamar, 'for Sarmiento, to govern is also to *depopulate* the nation of its Indians (and gauchos)' (Retamar, 1989: 23). Caliban threatens the creation of a *mestizo* society, a concept which is racially inimical to Prospero's colonial ideal for the island and radically contrary to the more sinister programme of depopulation.

The link between language and race has existed since the emergence of racialist theory in writers such as Buffon, and becomes a key feature of imperial discourse, as Macaulay's Minute indicates: the assumptions about language are encouraged and ratified by the political, cultural and racial assertions of a dominant group. This link is foreshadowed in the exchange between Caliban and Prospero and Miranda, although not explicitly, for it is important to remember that the formal categorization of races had not yet occurred in European thinking when the play was written. The language which enabled Caliban to 'name the bigger light and how the less' (I, ii, 337) and which therefore becomes commensurate with reality itself, is a language in which the consequent assumption of authority cannot brook any thought of racial (or linguistic) intermixing. In his play *Caliban*, Renan has Ariel say, 'Prospero taught thee the Aryan language, and with that divine tongue the channel of reason has become inseparable from thee' (1896: 18). There is a very deep investment in the link between language and culture in nineteenth-century thinking (when Renan wrote his play); indeed, it is the force of this link which carries over into assumptions about language today. Hybridity represents not merely a racial impurity, but, more profoundly, threatens to disrupt the link between language and race so important to racialist thinking, and hence to the civilizing mission of imperialism. According to Renan, if one is fortunate enough to speak 'Indo-European', one benefits from all the qualities of that race (*ibid.*: 145).

Indeed, the myth of the authority of the dominant (Aryan) tongue as a discourse of knowledge rests upon its inviolability. As George Lamming asks:

> Could Prospero really have endured the presence and meaning of a brown skin grandchild? It would not be Miranda's own doing. It would not be the result of their enterprise. It would be Miranda's and Caliban's child. It would be *theirs*: the result and expression of some fusion both physical and other than physical. (1960: 102)

It is these 'other than physical' possibilities that are the most far-reaching. For quite apart from issues of rape and miscegenation is the possibility of the emergence of a hybrid 'decolonizing' language which might completely transform the nature of the colonial relationship and, consequently Caliban's power over discourse and thus over the island itself.

However, the spectre of miscegenation is undergirded by the process of radical 'othering' by which the colonial subject is demonized as the very antithesis of the civilized imperial 'self'. This other is dark, pagan, superstitious, primitive, savage, monstrous. Caliban is the very embodiment of the 'Wild Man' of European fantasy. 'The figure of the Wild Man', says Greenblatt, 'and the Indians identified as Wild Men, serve as a screen onto which Renaissance Europeans, bound by their institutions, project their darkest and yet most compelling fantasies' (1990: 22). The threat of miscegenation is a threat to a racial purity which is firmly hierarchized in nineteenth-century thinking. To monogenesists like Buffon (all humans descended from Adam) or polygenesists like Voltaire (all human races are different species), the threat of hybridization is equally objectionable, for it is a threat to a divinely or naturally ordained hierarchy of values within which the discrimination between races is conceived.

Caliban is such an overdetermined focus of imperial othering, such a 'monstrous absence' in contrast to the 'civilized presence' of Prospero, that it becomes impossible to visualize him by the descriptions the play gives of him. The power of language to 'other' the colonized subject emerges from the arbitrary visual status accorded to Caliban. He is 'a strange fish!' (II, ii, 27); 'Legg'd like a man! and his fins like arms!' (II, ii, 34); 'no fish' (II, ii, 36); 'some monster of the isle with four legs' (II, ii, 66); 'a plain fish' (V, i, 266); and a 'mis-shapen knave' (V, i, 268). Morton Luce sums up this contradiction succinctly: 'if all the suggestions as to Caliban's form and feature and endowments that are thrown out in the play are collected, it will be found that the one half renders the other half impossible' (Hulme, 1986: 107).

The apparently confused and ambiguous representation of Caliban comes about because notions of race had not coalesced into clear physiological parameters when Shakespeare wrote, and were not to be so for a century and a half. The ambiguous directions, intimations and descriptions of Caliban in the play come about because, although the concept of the 'cannibal' had become entrenched in the European psyche as the absolute sign of the other, it had not yet been connected to the category of race. Caliban, in his contradictory and inexplicable monstrosity, demonstrates the European discourse of othering in the process of coming into being. Visually, Caliban is a kind of absence in the play, represented only by Prospero's discourse. He takes shape completely within the language of the colonizer, and by 'learning to curse' through that language (I, ii, 367) he fulfils the only expectations we may have of him. If we ask the question 'How would Caliban seem if it weren't for the consequences of his bondage and imprisonment?' we find that we cannot answer the question. In both his depiction as 'hag seed', monster, lying slave, filth, and his imprisonment in the colonial language by which this construction is borne, Caliban fulfils all prophecies of his debasement.

This process is demonstrated with beautiful symmetry in Prospero's play within a play, which is discussed by Peter Hulme. This play is a masque in which Prospero stages a fantasy version of the original conspiracy which exiled him, with the difference that this time he will defeat it. Within this orchestrated play, Caliban unwittingly plays the part of Antonio, who originally deposed Prospero, but this time will fail. 'Caliban is, as it were, playing himself, except that "himself" means the self that Prospero has cast for him – the treacherous slave' (Hulme, 1986: 122). Caliban, the racial other, enters the part that has already been set for him, the only script being the language itself. 'Caliban does indeed seize upon the part offered to him and plays it with gusto', says Hulme (*ibid.*: 123), and goes on to make the important observation that it would be difficult to deny that '*The Tempest* here has its finger on what is most essential in the dialectic between colonizer and colonized, offering a parable for that relationship probably never equalled for its compelling logic' (*ibid.*).

Caliban enters the part set for him – that of treacherous slave – because he does not have the power or means of controlling his own representation. Caliban's predicament is metonymized by the tension between the terms 'freedom fighter' and 'terrorist'. That which might otherwise be seen as a desperate attempt to claim justice, to fight for freedom, to usurp the invader of his island, is, in the play, an inevitable demonstration of his ungrateful, debased, uncivilized and monstrous nature. Linguistic colonialism, by this account, is not something embedded in the language but located in the nature of its use.

Beyond cursing: language and transformation

Miranda's response demonstrates the extent to which the filiative relationship with empire constructs the discourse of settlement, and to what extent she is placed in antagonism to Caliban through her ownership of language and her stewardship of education:

> Abhorred slave,
> Which any print of goodness wilt not take,
> Being capable of all ill! I pitied thee,
> Took pains to make thee speak, taught thee each hour
> One thing or other: when thou didst not, savage,
> Know thine own meaning, but wouldst gabble like
> A thing most brutish, I endow'd thy purposes
> With words that made them know. But thy vile race,
> Though thou didst learn, had that in't which good natures
> Could not abide to be with; therefore wast thou
> Deservedly confin'd into this rock,
> Who hadst deserved more than a prison. (I, ii, 353–65)

Miranda's language in this speech both embodies and describes the justification for the subjugation of the indigenous Caliban. Quite apart from his constitution as a rapist and miscegenator, he is an 'abhorred slave', 'savage', 'brutish', 'vile'. What is being enacted here is the power of Miranda's language to construct Caliban, a power which is coterminous with Prospero's very tangible control of his body, his actions, his destiny. Caliban is the very nadir of the natural man 'which any print of goodness wilt not take'. This is, of course, the inevitable retort of the civilizing mission to any rebuttals it might encounter from the colonized. The colonized subject cannot be endowed with the capacity for choice, can never be accorded the freedom to refuse incorporation. If he is recalcitrant, he must be constituted as incapable of improvement: as Prospero says, he is 'A devil, a born devil, on whose nature/Nurture can never stick' (IV, i, 188–9). The moral framework of the relationship is entirely constructed by the dominant party, the settler colonial Miranda, and it is a relationship dominated by a simple binary that remains central to imperial discourse.

The controversy surrounding this speech gives some insight into Miranda's own subjection to Prospero's discourse. The language has seemed to some to be too intemperate for Miranda and should more suitably be spoken by Prospero, to whom many productions of the play do, indeed, give this speech. But whatever Shakespeare's intentions might have been, it is clear that by entering so effortlessly into the diatribe of Prospero's language, Miranda reveals herself to be as formed by that language, by imperial discourse, as Caliban. Although she seems to further articulate the debasement of Caliban in which Prospero is engaged, her speech clarifies the link between the imperial and the patriarchal power. Miranda has clearly had a relationship with Caliban as a child, and assumes the nurturing aspects of colonial control by being responsible for teaching him language by which he can 'know himself', but her subjection to Prospero's discourse becomes more obvious when he commodifies her virginity to trade with Ferdinand in his plans to regain his throne.

Caliban's response to Miranda's diatribe is one of the most memorable in literature, and encapsulates the bitter reaction of many colonized peoples to centuries of linguistic and political control:

> You taught me language; and my profit on't
> Is, I know how to curse. The red plague rid you
> For learning me your language.

This statement has been used time and again as a cry of resistance: a recognition of the power of imperial language and the need for its rejection; but crucially, Caliban's response leaves him at an impasse, for he is provided with no way in which he can make the language work for him. The curse is not Miranda's language but the way in which he has been situated in it. We have seen in the scene itself that Caliban has the power of reply, he has the power of resistance, and he has the power to reject the self-representation which that language offers, but his inability to appropriate the language of Prospero confines him as securely as does Prospero's Art. It is this acceptance of the link between Prospero's language and his Art, and hence the subtle acceptance of his domination, which traps Caliban.

What Caliban might do with this language constitutes one of the most pressing issues in post-colonial writing, for what he *might* have done has indeed been accomplished in post-colonial literatures. Until the mid-twentieth century, says Vaughan, most critics implicitly sided with Prospero, blaming Caliban for his own linguistic limitations (Vaughan *et al.*, 1991: 166). However, language as a key to the relationship between Prospero and Caliban took a turn in George Lamming's essay 'A monster, a child, a slave' in 1960. When Lamming identified language as Prospero's 'prison', he posited an ambiguous prison which maintained its power productively: its 'imprisonment was effected in the way it could "produce" Caliban'. We do well to remind ourselves of Foucault's admonition to stop talking about power as negative and see it as productive (1977a: 194), because a recognition of the productive nature of power might change the ways in which it is engaged. When Lamming describes the language as 'a necessary avenue towards areas of the self which could not be reached in any other way' (1960: 109), he ascribes to Prospero's colonizing language more discursive power over the construction of subjectivity than it deserves. For that productivity, when we see it manifested in the production of post-colonial literatures, has been neither deterministic nor imprisoning.

No doubt Prospero remains convinced that his language is Caliban's prison, 'the very prison in which Caliban's achievements will be realised and restricted' (Lamming, 1960: 110). This is a ubiquitous argument about the function of a colonizing language, although it is not always expressed so subtly: that for those for whom it is not a mother tongue the language is inevitably and essentially limiting. Language will not allow Caliban's expansion beyond a certain point, says Lamming. 'This kind of realisation, this kind of expansion, is possible only to those who reside in that state of being which is the very source and ultimate of the language which bears them always forward' (*ibid.*); that is, expansion and true self-realization are only possible to those born into the language. Yet we must ask how that 'state of being' becomes the inherent property of a mother tongue. Why is Prospero's language prevented from 'bearing its speakers forward?' The history of post-colonial appropriation of the dominant language, and the numerous examples from post-colonial writers, including Lamming himself, would seem to suggest that language is a horizon into which all speakers may enter in different ways and along different trajectories.

Caliban 'can never be regarded as an heir of that Language', adds Lamming, 'since his use of Language is no more than his way of serving Prospero; and Prospero's instruction in this Language is only his way of measuring the distance which separates him from Caliban' (*ibid.*). This embraces a *non sequitur* which denies Caliban any agency. Certainly it is undeniable that the colonizing language is taught and disseminated in a way which entrenches difference: the colonized speak dialect or marginal varieties, while the colonizer speaks Standard English. It is also true that the play envisages no more than imprisonment and curses in Caliban's use of language, but the idea that colonized peoples are unable to use the colonizer's language as anything more than a way of serving the colonizing power is a myth about the function of language which falls into Prospero's trap.

Lamming's comments on language are a small section of his essay, but they express sentiments which were both influential upon and representative of a growing school of thought about colonial language. An alternative view was expressed by Janheinz Jahn, who in 1968, building on Mannoni's and Lamming's ground-breaking interventions, offered a different prognosis for Caliban. Jahn suggests that Lamming is right, that 'if Caliban is no more than a part of nature, he will never be able to break out of the prison of Prospero's language' (1968: 240); 'But suppose Caliban is also part of a culture, a different culture unfamiliar to Prospero?' (*ibid*.) asks Jahn. Suppose also that Caliban carries out his revolt, relying on his own resources rather than on the buffoons Stephano and Trinculo. In that event, the 'thousand twangling instruments', the music of his island which he explains to them, might be considered to be the voices of his culture rather than the voices of nature. Caliban emerges from a culture very different from Prospero's book culture but is able to utilize it.

> So he captures, in his own and Prospero's language, a culture Prospero did not create and cannot control, which he, Caliban, has recognized as his own. But in the process the language is transformed, acquiring different meanings which Prospero never expected. Caliban becomes a 'bilingual'. That language he shares with Prospero and the language he has minted from it are no longer identical. Caliban breaks out of the prison of Prospero's language. (*ibid*.: 242)

Furthermore, Prospero will be excluded from Caliban's language if he retains his old attitudes. He is 'bound to miss essential parts, nuances and references, everything that relates to that different cultural background, and so he will misunderstand Caliban's new language' (*ibid*.). Although perhaps still tied a little closely to *The Tempest* metaphor, this explanation offers a convincing alternative to Lamming's notion of the language as a prison. It accounts very well for the ways in which an authentic post-colonial culture is 'built' out of all the tools available, rather than resurrected from the past. In particular it apprehends the way in which the dominant language has been used in literary production.

Jahn explicitly dates Caliban's appropriation of Prospero's culture, the 'successful revolt from the prison of Prospero's language' (*ibid*.) from the rise of the Negritudinist literary movement between 1934 and 1948. According to Jahn, the escape was effected in three ways: in semantics, rhythm and subject matter. In particular, the use of French led writers such as Senghor, Damas and Césaire to construct a new literary culture which reconfigured Africa as 'no longer exotic and "primitive" but as a specific culture' (*ibid*.). The limitations of the Negritude Movement have been widely discussed, but clearly the appropriation of French by these writers preceded a flourishing African literature in English in the post-independence 1950s. Caliban remained in Prospero's prison of language only as long as he could be deceived into believing it was a prison. The transformation of post-colonial literatures, which began in the Negritude Movement, was one which saw that language was not the repository of culture but its agent.

The power of the book

From the position of inconsolable despair with which Caliban concludes his 'learning to curse' exchange with Prospero and Miranda, he is relegated to the role of comic foil for Stephano and Trinculo. However, this comedy comes to revolve around an important accessory to Prospero's language, his books, which Caliban identifies as the source of his power, and which he entreats the two clowns to destroy. The play's location of Caliban hinges on a subtle connection between the imperial language, which teaches Caliban 'how to name the bigger light and how the less', Prospero's Art, by which he keeps Caliban under control, and the books which Caliban 'recognizes' as the source of Prospero's power. This relationship elaborates the very important link between language and writing in the colonial exchange.

The power of writing in modern times stems from the ease with which it lends itself to commodification; books, writing, print in their material presence are more obviously exchangeable repositories of cultural capital. Obviously oral knowledge and skill works as cultural capital as well, but not as authoritatively in the post-Enlightenment reification of written discourse in Europe. The written assumed power over the oral in Western society when the 'will to truth', as Foucault puts it, ensured that the 'enunciated' assumed precedence over the 'enunciation'. Once the power of the orator's discourse was overtaken by the 'will to truth', when the veracity of *what was said* assumed greater importance than the persuasiveness or eloquence of its delivery, the written text became privileged as a means of fixing what was said. The conviction of the power of the written word in Western thinking becomes linked to its teleological notions of the 'improvement of mankind'. Lévi-Strauss, a consistent critic of the idea of historical progress, still asserted that the invention of writing made it possible to accumulate the knowledge of each generation as 'working capital' for the next (Lévi-Strauss, 1969).

The discursive power of Western imperialism lies not so much in the power of the written over the oral but in its power to convince colonial subjects that the written is more authoritative than the oral. The tangibility of print, the rendering of the aural into a visual icon of authority, learning or scientific perspicacity, assisted this hegemonic process, since it could be supported by force. In addition, the relative permanence and transportability of print facilitated an atomistic, rationalist and teleologically structured view of the world, as well as lending a relative permanence to the details of legal or bureaucratic directives.

This ideological assumption of the power of print is replicated in *The Tempest* in the power that accrues to Prospero from his books. The play imprisons Caliban in a colonialist view of the colonial subject in two ways: first, it describes Caliban's unquestioned acceptance of the fact that Prospero's power, his 'superior technology', is located in a superior culture which is embodied in the written word, in his books; second, it denies Caliban any opportunity to appropriate Prospero's technology. He is constituted by the play as bestial, ugly, monstrous, lowly, little more than an object of the civilizing influence of Prospero's Art. The play specifically denies him the opportunity to be nurtured by this Art, because, as an unreconstructed natural man, a 'devil', he is one 'on whose nature Nurture can never stick'.

When plotting to overthrow Prospero, he advises Trinculo and Stephano:

> Why, as I told thee, 'tis a custom with him
> I' th' afternoon to sleep: there thou mayst brain him,
> Having first seized his books; or with a log
> Batter his skull, or paunch him with a stake,
> Or cut his wezand with thy knife. Remember
> First to possess his books; for without them
> He's but a sot as I am, nor hath not
> One spirit to command: they all do hate him
> As rootedly as I. Burn but his books. (III, ii, 85–93)

In a sense Caliban is here playing out the part set out for him, not only by the play but by Prospero and imperial discourse. First, his resistance falls into the trap of violence, and thus he acts out his representation in discourse; second, if he seizes Prospero's books he will do nothing but burn them. While it is language which has unmanned him, made him less than human, excluded him from culture, taught him how to curse, it is nevertheless Prospero's books which are the source of his colonizing Art and thus the source of the power of his language. As Macaulay put it, knowing English gives anyone access to a 'vast intellectual wealth', a literature that is intrinsically more valuable than any other, a corpus of arts and sciences which cannot be matched. The capacity to transfer this *belief* is the capacity to rule.

In his play *Caliban*, Renan elaborates the connection between Prospero's books and the power of his language, adding the extra dimension of those scientific instruments by which Prospero has effected his Art and representing what, to Renan, is the ultimate secret of European supremacy.

> Those books of hell – ugh! how I hate them. They have been the instruments of my slavery. We must snatch and burn them instantly. No other method will serve but this. War to the books! They are our worst enemies, and those who possess them will have power over all their fellows. The man who knows Latin can control and command the people to his service. Down with Latin! Therefore, first of all seize his books, for there lies the secret of his power. It is by them that he reigns over the inferior spirits. Break, also, the glass retorts and all the materials of his laboratory. (1896: 42)

There is both a class and a race dimension to Caliban in this play. The slave has been taken back to Milan with Prospero and his vengeful nature has become the instigator of rebellion among the disaffected classes in this 'civilized' duchy. Once Caliban has assumed power as the result of the revolution, his rule also assumes the moderation of princes, but Prospero's counter-attack through Ariel is fruitless because, as Ariel suggests, the power of Prospero's art lies in its capacity to persuade people of its reality.

> Whence did it come that our magic prevailed so easily over our adversaries in the enchanted island? It lay in the fact that Alonzo and those minds who were so accessible to it perceived and believed in it. . . . The people do not admit anything of all that, and the winds and tempests can roar together, without producing any effect. Our magic is of no more use. The revolution is a realism, and all that is evident to the finer senses; all that is ideal and insubstantial, does not exist for the people. They admit only the real. (Renan, 1896: 53)

Prospero's cultural power founders in Milan because he fails to convince the ruled that the power lies with him. More significantly, once Caliban assumes power, his fear of Prospero's books wanes.

The actual relationship with these books is a source of extreme ambivalence in the colonial relationship. Ideologically, when Macaulay says that English gives one access to a 'vast intellectual wealth', he is merely intoning one of the cultural assumptions which interpellate colonial subjects the way Prospero's discourse interpellates Caliban; but *strategically*,if Caliban were to acquire those books rather than burn them, would he not have access to an empowering counter-discourse? Because Caliban is the unreceptive object of Prospero's civilizing ministrations rather than a subject capable of engaging colonial dominance, this opportunity is denied him. The underlying Eurocentrism of the play abandons Caliban to despair: all Prospero's and Miranda's language can teach him is how to curse.

The example of post-colonial literatures reveals that however cursed may be the linguistic relationship of colonizer and colonized, the response available to Caliban is to take hold of the language and reconstitute it as a tool of empowerment. This is because it is not just language with which Caliban has to contend. Language is one key feature of a set of relations of power which constitute imperial discourse. Rejecting the language will not alter the fundamentally productive power of the discourse itself. The future of Caliban's language is not cursing but transformation. By appropriating Prospero's language, his books, indeed the whole technological edifice of his 'Art', Caliban may determine not only his own future, but Prospero's as well.

Notes

1. Interestingly, the possibilities for reading this play in terms of the political and cultural relationship between Caliban and Prospero date from the nineteenth century. J. S. Phillpot's introduction to the 1873 Rugby edition of Shakespeare notes that 'The character may have had a special bearing on the great question of a time when we were discovering new countries, subjecting unknown savages, and founding fresh colonies. If Prospero might dispossess Caliban, England might dispossess the aborigines of the colonies' (Furness Variorum Edition: 383). This edition precedes the rise of classical imperialism which culminated in the 'scramble for Africa' in 1882. Curiously, the colonial importance of Prospero and Caliban was not revisited until 1950 when the major European empires were beginning to be dismantled.

2. Chantal Zabus (1985) extends Lamming's reading of *The Tempest* to show how writers throughout the post-colonial world, particularly writers of the Anglophone and Franco-phone white and black diasporas, have written answers to *The Tempest* from the perspectives of Caliban, Miranda and Ariel. Lamming himself has rewritten *The Tempest* from a post-colonial perspective in his novels *Natives of My Person* and *Water with Berries*. Diana Brydon's 'Re-writing *The Tempest*' (1984) surveys a number of Canadian rewritings of *The Tempest* and argues that in the Canadian context the play is internalized in a different way to the usual externalized post-colonial response in which an identification of the colonial with Caliban occurs. For Canadian rewritings, at least in Canadian English, the emphasis has been on Miranda. Brydon suggests that this is consistent with English-speaking Canada's view of its colonial relationship with the Motherland as 'dutiful daughter'. Significantly, Quebecois rewriting, as she notes, follows African, Afro-American and West Indian readings in externalizing the colonizing power as Prospero and identifying with Caliban (Brydon, 1984).

CHAPTER 7

Fractured paradigms

The fragility of discourse

Caliban's capacity to create a future for himself by transforming the colonial language depends very much on his ability to confront the imperial discourse that inscribes him. This leads us to consider the power of discourse itself. How firm are the boundaries of a discourse? How corrigible are its norms? Are they only as authoritative as the subject allows at any given moment? The sovereignty of a discourse over the subjects it constructs or inscribes is a crucial issue for post-colonial politics and for any counter-discursive political relationship, for counter-discourse reveals that the fractures in dominant discourses may be more numerous and wider than one would expect. According to Foucault's description in 'The orders of discourse' (1971: 8–10), discourses have firm rules of inclusion and exclusion, but we know these rules may be modified over time: take, for instance, the grudging and gradual acceptance of acupuncture into Western medicine. Yet how much authority does a discourse actually have over a subject's behaviour and experience? This is an extremely important question for any investigation of post-colonial subjectivity, since discourse is regarded as a system within which, and by which, subjectivity is constructed. The sovereignty of a discourse, therefore, must be balanced against the agency of the subject which it purportedly constructs.

The authority and hegemony of colonial culture, extensive as it is, begins in the discursive control of subjectivity. When we think about the transformation of colonial culture, the question of the agency of the subject in engaging the discursive framework(s) of colonialism is central. The study of colonial discourse flourished in the 1980s in the work of Bhabha and Spivak, but the most controversial aspects of their theory concerned the uncertain place of the subject in a system that seemed to bear the seeds of its own demise. This, of course was the problem which motivated critiques such as that of Benita Parry, who sought, in a Fanonesque way, to re-install the effectiveness of the resisting subject. The questions we need to ask are: Does a place exist for a conception of a subject which is not completely autonomous, yet which is active within, and against, the boundaries of discourse? How sovereign is discourse itself?

A fascinating perspective on this question can be gained by returning to an older conception of discursive formations. This takes us into strange territory for post-colonial studies, but it places the issue of discourse and individual agency in a wider context. In his book *The Structure of Scientific Revolutions* (1967), Thomas Kuhn argued that scientific research and thought are defined by 'paradigms', or conceptual world-views, that consist of formal theories, classic experiments and trusted methods. Scientists operate within the general world-view of this paradigm until theoretical problems or experimental anomalies expose a paradigm's inadequacies or contradictions. This triggers a crisis that can only be resolved by an intellectual revolution that replaces an old paradigm with a new one. The overthrow of Ptolemaic cosmology by Copernican heliocentrism is one example of such a shift. Another occurred at the beginning of the twentieth century – the shift from Newtonian to quantum physics. The quantum shift has disrupted our view of physical reality perhaps more profoundly than any shift before it – at least potentially. When we classify a 'paradigm' as a discourse, this quantum paradigm shift raises a fascinating question about its discursive authority: To what extent does a paradigm actually affect the behaviour of subjects? Have people really abandoned the Newtonian world-view?

On the face of it, the repeal of this world-view at the turn of the century was absolutely cataclysmic. In 1900 Max Planck conducted an experiment which turned out to be a catastrophe for Newtonian science: when matter is heated the atoms emit and absorb energy in specific amounts, radiating energy in spurts or quanta, revealing that the basic structure of nature is *discontinuous*, and discontinuity conflicts with (or at least reinterprets) Newtonian science (see Guillemin, 1968: 50–1). This experiment might be said to be the founding moment of postmodern science,[1] and the first step initiated a stampede. Where Planck described the processes of energy absorption and emission, Einstein theorized in 1905 that energy itself is quantized. He proved this by referring to the photo-electric effect, which showed that when light hits the surface of a metal, it jars electrons loose from the atoms in the metal and sends them flying off. This was revolutionary enough, but it also contradicted the prevailing knowledge that light was a wave formation. In 1803 Thomas Young had settled the question of the nature of light, it seemed, with a simple and ingenious experiment called the double-slit experiment which proved that light was made up of waves.[2] So how could light be both particles and waves? This was the end of the line for classical causality and it was explained by Niels Bohr as a process of 'complementarity': the apparently mutually exclusive wave and particle characteristics are not properties of light but of our *interaction* with light (Bohr, 1934: 53). Put another way, it indicated that waves and particles are themselves signifiers rather than signifieds. This is something which distinguishes the quantum physics paradigm from all others, for it cut to the heart of scientific certainty itself: the certainty of an observable and verifiable world. Eventually, the metaphorical status of the language of science was confirmed when it was 'discovered' in subsequent experiments that particles *are* waves.[3]

The official overturning of Newtonian science was the Copenhagen Interpretation of Quantum Mechanics formulated in 1927, which essentially rejected the assumption that nature could be understood in terms of elementary space–time realities.[4] The fact that science now verified something that had been considered contradictory and inconceivable amounted to a crisis in European thought. The notion of crisis itself forms part of the apparatus of historical method, a recursive construction upon which paradigm shifts might hinge, but 'crisis' it was considered to be. Edmund Husserl, the founder of modern phenomenology, launched, in response, the last and most heroic effort to restore science to its status as chief arbiter of the real. His aim was to restore Cartesian certainty to knowing by uncovering the access of consciousness to the 'thing-in-itself' – the 'real object' existing in time and space outside our relationship with it. Husserl's failure to do this was virtually a failure of the intellectual empire of modernity itself. Not only did it present a crisis in rational thinking, in scientific certainty about our relationship with the world, but it implied an undermining of the dominance of European rationalism, the very foundation of modernity.

Quantum physics appears to be a remarkably coherent example of a new discourse, but the most remarkable feature of the revolutionary quantum paradigm was that it hardly seems to have affected most scientists' ordinary acceptance of the centrality of the object, the neutrality of observation, the stability of the earth's co-ordinate system, and the tenacious belief that they are simply 'discovering' what is 'there'. If the quantum paradigm shift failed to filter down to scientists' mundane perception of their own activity, even less did it affect the thinking of ordinary people about the world in which they live. This amounts to a staggering problem both for the theory of paradigm shift and the theory of discourse. If people can accept the validity of a discourse without it affecting the way they actually inhabit the world, then discourse itself may be presumed to be highly provisional in its 'sovereignty'. This has far-reaching implications for discursive analysis, for it demonstrates that people may live comfortably between competing and even radically contradictory discourses, negotiating those discourses at will. This is constantly borne out around the world where individuals have no trouble negotiating the apparent gap between the essentially secular world-view of global culture and the mythic horizon of their own local cultures.

The reason the paradigm shift did not radically alter mundane perception of the scientifically observable world is first a problem of language. The central shift in quantum physics was the realization that the material nature of the observable world was a function of the ways in which it was observed and talked about. In 1938 Einstein made the revolutionary statement that physical concepts are free creations of the human mind:

Physical concepts are free creations of the human mind, and are not, however it may seem, uniquely determined by the external world. In our endeavour to understand reality we are somewhat like a man trying to understand the mechanism of a closed watch. He sees the face and the moving hands, even hears its ticking, but he has no way of opening the case. If he is ingenious he may form some picture of a mechanism which could be responsible for all things he observes, but he may never be quite sure his picture is the only one which could explain his observations. He will never be able to compare his picture with the real mechanism and he cannot even imagine the possibility of meaning such a comparison. (Einstein and Infeld, 1971: 31)

This statement indicates the fundamentally metaphoric, discursive, and indeed, *interactive* view of nature which quantum mechanics introduced to physics. Yet Einstein cannot talk about the situation without inferring the presence of a 'real' watch, of a reality which transcends the explanations we make about it. Language does not appear to provide terms in which such a situation could be adequately expressed; that which *is* exists as a function of our explanations rather than exterior to them. The ground rules had been set by Newton, whose premise was that physical laws are based on experimental evidence and nothing else. If it could be verified experimentally, it was true. Experiment obviated the variable of the experimenter's consciousness entirely. Truth did not become revealed as a *product* of the experimental method until it was found that in the realm of atomic matter, Newtonian mechanics simply doesn't work.

Indeed, the transcendent reality of the objective world could be protected by a simple division between sub-atomic phenomena which may be 'tendencies to exist', and super-atomic phenomena which are 'observable' realities. In other words, Newtonian theory works 'well enough' for explaining the phenomenal world. The fracture in scientific practice has been formalized ever since by this arbitrary empirical division. Yet the outmoded 'Newtonian' planetary model of atoms conceived by Bohr and Rutherford has long outlasted the more paradoxical view of particles as standing waves precisely because it is a *picture*, for pictures reproduce a principle of representation which is deeply embedded in Western epistemology – that of ocularcentrism.

Despite the refusal of scientific practice to examine itself in the way the new paradigm seems to have demanded, quantum physics underwent a process which is more familiar in philosophical and literary theoretical thought. The first step was a view of the observing or experimental process which broke down the classical dichotomy between the subject and object. This is explicit in Bohr's views of complementarity, but is most neatly encapsulated in Heisenberg's Uncertainty Principle, which states that the very act of knowing something about the sub-atomic phenomenon changes it (Heisenberg, 1958). An object moving through space has both a position and a velocity which can be measured. In classical physics the measurement of these objects is a relatively simple affair, but in the sub-atomic realm we cannot know both the position and the velocity of a particle with absolute precision. We can know both approximately, but the more we know about one, the less we know about the other. We can know either of them precisely, in which case we can know nothing about the other. We must choose, by the selection of our experiment, which one we want to measure most accurately – position or velocity. Specific events cannot be predicted, only their probabilities.

The initial achievement of quantum mechanics was to reinstate the subject in the process of objective measurement. The observing system is the environment which surrounds the observed system, including the physicists studying the experiment. While the observed system is travelling undisturbed, it develops according to the Schrödinger wave equation. The wave-like properties of a particle constitute a wave of probabilities described by this equation; that is, the wave-like characteristics are 'primarily and essentially possibility of being'. The wave of probabilities continues in perpetuity until the participation of the observer 'collapses' one of the possibilities contained in the wave function into a physical 'reality'. This is called the quantum leap, when the multifaceted potentiality contained in the wave function collapses into a single actuality.

The implications of this emerged more fully in Einstein's theories of relativity (Einstein, 1920). Once sub-atomic particles had been shown to be patterns of standing waves, tendencies to exist, the path was set for Einstein to evolve the theory of the interrelation of space, time and matter itself.[5] The special theory of relativity offers several propositions: first, a moving object appears to contract in the direction of motion as its velocity increases, until, at the speed of light, it would disappear altogether;[6] second, a moving clock runs more slowly than a clock at rest until, at the speed of light, it stops running altogether; third, the mass of a moving object increases as its velocity increases. The most popularly known aspect of the special theory is that mass and energy are versions of the same thing: $E=mc^2$. Mass and energy are patterns of subatomic interrelation no different from the individual patterns which characterize different states of matter. In short, both space/time and mass/energy are continua rather than separate phenomena.

The three characteristics of quantum mechanics – its acceptance of the essentially metaphoric nature of the language of scientific description; the recognition of the importance of an 'observing system' in actually bringing sub-atomic phenomena into being; and the realization that the patterns of sub-atomic phenomena defied all notions of material essence – lead to a proliferation of the discovery of particles. The original aim of particle physics was to find the ultimate building blocks of the universe, but what physicists actually found is that if there is any 'stuff' of the universe, it is energy. Yet 'energy' is itself a description of the experimental perception of motion, and motion is nothing more than a correlation of space and time. At the sub-atomic level there is no longer any distinction between what is – authentic being – and what happens. Matter, or particles, are continually created, annihilated and created again.[7]

It is quite possible that nothing has equalled quantum mechanics in revealing the linguistic nature of experience, for, after all, what actually collides in a bubble chamber? Despite the term, sub-atomic particles may have no objective existence apart from their interaction with a measuring device. Particles are better described as *interactions between fields* which appear particle-like because the fields interact very abruptly in minute regions of space. In other words, they cannot be held to refer to any substantive thing; but of necessity, quantum physicists talk about these phenomena as though they are little bits of matter because they have encountered the infinite regression of objective meaning – both the terms 'energy' and 'interacting fields' are equally metaphoric. Just as Heidegger could say, 'Language speaks. Man only speaks insofar as he artfully complies with language' (1971: 73), the quantum physicist can say that 'space–time is, man only understands space–time insofar as he artfully participates in its intricate web of changing relationships'. In that infinitesimal moment between one particle becoming another, where might lie the essential truth of matter and of language, we find ourselves staring straight into the Abyss – for there is nothing there.

The conclusion we reach upon observing the quantum revolution is that it not only parallels the overthrow of modernity, which occurred from the beginning of this century in the humanities, but it may be seen to be an arm of postmodernity itself. This interaction is best seen in the uncanny link between Einstein and Derrida. For Einstein, reality is not a three-dimensional state but four-dimensional, the fourth dimension being time.[8] According to him there is no such thing as space and time, only space–time. Space signifies difference, time signifies deferral. Einstein's union of the two pre-dates Jacques Derrida's concept of *différance* by seventy years. 'Différance indicates on the one hand difference as distinction, inequality or discernibility; on the other it expresses the interposition of delay' (Derrida, 1967: 129). Derrida's interposition of deferral, the temporalizing dimension, into the structure of difference, precisely mirrors Einstein's addition of the dimension of time to the pattern of relationships of which sub-atomic phenomena are constituted. Space, time, mass and energy are merely uses of language to conceptualize certain patterns of interrelationships in experience. They bear the same relationship to the term 'material existence' as they do to the word 'language'. Although Einstein himself would not say this, the special theory of relativity implies that material existence at the sub-atomic level is located within language rather than represented by it.

The fractures in discourse

Seeing scientific paradigms as discourses uncovers the very provisional hold a particular discourse might have over its subjects, but at the same time it reveals that human action inevitably occurs within *some* discourse. In the case of science, the failure of the quantum physics paradigm to gain control of ordinary thinking (despite its apparent ubiquity in popular imagination) stems from its failure to develop a language which dispenses with the idea of a concrete observable reality. That language, arguably, may have been developed by post-structuralism. Yet scientists and non-scientists, at least in their everyday activity, still operate within a different discourse – Newtonian physics – one that functions within the frame of the familiar language of Enlightenment rationalism. Nor, for that matter, does post-structuralist language have any greater sway in everyday speech. This phenomenon disrupts Foucault's earlier notion of an *episteme* – the idea that a particular world-view prevails universally in a culture in a particular epoch. More specifically, it disrupts any assumption that such *epistemes* are totalizing and universal. Contesting discourses may operate alongside one another, either in conflict or, as in science and most other discourses, in a state of *rapprochement*. This also offers a more subtle view of political and cultural control, for that control is constantly rendered provisional by the interaction of contesting views.

Such a state of shared dominance describes extremely well the co-existence, and interrelation, of many dominant discourses, such as modernity and postmodernity. Just as the scientist conducts his or her discipline as if the world is 'there', so the postmodern critic always faces some intransigent considerations – that writers write and readers read; that texts issue from, and produce particular material effects in, the world; in short, that they are 'worldly' (Said, 1983). Post-structuralism finds itself located squarely on the paradoxical intersection of modernity and postmodernity: the fundamental concepts which make meaning possible are undermined by Derrida and dispersed by a discourse which *confesses it must make use of these concepts at every turn* (Kellner, 1987: 5). We find that the postmodern paradigm has gained as little hold over ordinary thinking as that of quantum physics. For while people may readily grant the existence of 'the postmodern', it is still a *way of speaking* rather than an observable reality: ordinary individuals clearly conceptualize their own life in terms dictated by Enlightenment epistemology.

This situation confirms something which ought to have been quite obvious to us: that people may enter and leave a discourse at will. Just as a scientist may oscillate between a Newtonian and a quantum view of the world, depending on the occasion, ordinary individuals may see the world, at different times, in quite distinct, and even contradictory, ways demanded by the constraints of a particular situation. The crucial point here is that they enter one discourse and leave another, cross the boundaries between discourses, and accommodate the apparently comprehensive demands of different discourses *at will*. This is because those discourses are *a way of speaking* about experience. Yet such a perception of subjects' relation to discourse seemed at odds with Foucault's perception of their insidious and permeating effects, their 'capillary' form of existence:

> When I think of the mechanics of power, I think of its capillary form of existence, of the extent to which power seeps into the very grain of individuals, reaches right into their bodies, permeates their gestures, their posture, what they say, how they learn to live and work with other people. (Foucault, 1980: 39)

The resolution of this apparent paradox becomes absolutely crucial to any examination of the construction of subjectivity, because the discursive mobility of the subject compels us to take agency into account within this arena of competing discourses. Is it possible for discourses to be permeating, totalizing and negotiable at the same time?

The relevance of post-colonial analysis to this question is hinted at when Foucault speaks of the imperialism of the discourse of sexuality: 'the singular imperialism that compels everyone to transform his sexuality into a permanent discourse' (1978: 33). Post-colonial experience demonstrates the actual negotiability and provisionality of 'imperial' power, despite its obvious compulsion and extension. Colonial discourse may be something with which ordinary individuals concur at certain moments in their daily life, negotiating a path between institutions of power without their personal lives being deeply affected. This is how de Certeau describes the strategies of ordinary living in *The Practice of Everyday Life* (1984). If this is the case, can subjects also adopt this utilitarian and provisional attitude to a colonizing language? For the forced imposition of a dominant language's world-view is taken to be an inescapable consequence of its use to those who believe that to use the colonial language is to remain colonized.

When we consider Caliban's response to Prospero's language (Chapter 6), the inability to use it for anything but cursing, we understand that for Shakespeare, the possibility of the integrity and agency of natural man does not exist. Caliban simply disappears from the play once his role as an object of Prospero's power is fulfilled. Paradoxically, this assumption, that the power of Prospero's discourse is incontrovertible, underlies many conceptions of colonial resistance. However, if we were to follow Caliban through history, as it were, seeing how the colonized subject has coped with Prospero's discourse, we would discover something that has been made very clear by the provisionality of the quantum paradigm: Caliban can move between discourses, languages and their attendant social worlds at will, no matter how powerful or all-encompassing they appear to be. These discourses become permeating and totalizing only to the extent that Caliban believes that experience, and a particular way of speaking about it, are one and the same.

Even the most influential and universal, and possibly the most 'capillary' mode of existence – European rationality – can be seen to be provisional in ordinary experience. If sub-atomic particles are tendencies to exist, if the observed reality in a bubble chamber depends entirely on the deployment of the observing system, we may infer that other methods of describing reality, other forms of 'real experience', may have an equal validity in accounting for the world. This is the point at which post-colonial theory intervenes in this paradigm conundrum. The impact of imperial culture upon colonized societies is equivalent to a paradigm shift in science, in terms of its power, ubiquity and the epistemological consequences of its effect upon thinking. Yet colonized societies may, on the one hand, have conceptions of human existence which contradict the 'universally' held assumptions of Western rationality, but also maintain a heavy investment in the materiality of the real world. This dilemma is encountered and negotiated continually by post-colonial discourse, as it is by any human experience in which political considerations are a prominent concern. The provisionality of paradigms is important to post-colonial studies because it reveals that such paradigms are both negotiable and transformable.

This discovery uncovers several important facts about discursive formations: contesting discourses may co-exist; one discourse may strategically appropriate another, dominant discourse, for its own purposes; and different discourses may be deployed on different occasions by a single subject. Most importantly, Foucault pointed out that power itself, a force which is transmitted by discourse, does not emanate from centres of power. 'We must cease once and for all,' he says, 'to describe the effects of power in negative terms: it "excludes," it "represses," it "censors," it "abstracts," it "masks," it "conceals,". In fact, power produces; it produces reality; it produces domains of objects and rituals of truth' (1977b: 194). Power is positive in that it *produces* subjects, but we discover that power does not *inevitably* produce subjects, nor does it immobilize the subjects it produces. A discourse is comprehensive in its effects but fragile in its structure.

There is a further issue of particular interest to post-colonial discourse: in a binary structure of shared dominance, such as we find in the scientific model, with Newtonian science and quantum science sharing the field, or in a political model, with imperialism and nationalism alternatively dominant, how does *counter-discourse* operate? Subjects may move from one discourse to another at will, but here we discover a strategy of a totally different kind. For how does the subject accommodate a discourse and a contesting discourse *at the same time*? The answer lies in the existence of fractures within both these discourses in their hold on individual subjects. The very fact that discourses may exist in contestation, that cracks may appear in discourse through which agency may operate, confirms the provisional hold actually exerted by discursive formations. Post-colonial discourse may find itself at odds with *all* these dominant formations at different times: it may contest both New-tonian and quantum physics, imperial discourse and nationalist rhetoric, modern rationality and postmodern uncertainty. However, the most effective way of doing this is not through a structure of binary opposi-tions, but an interaction, a counter-discourse, which is not one of exclusion and polarization, but of engagement and rearticulation.

These fractures in discourse, therefore, define the spaces in which post-colonial resistance moves. Indeed, it is the territory of discursive rules, the borders which determine 'what can be said' and what cannot, where the fractures, overlaps and slippages of discourse operate most subtly. Hairline fractures open up within discourse at the boundaries of its determination, where the 'rules of exclusion' and 'rules of inclusion' are negotiated. Discourses are never absolutely delineated, but are surrounded and penetrated by these porous borders, in which the tactics of choice, difference and resistance may come into play. Forms of post-colonial discursive resistance have always had to live in this 'epistemic' fracture; they have always had to negotiate this space in discourse itself, occupying the *other space of reading.* The fractured paradigm is not simply a fracture opened up between theory and practice, between words and things, nor even the profound political fracture between the material and discursive, although it is all of these. Rather it dramatizes the fracture which is the very condition of post-colonial subjectivity.

The fractures and slippages, the epistemic lags and shifts of colonial discourse, identify the conditions of possibility for post-colonial resist-ance, not as a condition of permanent exclusion and recalcitrant opposi-tion, but as the condition of its empowerment. The power of the post-colonial lies not in an opposing structure of actions, an opposing but dominant discourse (which might be the case if the 'post' in post-colonial were a chronological marker), but in its transformation of colonial culture. Transformation is achieved in many ways, but it always results from the *interpolation* of the dominant discourse through those fractures and slippages which both define and delimit that power.

The resistance of the post-colonial is better defined by what de Certeau refers to as 'tactics' rather than 'strategies'. Strategy is 'the calculation . . . of power relationships that becomes possible as soon as a subject with will and power (a business, an army, a city, a scientific institution) can be isolated' (de Certeau, 1984: 36). A 'tactic', on the other hand, is 'a calculated action determined by the absence of a proper locus' (*ibid.*: 37). 'The space of the tactic is the space of the other. Thus it must play on and with a terrain imposed on it and organized by the law of a foreign power' (*ibid.*).[9] 'In short, a tactic is an art of the weak' (*ibid.*). Post-colonial tactics are not, of course the only ones operating in the fissures of discourse; indeed, you cannot have a *formal* tactics, only an ensemble of which particular tactics are deployed for specific purposes. Thus the post-colonial subject shares tactics with other kinds of resistance (or conversely we could say the post-colonial discourse is not the only one in which the subject employs tactics). Tactics only operate 'contingently'. This is perhaps their most fascinating feature: the very existence of tactics arises from the fragility of discourse, rather than a formal programme of opposition.

The fractures which open up in the liminal regions of discourse emerge most clearly at the level of language itself, where post-colonial interpolation occurs most directly. The post-colonial *experience* of language has always had to accommodate an apparent fracture in the sign, a fracture between the word and the thing, because it deals with imperial language, which in many senses never seems to quite 'fit' the material experience of the speaker. This is not only true for those colonized peoples whose mother tongue is different from the colonizing language, but also for those 'settler' colonials whose experience of place is never properly accommodated by the imported language. Authentic being is neither purely a feature of language nor of physical reality. The word is like the sub-atomic particle in the physicist's bubble chamber. We are tempted on one side to look at the particle as the ultimate bit, essential presence, while on the other to see it, rather, as the essential 'absence', the final sign of our inability to know the world; but language is our mode of knowing the world, not merely its intermediary. The meaning of the word is not the 'actual' fixed centre of a number of possibilities, a substantive existence; it is like the rule connecting a mathematical series, something which is determinate in its application, but which is always capable of being extended to some further application. The word is the rule of its emerging series of possibilities, not external to the series but determinate in it.

Perhaps the most adept management of the conditions of post-colonial language, the most cunning resolution of the fracture between the word and the thing, is the installation of the fracture into the post-colonial text in the form of what we may term the 'metonymic gap'. This is the gap of silence installed in the text when some aspect of the operation of the mother language is imported into the text as a cultural synecdoche. Language used in this way allows the post-colonial to mediate the apparent fracture between signifier and 'referent' through a constitution of the text as a transitive and transformative field of work. The abrogation of the ideology of a standard grammar which accompanies the appropriation of the colonial language is perhaps the most practical step in this process. Language is always an *act*, a message event, in which signification is the constitutive achievement of the writer and reader functions, the field on to which the text tactically inserts its urgent material and political representations.

The process modelled by language occurs within the various master discourses by which colonial dominance is maintained – history, philosophy, geography, linguistics, literature – and also in cultural production of various kinds. In every case the power of the dominant discourse is both provisional and ambivalent. This provisionality is perhaps best demonstrated by the tenuous hold maintained over mundane practice by scientific paradigms, and the curious inability of the quantum paradigm shift to take hold of quotidian experience. This provisionality results not so much from opposition, but from the recalcitrant ability of everyday practice to deploy discourses as tools rather than as imprisoning world-views. Exactly the same provisionality occurs in the hegemony of imperial discourse, which may not make much impression on many aspects of quotidian colonial life. But the most important observation in this process is the capacity of 'resistance' activity to operate within the fractures and fissures opened up in discourse, interpolating that discourse for its own ends, appropriating its technologies for self-empowerment, and ultimately transforming it.

Notes

1. Indeed, we could say that this was the founding moment of both modern and postmodern science. The disruption of scientific assumptions that had seemed to be foundational to Enlightenment thinking lies at the core of the quantum shift, making it the scientific accompaniment to the modernist revolution at the turn of the century. Yet its similarity to postmodern and poststructuralist ideas of meaning and understanding is uncanny. This itself demonstrates that we may best understand postmodernism by seeing how deeply it is embedded in modernism. The postmodernism of quantum physics becomes developed and extended in chaos theory which is an even greater assault on Newtonian physics.

2. Thomas placed a screen with two vertical slits in it in front of a light source. Each slit could be covered with a piece of material. On the other side of the double-slit screen was a wall against which the light coming through the double slits could shine. When one slit was covered, the wall behind the other would be illuminated as would be expected. But when both slits were uncovered, instead of a sum of the light from both slits, the wall was illuminated with alternating bands of light and darkness. These alternating bands result from a well-known phenomenon of wave mechanics called interference. Interference results when the waves of light diffracting from the two slits interfere with each other. In some places these waves overlap and reinforce each other, in other places they cancel each other out. Using Newton's laws of motion we can predict where the photon will land on the photographic plate if *one* slit is open, but there is no logical way, using classical mechanics, to account for the different performance of the photon if two slits are open.

3. The Davisson Gerner experiment showed that when a beam of electrons is sent through tiny openings, like the spaces between the atoms in metal foil, which are smaller than the wavelengths of the electrons, the beam diffracts exactly the way a beam of light diffracts. Eventually Schrodinger's view became accepted that particles are *standing waves* like the waves formed on a vibrating guitar string or the surface of a liquid (Schrodinger, 1961: 50). The standing waves can only be increased or decreased discontinuously and are therefore quantized. With a view of particles as standing waves, understanding of the atom was opened to perceptions inconceivable in classical physics, such as that the constituents of an atom operate within hundreds of different dimensions.

4. The term 'Copenhagen Interpretation' reflects the dominant influence of Niels Bohr (from Copenhagen) and his school of thought.

5. One of the great puzzles of Einstein's day was that the speed of light was found to be constant under any circumstances. Whether one is stationary or travelling towards a light source at 100,000 miles per hour, the speed of light is always 186,000 miles per second. In a quantum leap of his own, Einstein simply took the puzzle of the constant velocity of light and called it the *principle* of the constant velocity of light. In other words, common sense must be wrong. If the speed of light remained constant, *everything else must change*

(Einstein, 1920, 1936). Classical transformation laws stated that the speed of light must be its velocity from a light source plus or minus the velocity of the observer. By bracketing out all assumptions exterior to the text of this problem, Einstein deduced that if the speed of light as measured by stationary observers and those who are converging on the light source is the same, then somehow the measuring instruments change from one frame of reference to another sufficiently to maintain the constant velocity of light. In other words, by bracketing the genre of Newtonian science, Einstein was able to uncover the conditions of the possibility of the 'constant speed of light', the rules by which such a statement could be made, and such rules constituted a separate discourse.

6. This is theoretical, since matter cannot travel at the speed of light.

7. Particles live much less than a millionth of a second and are too small to be observed directly, so their trails are located inside a bubble chamber positioned inside a magnetic field. These trails are signs or 'traces', an emptiness signifying a something which has no autonomous existence but which is distinguishable only by its difference from other trails. When a particle called a negative pi meson collides with a proton, both pi meson and proton may be destroyed (or other processes occur) and if so, two new particles are created in their place: a neutral k meson and a lambda particle. Both of these particles decay spontaneously into two additional particles, two of which are the same particles with which we started. Matter is not even energy but a continual movement between states. A proton never remains a simple proton. It alternates between being a proton and a neutral pion on one hand, and being a neutron and a positive pion on the other. The identity of a sub-atomic particle is inextricable from its potentiality as a range of other particles.

8. It is believed that more than ten dimensions of the universe exist with all but four curled up in a manifold. The other six or more dimensions have been of marginal significance since shortly after the big bang.

9. Catachresis is one tactic by which the dominant discourse may be invaded. The strategic catachresis of an aboriginal *nation*, for instance, is an interesting example of the tactical occupation of the 'space of the other'. Until it becomes *institutionalized* as such, the idea of nation can operate quite apart from the burden of nationalism and can be a successful tactic in organizing resistance. However, if institutionalized, its strategic space is delimited and controlled by the imperial power which it comes to reflect. Its agency is subsumed back into the imperial structure.

CHAPTER 8

Post-colonial excess and colonial transformation

The transformation of colonial cultures often occurs, as we have seen, when colonized subjects occupy fractures in the discourses which frame those cultures. A primary form of this tactic is one we could call 'interpolation'. The ability to interpolate institutions of power – as occurs when post-colonial writers use global systems of publishing, or when intellectuals use dominant discourses such as history, philosophy or politics to reshape those discourses – can be regarded as a form of tactical occupation. The appropriation of dominant forms of representation for their use against their culture of origin, and to control self-representation, is a primary function of this tactic. The fractures that always exist in discourse are a prime site for the intervention of the theoretically 'weak' (as de Certeau puts it) in their task of redeploying power and reshaping what appears to be an unassailable cultural dominance.

However, there are some institutions, such as the post-colonial nation-state, where transformation has very often failed to take place. Invariably, sovereignty has been transferred without being transformed. Founding fathers, reversing the construction of the colonized subject as 'child', institute patrimonial states that often seem to be unshakeable in their continuance of imperially established structures of power. The tactics of interpolation seem to gain no purchase here because the strategic movement of independence has simply occupied the field of battle without changing it. The presence of such problematic resistances to transformation suggest the need for a different kind of tactic, one that does not simply occupy the fractures of discourse but exceeds the boundaries of the discourse itself.

Such excess seems, in many cases, to be more than a tactic, but rather a fundamental characteristic of post-colonial experience. In a conversation between Edward Said and Salman Rushdie about Said's book on the Palestinians called *After the Last Sky* (Said, 1986), Said comments on the 'excess' with which the Palestinian, and particularly Palestinians together, insist upon the reality and autonomy of the Palestinian experience. It is an excess which can reveal itself in many other ways as well, such as parody and mimicry, but it always seems, according to Said, 'too much'. The reason for this is obvious: the Palestinian is riven by incompletion, marginality, fragmentation, in a world in which the individual Palestinian is consistently represented as the threatening other of the Western imagination. This is the 'uniquely punishing destiny' about which Said often speaks (1978: 27). Exclusion and relegation constantly confront one's sense of being. Excess, therefore, is sometimes a necessary feature of the attempt to make a space for oneself in the world. 'Excess', says Georges Bataille, is 'that whereby the being is firstly and above all else conveyed beyond all circumscribing restrictions' (Bataille, 1956: 145). For the post-colonial subject it often seems as though the breaching of such boundaries and restrictions – perhaps above all, the restrictions of the colonizing discourse – sometimes requires a strategy of excessive statement simply to establish identity.

Excess provides us with another strategy by which the counter-discursive may transform the influences of a dominant discourse. Excess is a fascinating feature of a power relationship, for the excess of the dominated subject is not so much oppositional as *supervening*. While the post-colonial (and any discursively 'produced') subject may occupy the fractures in discourse, may negotiate entry to, and exit from, a discourse, and may render it provisional in its effects, it may also *exceed* the boundaries of that discourse in various ways. A discourse is always buttressed by the regulatory and disciplining presence of other subjects. 'The judges of normality are present everywhere', says Foucault

> We are in the society of the teacher-judge, the doctor-judge, the educator-judge, the 'socialworker' judge; it is on them that the universal reign of the normative is based; and each individual, wherever he may find himself, subjects to it his body, his gestures, his behaviour, his aptitudes, his achievements. The carceral network, in its compact or disseminated forms, with its systems of insertion, distribution, surveillance, observation, has been the greatest support, in modern society, of the normalizing power. (1977b: 304)

Although speaking of the prison, and its extension of the carceral structure of society, the pervasive pressures of 'normality' upon all social subjects effect themselves through the 'capillary' movement of discourse. As we have seen, pervasive though it is, discourse is fragile and negotiable, but the very weight of 'normality' – in Said's case the widespread US assumption that all Palestinians are terrorists – seems to demand an excessive response. Here we find a tactic somewhat different from the occupation of the 'fractures' of discourse; yet the two go hand in hand, in the sense that counter-discourse generates various tactics, all of which are geared to deal with power on its own terms.

There are many discussions of excess in contemporary literary analysis,[1] but the examples of Rushdie and Said present significant though very different examples of the tactic. There is no more visible or more vocal spokesperson for Palestinian affairs in the USA than Edward Said. The excess of repetition, insistence, pervasiveness, and, occasionally, vociferousness, characterizes his contributions in the press, in debating forums and in more academic analyses. This excess marks his perpetual and celebrated campaign to 'speak truth to power' (1994: 85–102). The only guarantee that power might listen, however, is that it is addressed on its own terms, that the excessive confirmation of Palestinian identity occurs within the dominant discourse. Salman Rushdie's irrepressible fictional exuberance, his extravagant fabric of ethnic hybridity and discursive insurrection, present a different but equally forceful example of excess. As Saleem says in *Midnight's Children*, 'there are so many stories to tell, too many, such an excess of intertwined lives events miracles places rumours, so dense a commingling of the improbable and the mundane!' (Rushdie, 1981: 9). Both figures suggest three interrelated modes of this phenomenon in post-colonialism: the excess of insistence; the excess of supplementarity, and the excess of hybridity. The literature of excess is obviously not limited to the post-colonial, neither is all post-colonial literature what we might call 'literature of excess', but it is not too much to claim that at least one of these modes of excess is always present in post-colonial writing, both 'creative' and 'theoretical'.

Insistence

The energy of insistence is clearly demonstrated in that excessive and voluble affirmation of Palestinian experience which characterizes Said's profile as a public intellectual, but this has its clear correlative in post-colonial theory. Said appears to infer that excess is somehow the historical lot of the Palestinian, but an 'excessive' insistence is a common tactic of the marginal and displaced. As the Palestinian example forcibly reveals, excess can become the *place* in which the post-colonial is located. There is possibly no better demonstration of the agency of the carceral subject than the insistence and repetition of the voice of dissent. If this is the 'place' in which the post-colonial subject dwells, then that place exists, above all, in language, for it is in language that the agency of the subject is realized by insistence.

We can see an interesting conflation of agency and insistence in psychoanalytic language. The word *instanz* in Freud is translated as 'agency', in 'the agency of the ego in the unconscious'. But Lacan mimics this word with the homonym *instance* which in French means 'insistence'. Thus, for Lacan, 'insistence' and 'agency' are synonymous. His paper 'The insistence of the letter in the unconscious' is also translated as 'The agency of the letter in the unconscious' (Lacan, 1977: 146–78). Similarly, we can say that the excess of *insistence* in post-colonial discourse is a strategic site of *agency* for the post-colonial subject (see translator's note in Lacan 1977: vii–viii). Not only do the two go hand in hand, but this conflation provides an important key to the subject's ability to resist the interpellation of ideology and the subject formation of discourse.

When we are thinking about transformation we need to articulate the subtle difference between insistence and resistance. Resistance that defines itself as opposition is merely defensive, whereas insistence is productive, assertive and excessive. It is in the excess of *instanz* that the agency of the resisting subject is confirmed. Agency is most productive when it is involved in fashioning the self. Such self-fashioning is *transformative* when it takes hold of the dominant language, genre, technology, and uses it for that purpose, for, as we have seen, this process invariably transforms the discourse itself. The post-colonial 'recapture' of representation, in various modes of creative production, for instance, demonstrates precisely the kind of 'insistence' by which the agency of the subaltern subject is realized. Those cultural representations which can be termed a 'tactical occupation' of the fractures of discourse can only really come into being through the agency of insistence.

Curiously, in a discourse which can be prone to several kinds of excess, this insistence is often an insistence upon *reality*, the reality and materiality of post-colonial experience. J. M. Charcot once suggested that 'Theory is good, but it doesn't prevent things from existing' (cited in Brooks, 1990: 2). This becomes very pertinent in post-colonial writing, because the ultimate horizon of that materiality on which it insists is death itself. We could detail the history of oppression and death that has attended many writers' careers to elaborate this, but we need look no further than to one of our conversants – Salman Rushdie. The *fatwa* declared against Salman Rushdie by the Ayatollah Komeini, for alleged sacrilege in *The Satanic Verses* against the wives of the prophet Mohammed, brings us face to face with the worldliness of the text – and the material reality of the author. In an immense contemporary drama of reading, we see the excessive insistence of Rushdie's text collide with the unswerving judgement of a fundamentalist reading, an encounter with the terrorism of absolute meaning. Suddenly we have lurched beyond the comfortable consideration of textuality, of the author as simply a 'function of the text', and find ourselves facing the clear denominating line of post-colonial reality: the author's death. The irony of this is deeply symptomatic of the protean adaptability of power: Islam, the oriental 'Other' of the West, becomes the totalitarian and 'imperial' regulator, the master narrative which punishes and (very effectively) incarcerates the writer. This incident becomes a very clear, if ironic, metonym of the operation of colonial power.

The contest between reality and discourse which death appears to adjudicate can be examined by a consideration of Foucault's discussion of the emergence of the author-function in 'What is an author?' (1969). Authors emerged when owners needed to be found for texts, and subjects found responsible for their transgression. 'How can one reduce the great peril, the great danger with which fiction threatens our world', Foucault asks. 'The answer is: One can reduce it with the author' (*ibid.*: 158). In his connection of writing and death we find a precise moment in which the real and the deferred coincide. Foucault points out that writing leads to death: 'The work, which once had the duty of providing immortality, now possesses the right to kill, to be its author's murderer, as in the cases of Flaubert, Proust and Kafka' (*ibid*.: 142). He goes on:

> That is not all, however: this relationship between writing and death is also manifested in the effacement of the writing subject's individual characteristics ... the mark of the writer is reduced to nothing more than the singularity of his absence; he must assume the role of a dead man in the game of writing. (*ibid*.: 142–3)

That is all well and good, we might say, but we must add a supplement to it; we must say to Foucault: 'And yet ... Rushdie may die!' Rushdie's possible death has meaning in a number of possible discourses. It is metonymic rather than metaphoric; metonymic of post-colonial writing itself. Its reality is transdiscursive. This is, perhaps, what makes it 'really real'. 'Nevertheless', we insist, 'Rushdie may die!' The author may be reduced metaphorically to the 'singularity of his absence', as Foucault puts it, but in Rushdie's case we are made painfully aware that writers are more than absences, that the production of the text occurs in some material space. In this battle we exceed any mere role-playing of the author's death. Excess is an encounter with real life.

Indeed, the Rushdie example highlights a crucial feature of post-colonial and other political discourse. While we may accept the function of discourse or language in the construction of the subject, we are still left with very material parameters to experience, parameters which define a view of the real: death on the one hand and an *insistence* upon identity on the other. It is, perhaps, this dichotomy which makes the insistence of the post-colonial subject so potent and perhaps so important, for it is out of this excess that a sense of the reality of experience can be recovered.

Supplementarity

Another mode of post-colonial excess is one we may call 'supplementarity'. The most recognizable use of the concept of supplementarity occurs, of course, in Derrida's deconstruction of signification, in the concept of *différance* in which the supplement of the sign always exceeds the closure of the signified. Indeed, the 'supplement' of meaning, by which signifieds are always further signifiers, is a central feature of the post-structuralist revision of Saussure's theory of signs. However, there is a sense in which supplementarity can be used quite differently, to refer to a mode of post-colonial excess.

In his book *The Accursed Share* (1967), Georges Bataille proposes a theory of excess which stems from a general economy of energy, which asserts that, 'if the demands of the life of beings (or groups) detached from life's immensity defines an interest to which every operation is referred, the *general* movement of life is nevertheless accomplished beyond the demands of individuals' (Bataille, 1967: 74).

Bataille's economy hinges on the need for a system to use up that excess energy which cannot be used for its growth. Thus the unproductiveness of *luxury* of all kinds; the apparently meaningless expenditure of *sacrifice*; the tradition of gift-giving called 'potlatch'[2] which demands the maintenance of honour by the return of a greater gift, all maintain a system's balance by using up surplus wealth. Within this general economy the sexual act is a pre-eminent form of non-utilitarian expenditure of energy, war is almost essential, while death itself is the ultimate moment of 'luxury' in the system. Bataille summed up his general economy with the resonant statement that 'the sexual act is in time what the tiger is in space' (1967: 35). The eating of one species by another (represented in the tiger) is the simplest form of luxury (*ibid*.: 33), but 'sexual reproduction is, together with eating and death, one of the great luxurious detours that ensure the intense consumption of energy' (*ibid*.: 35).

If we accept at least the general proposition of this trans-phenomenal and transdiscursive movement of energy, we may detect a fascinating feature of the imperial process. Imperial power expends its excess wealth through war (i.e. the military force employed in colonial expansion and the subjugation of colonial possessions), to create greater wealth which is then diffused as luxury, further military expansion and so on. Though it is a centred system, it is never a closed system: the dissipation of the excess always increases wealth. We can see here the very close connection between capitalism – which Wallerstein claims is *the* world system and has been since the sixteenth century (1974a, 1974b) – and the relentless establishment and expansion of empire by the various European powers.

However, when we look at the colonial world, we see that the excess of 'luxury' is ideally exported as high culture. Culture, and the non-productive superstructure it supports, is an extremely prodigal expenditure of surplus energy originally accumulated as wealth. As post-colonial theory has long known, the expenditure of surplus energy through cultural hegemony long outlasts the 'luxury' of war, invasion and annexation, and maintains the production of wealth which is always distributed in a centripetal way. In other words, cultural hegemony maintains the economy of wealth distribution.

This process leaves the system of imperial hegemony intact. An instance of this hegemony may be seen in the export of theory, and this of course works on its own momentum long after the official end of imperialism. Thus whereas surplus value creates wealth for the centre in a fairly obvious way, so the cultural surplus works to the same end. Even when manifested in apparently subversive and heterogeneous formations such as post-structuralism (with its own ironic doctrine of the surplus of the sign), this cultural surplus works through language to defuse opposition and preserve the system of wealth creation.

According to Bataille, true opposition is best effected by the one who spurns the very system in which wealth has its meaning. This is of crucial significance to post-colonialism since, by means of various strategies, it resists, subverts, interpolates, and generally evades the centrality of the wealth system it engages, even when that engagement is effected through mimicry.

> The true luxury ... of our times falls to the poverty stricken, that is, to the individual who lies down and scoffs. A genuine luxury requires the complete contempt for riches, the somber indifference of the individual who refuses work and makes his life on the one hand an infinitely ruined splendour, and on the other, a silent insult to the laborious lie of the rich ... henceforth no one can rediscover the meaning of wealth, the explosiveness that it heralds, unless it is in the splendour of rags and the somber challenge of indifference. One might say, finally, that the lie destines life's exuberance to revolt. (Bataille, 1967: 76–7).

Post-colonial excess reveals itself in the exuberance of life which is destined to revolt. The option of lying down poverty stricken to scoff is one taken by Wilson Harris (very successfully) when he refuses to be called a theorist. This act of course deconstructs the very term 'poverty stricken', but such an end may also be accomplished less cataclysmically in the strategy of appropriation. The appropriation of that surplus wealth represented by theory itself is not just a cunning strategy, but one of a quite limited number of ways to recirculate the energy stolen from the colonized world in the first place.

The discourse of decolonization appropriates the cultural surplus, whether as genre, form, style or theory itself, and redistributes it as excess. This means that the appropriated form of life or language game is immediately 'blown apart', so to speak, by the perpetual supplement of hybridity, marginality, supplementarity, the open horizon of post-colonial ontology. In a sense this can be the option of the poverty stricken to 'lie down and scoff' because the selective mimicry of appropriation mocks the riches of the system. Excess is, in this sense, the continual supplement of the surplus (i.e. a surplus can be finite, but excess is not). There are many ways of conceiving this, of course. The selective mimicry of appropriation is a transgression in which the bandit post-colonial mounts raids across the porous borders of discourse. This poverty and transgression in the gaze of the centre puts post-colonial discourse beyond the apparent riches of an alternate but symmetrical centre. Such scoffing rejects the system itself, and with it the hope of resurrecting some seamless and unproblematic cultural identity. Indeed, the very opposite is the case; post-colonial 'ontology' itself is located in the excess of hybridity.

Also available to post-colonialism is a programme of recuperation, in which the immense wealth of theory generated in the post-colonial creative text is recovered (the 'excess' of this essay is itself taken from a conversation). Such a recuperation of theory could enhance the construction of a non-symmetrical and non-reactive oppositional system which hinged on a kind of hybrid excess of theoretical profusion. In this way, post-colonial theory might better avoid an 'opposition' that is simply a response to the 'position' of Eurocentric theory.

Nevertheless, the *centripetal* impetus of hegemony works feverishly against the exuberance of post-colonial life in many ways, both from without and within. The Rushdie sanction is the grimmest example of external force; and it also operates when Wole Soyinka, Patrick White, V. S. Naipaul or W. B. Yeats are reincorporated into the system by the 'disinterested' approbation of the canon. However, the same principle works 'from within', so to speak, when Joseph Furphy or Robbie Burns, say, are incorporated by nationalist ideology. Opposition can itself be a form of luxury which merely maintains the total system by conserving a symmetry of oppositions. It is the excess of post-colonialism which avoids this symmetry.

Hybridity

The ultimate goal of counter-discursive interpolation is not simply to fracture a discourse but to exceed its boundaries. The most resilient boundary established by a discourse is the binary between colonizer and colonized, which generates variations such as black/white, teacher/ pupil, adult/child. As we have seen, the first trap of resistance discourse is the reversal, but retention of the binary in a way that transfers power without transforming it. One way in which post-colonial theory has addressed this trap is to focus on the concept of hybridity, a term that has come under suspicion as quickly as it came into vogue. Popularized by Homi Bhabha, it has been criticized for its suggestion that cross-cultural exchange occurs on a level political field rather than one characterized by great inequalities of power. Robert Young argues that it was a popular term in imperialist discourse and accompanied con-scious assimilationist strategies (1995). Yet even he admits that there is a difference between the unconscious processes of hybridity and a delib-erate political disruption of cultural identity. While the concept can lead to a dangerous levelling out of cultural power, hybridity is still an important feature of post-colonial attempts to disrupt colonial binaries. In its 'excessive' disruption of the certainties of essentialist categorization it is a consummate example of excess.

Hybridization takes many forms: linguistic, cultural, political, racial and religious. Linguistic examples include pidgin and creole languages, and these echo the use of the term by Bakhtin, for whom it denotes the disruptive and transfiguring power of multivocal language situations and, by extension, of multivocal narratives. The idea of a polyphony of voices in society is implied also in Bakhtin's idea of the carnivalesque which emerged in the Middle Ages when 'a boundless world of humorous forms and manifestations opposed the official and serious tone of medieval ecclesiastical and feudal culture' (Holquist, 1984: 4).

Young notes that, for Bakhtin, hybridity is politicized, made contestatory, so that it embraces the subversion and challenge of division and separation. Bakhtin's hybridity 'sets different points of view against each other in a conflictual structure, which retains "a certain elemental, organic energy and openendedness"' (1995: 22). It is this potential of hybridity to reverse 'the structures of domination in the colonial situation' (*ibid.*: 23) which Young recognizes that Bhabha also articulates.

> Bakhtin's intentional hybrid has been transformed by Bhabha into an active moment of challenge and resistance against a dominant colonial power ... depriving the imposed imperialist culture, not only of the authority that it has for so long imposed politically, often through violence, but even of its own claims to authenticity. (*ibid.*)

Bhabha contends that all cultural statements and systems are constructed in a space which he calls the 'Third Space of enunciation' (1994: 37). Cultural identity always emerges in this contradictory and ambivalent space, which for Bhabha makes the claim to a hierarchical 'purity' of cultures untenable. For him, the recognition of this ambivalent space of cultural identity may help us overcome the exoticism of 'cultural diversity' in favour of the recognition of an empowering hybridity within which cultural difference may operate:

> It is significant that the productive capacities of this Third Space have a colonial or postcolonial provenance. For a willingness to descend into that alien territory ... may open the way to conceptualising an *inter*national culture, based not on the exoticism of multiculturalism or the *diversity* of cultures, but on the inscription and articulation of culture's *hybridity*. (*ibid.*: 38, emphasis in original)

It is the 'in-between' space which carries the burden and meaning of culture and this is what makes the notion of hybridity so important.

The most tenacious aspect of anti-colonial binarism is the tendency to make a distinction between 'bad' colonizer and 'good' colonized, demanding a rejection of everything colonial. Such a position, although rhetorically satisfying, does nothing to describe the complex range of engagements and strategies which colonized subjects employ in their engagement with the dominant power, nor does it give even an inkling of the Third Space of enunciation in which the polyphony of colonial resistance operates. Thus when V. Y. Mudimbe advocates the repudiation of Western rationality, Abeola Irele points out the contradiction of using Foucault to support his argument.

> What we really want to know is whether the Western system provides useful ideas, and I do not see Foucault (on whom Mudimbe depends

for his deconstructive analysis of Western – that is, colonial – discourse on the idea of Africa) as having undermined that basic point. (Irele, 1995: 296)

Clearly, the emancipatory energy of post-colonial discourse can find much that is useful in the colonial dominance it is resisting, and indeed can use it in the act of resisting.

The difficulty many post-colonial writers have with this apparent ambiguity stems from an essentialist perception of identity. D. A. Masolo perceptively reveals a common misconception in much post-colonial criticism: the assumption

> first, that all formerly colonized persons ought to have one view of the impact of colonialism behind which they ought to unite to overthrow it; second, that the overthrow of colonialism be replaced with another, liberated and assumedly authentic identity. So strong is the pull toward the objectivity of this identity that most of those who speak of Africa from this emancipatory perspective think of it only as a solid rock which has withstood all the storms of history except colonialism. Because of the deeply political gist of the colonial/postcolonial discourse, we have come to think of our identities as natural rather than imagined and politically driven. (Masolo, 1997: 285)

The assumption of the 'solid rock' of authentic identity is habitually contradicted by the actual transformative processes of post-colonial experience, for the 'solid rock' itself is fluid, a continual state of becoming. It is 'post' colonial, constructed, political, even at its most authentic, because it is being formed within the inescapable historical reality of colonization and its consequences. In some cases, as in the assumption of an authentic African identity, the construction process has assumed mammoth proportions. As Anthony Appiah says:

> To speak of an African identity in the nineteenth century – if an identity is a coalescence of mutually responsive (if sometimes conflicting) modes of conduct, habits of thought, and patterns of evaluations; in short, a coherent kind of human social psychology – would have been to give 'to give to aery nothing a local habitation and a name.'
> Yet there is no doubt that now, a century later, an African identity is coming into being. I have argued . . . that the bases through which it has largely been theorised – race, a common historical experience, a shared metaphysics – presuppose falsehoods too serious for us to ignore. (1992: 74)

African identities are diverse and pluralist. Just as culture itself is fluid, so identities are always 'hybrid' in the broadest sense. This contradicts the assumptions of both pan-Africanist ideology and much Western ethnology. The heterogeneity, or hybridity, of post-colonial identities, like all identities, lies in the ways in which subjects inhabit the various locations of those identities.

The emancipatory drive of post-colonial excess, the drive to re-empower the disenfranchised, is too often conceived in terms of a simplistic view of colonization, of post-colonial response, and of post-colonial identities. The consequent exhortatory tone of decolonizing theory runs the risk of theorizing how the world should be rather than how the world *is* in the ordinary actions of individuals. Transformation is a dominant mode in the post-colonial response to those colonizing forces which appear constantly to suppress and control. Recognizing this fact is all the more urgent given the complete failure of Marxist programmes of 'liberation' in Africa and other post-colonial states.

The 'excess' of transformation gives us a different way of looking at what Bhabha calls the ambivalence of colonial discourse. For, rather than a kind of flaw in the operation of colonial discourse, a self-defeating need to produce in the colonized subject an imitation which must fail, because it can never be an exact copy, ambivalence may be regarded as a much more active feature of post-colonial subjectivity. It may be seen to be the *ambivalent* or 'two-powered' sign of the capacity of the colonized to 'imitate' transformatively, to take the image of the colonial model and use it in the process of resistance, the process of self-empowerment. Ambivalence is not merely the sign of the failure of colonial discourse to make the colonial subject conform; it is also the sign of the agency of the colonized – the two-way gaze, the dual orientation, the ability to appropriate colonial technology without being absorbed by it – which disrupts the monologic impetus of the colonizing process.

This ambivalence is a very different thing, however, from the rigid opposition of colonizer and colonized which can lead to what Eze calls the 'radically mythical'. Informed by a friend that Nigeria's economy was in 'deep depression', the farming, banking and manufacturing industries in 'distress', he remarks:

> In depression and distress and always on the verge of the tragic, our engagement with the West becomes susceptible, and in fact readily transposes itself, to the realm of the radically mythical: the West is against us, yet the West is our savior. In this role the West becomes not just the (objective) West, but the Absolute West – which repels and fascinates us all at once. (1997: 343)

If the ambivalence of post-colonial reality descends to a schematization of the West as 'mythical and phantasmagoric', then its transformative capacity is truly lost. Such a mythical schematization is not the result of ambivalence, but of the tendency to fall into the habit of absolute dichotomy – the Absolute West vs. the Rest. In such an opposition there is no resolution to the paradox of the West as oppressor and saviour. In the face of this opposition the concept of hybridity is truly 'excessive'.

Yet nowhere has the 'oppression of the saviour' been demonstrated as clearly as in the development economics pursued in Africa. All societies possess specific preconceptions, methods and strategies of economic organization, but when these have been too completely suppressed by the modern economics of neo-colonialism the result has been disastrous at worst, tardy at best. 'Africa has not "taken off" and developers still stumble over a rationality which is not that of their programs. The growth in productivity that Africa so urgently needs has therefore not been achieved' (Verhelst, 1990: 25). This is partly because the rigidity of economic assumptions and developmental practices has prevented them from utilizing the natural adaptability of ordinary people and their everyday economic practice. 'The African peasant's economic behaviour patterns' says Verhelst, 'seem to involve a delicate balancing act between the economic rationality prevalent in the West and certain non-rational social pressures or even beliefs which escape the more utilitarian, materialistic and individualistic logic of Western capitalism' (1990: 26). It is only when this balancing act is unbalanced in favour of the methods of the local that transformation can begin. Unfortunately, national politics too often block such developments, since their own policies are determined by the demands of the World Bank and the IMF.

Indisputably, the theoretical purchase of hybridity has been undermined by its link with notions of race and biology. However, if we dispense with the assumption that hybridity describes an ontological condition (in much the same way that we must reject 'post-colonial' as an ontology), and see it as another term for the range of strategies and interactions by which colonial cultures are transformed, we will gain a better idea of the excessive and complex agency of post-colonial engagements with colonial power. Post-colonial transformation is not linear but discontinuous, rhizomic, intermittent, excessive. If we understand hybridity as a potential for change, or, in Bakhtin's terms, a 'polyphony', rather than a static heterogeneity of being, we will more clearly see its place in this transformative process, alongside 'supplementarity' and 'insistence' as a strategic mode of post-colonial excess.

Notes

1. American critics such as Weiss (1991) and LeClair (1989) investigate the aesthetics of excess in the work of writers like Thomas Pynchon, Joseph Heller, John Barth, Robert Coover. For Tom LeClair, excess is a feature of those writers who demonstrate 'mastery' – 'a combination of quality and cultural significance' (1989: 1). Since this engaging phrase occurs on page 1 of LeClair's book, post-colonialists not interested in systems theory need read no further. The work of Georges Bataille (1967, 1985) is more useful for this discussion. For Bataille, excess takes many forms. Mostly the excess is an excess of the iconoclastic, the taboo, the breaking of restrictions to the realization of full being.

2. This originally referred to a ceremonial feast of the American Indians of the north-west coast marked by the host's lavish distribution of gifts or sometimes destruction of property to demonstrate wealth and generosity with the expectation of eventual reciprocation. The word is analysed by Marcel Mauss in *The Gift* (1954).

CHAPTER 9

A prophetic vision of the past

History and allegory in Peter Carey's *Oscar and Lucinda*

There is possibly a no more contentious area of discussion in post-colonial studies than the status of settler colonies. The relevance of the cultural hegemony of empire is obvious to anybody who grows up in these countries, but to others, their relative prosperity and officially monolingual character excludes all except their indigenous inhabitants from post-colonial discourse. This is largely because attitudes to decolonization are invariably, if often unconsciously, infected by the imperial binaries of 'us and them', 'colonizer and colonized', 'black and white', 'civilized and primitive'. Indigenous politics get drawn into these binaries so quickly that they are assumed to be these societies' only engagement with colonization; yet settler colonies disrupt, confuse and destabilize these binaries at all levels. They demonstrate some of the supreme examples of post-colonial transformation because they are by definition ambivalent, contradictory, torn between identity stereotypes and imperial cultural affiliations, marked by the stresses and tensions of affiliation which exist in all post-colonial societies, but which are ignored in favour of egregious polarities.

In their appropriations of language, their ambivalent construction of place and their various transformations of colonial discourse, settler colonies reveal the complexity and the ambiguous rhizomic nature of the operation of imperial power. They demonstrate in clearer form what is true of all post-colonial societies: that the colonized can be the colonizers, the marginalized can be the marginalizers, that imperial power circulates and produces rather than simply confines. When we understand that 'being colonized' does not indicate a coherent and predictable state of being but a wide range of cultural, political relationships, we are better able to see the network of strategies that constitute the 'condition' of post-coloniality. Settler colonies develop strategies of resistance and transformation that are similar in *process* to those of other colonized societies while being very different in content. The struggle between filiation and affiliation; the struggle to represent self and thus obtain cultural agency; the inheritance of forms of subject formation such as nationalism and ethnicity; the ambivalent and contested representation of place: these experiences outline spaces of contestation shared by all colonies.

We may demonstrate the operation of post-colonial discourse in various ways, but it is in the attitude to history, the 'interpolation' of historiography conducted by literary writers, that some of the most resonant transformations occur. No other discourse has such an investment in a particular kind of future. History, so powerful an instrument of Europe's construction of world reality, not only records 'the past' but outlines a trajectory which takes in the future. The teleology of historical method is obvious, but it is nowhere more determining and coercive than in the ideology of imperial history. Such history locks the 'postcolony' into a future determined by the civilizing mission of empire. There are various ways of encountering the prescriptions of history. The OED gives one definition of history as: 'a written narrative constituting a continuous methodical record, in order of time, of important or public events, especially those connected with a particular country, people or individual.' Each one of these elements – its written form; its weddedness to chronological time, its will to truth, its continuity, its teleology, its narrativity, its aspiration to be a scientific record of events; its articulation of what constitutes events of historical value – is important in the imperial function of history over the last two centuries. History occludes local pasts in various ways, sometimes by nominating the pre-colonial as 'primitive' and 'prehistoric', sometimes by overshadowing it with the prestige and status of modern history's scientific method. In settler colonies the suppression of the local history is more subtle: post-colonial history (other than the officially 'national') is regarded as having no value or importance because 'nothing significant' has occurred: Australian colonial history is simply an extension of British history. Whatever the particular way in which history dominates the local, it is fictional narrative which provides the most flexible and evocative response, principally because fiction is best able to reproduce the fundamentally allegorical nature of history itself.

Because post-colonial societies of all kinds have been marginalized from the disciplinary structures of European discourse, their access to those structures has often occurred by means of *literary* writing. The reason this is so efficacious is that 'the actual experience of life in a colonial or post-colonial culture has been, and continues to be, "written" by the texts of colonial discourse' (Slemon, 1987: 10). The dominant mode of this 'writing' has been allegorical, making allegory itself a site of struggle, and a mode of counter-discourse in all forms of colonial occupation. The 'great' literary allegories of the English literature canon have been the most influential formulators of what it is to be human and to have thus become the particular objects of counter-discourse. Thus, 'allegorical writing, and its inherent investment in history provides the post-colonial writer with a means' not only of proposing that history can be 'opened up to the transformative power of imaginative revision', but 'also of building it into the structuring principle of the fictional work of art' (Slemon, 1988: 159).

Of course, post-colonialism cannot lay an exclusive claim to the allegorical mode. To Roland Barthes, both history and narrative have a mythic dimension realized in the conversion of history into nature and 'the essence of the myths of our own day is the process by which the dominant cultural forces transform the reality of the world into images of that world' (Barthes, 1957: 215, 229). For Barthes, myth is an allegory in that it gives structure to a gap between its surface and its content, and history is mythologized by its subservience to 'irresistible' narrativity (*ibid*.: 200). Hans Kellner, at the conclusion of a meticulous discussion of theories of narrativity in history, concludes that allegory may be seen as the crucial instrumentality of the reality function of history. The allegorical nature of narrativity is the trope which unites the post-structuralist with otherwise widely divergent theories of history. As he says, 'The link, or at least *a* link between the post-structuralist critique of historical thinking and the narrativity which makes historical writing "historical" in a disciplinary sense is their sense of the *allegorical* nature of historical writing' (Kellner, 1987: 27). Contemporary anti-narrative theories such as quantitative history, cliometric history, theory-oriented history and psycho-history are more self-consciously allegorical than traditional narrative histories, but this merely serves to articulate the allegorical nature and function of narrative itself (*ibid*.).

> Ultimately, allegory questions its own authority by inescapably drawing attention to the *will* exerted in its creation; this will to represent is revealed as a human need, the product of desire or 'Care' and can be understood only within the authoritative confines of . . . another allegory. (Smith, 1982: 113)

When we turn to the allegorical trope in post-colonial history we see a peculiar employment of the 'will' to truth. Post-colonial allegory is not the figurative reference to some kind of 'totality', a real history which exists beyond or in the direction of the story. It recognizes that the history exists in the narrative and that the allegorical, by its very self-referentiality, disturbs the referential hegemony of imperial history. It is the insuperable problem of this inferred totality which 'keeps history in the narrative business', as Kellner puts it (1987: 27), but it is through allegory that the interpolation of the post-colonial into this narrative creates its own form of oppositional disturbance. The tactic of *interpolation* therefore distinguishes the allegory of post-colonial history from the allegorical nature of other historical writing, because interpolation *is* a mode of disturbance.

The significance of allegory for post-colonial accounts of history is the opportunity it opens up for what Edouard Glissant calls a 'prophetic vision of the past'. Talking about the difficult phenomenon of Caribbean history, the history of a people robbed of a prehistory, taken out of their own history, so to speak, and then denied a reality within early accounts of plantation society, Glissant conceives a history in prophetic terms: a past conflated with the present that the writer must continually strive to capture. 'The past' he says, 'to which we were subjected, which has not yet emerged as history for us, is, however, obsessively present. The duty of the writer is to explore this obsession, to show its relevance in a continuous fashion to the immediate present' (Glissant, 1989: 64). This prophetic vision, he explains, is neither a nostalgic lament nor a narrative locked into the scientific method of history. It enters the allegory of historical narrative in order to re-vision the future. A striking example of this, according to Wilson Harris, is the ubiquitous limbo dance found in the carnival life of the West Indies which is an allegory of the slaves' passage from Africa to the Caribbean, a continually and allegorically performed history, prophesying regeneration and renewal. This is a compelling image of a history that functions in the present, that not so much forms a dialectic between memory, future time and the present, as *enacts* the presentness of history.

Such a prophetic vision of the past radically revises our understanding of the continuity, teleology, chronology and methodology of history. For the simple scientific record of events becomes a tale with a future, either for empowerment, or, as in the case of *Oscar and Lucinda*, as a cautionary prophecy of the continued trajectory of imperial power in post-independence times. The allegory in *Oscar and Lucinda* is the allegory of imperial history itself: the classic journey of civilization into the wild on its historic mission to bring light into the darkness. On the face of it, the novel is an engaging story about a naive religious boy who follows what he believes to be God's will, leaves his father's church and makes his way across the terrifying sea to Australia, where he conceives and executes a fantastic plan to build a glass church and sail it up the Bellinger River as a vicarious act of love for Lucinda; but Oscar's journey is an ambivalent subversion of our usual assumptions about the progress of civilization from Europe to Australia. The allegorical journey not only disrupts the fixity of history but also dismantles the teleology of history.

Imperial/empirical history is a story of development towards a par-ticular end. This is one meaning of the term 'historicism', but its teleological impetus is one which is centripetal, that is, it constantly moves towards the centre, and establishes an order which is the essential aspect of the imperial – it orders reality. This elaborate story of Oscar's floating church, representing as it does the movement of white society into the unknown, the importation of spiritual solace, the improvement of society and the gradual movement towards order, is itself a parody of the allegory of imperial history. Such history is grounded on the imperial *telos* of progress and civilization, the *telos* of order. The idea of a *telos* – an end or goal to which the great transcendent movement of history is directed – is implicated in the idea of the sequential itself. For out of the notions of contiguity and temporal sequence emerges the principle of *cause*, which can in turn be seen to be a product of narrative structures once the world is considered as a text.

The teleological view of history which emphasized the constancy of progress is, not surprisingly, a strong feature of the school of British historians who wrote during the emergence and growth of Britain's empire. E. A. Freeman voices the clear conviction of imperial history when he says, in *The Growth of the English Constitution from the Earliest Times*:

> Each step in our growth has been the natural consequence of some earlier step; each change in our law and constitution has been, not the bringing in of anything wholly new, but the development and improvement of something that was already old. . . . Let ancient customs prevail; let us ever stand fast in the old paths. But the old paths have in England ever been the paths of progress. (Williams, 1972: 41)

English historians in the mid-nineteenth century share a strong conviction of the special calling of the nation to the civilizing mission. Perhaps the best-known expression of this belief is Macaulay's view in his 1835 Minute that 'whoever knows [the English language] has ready access to all the vast intellectual wealth, which all the wisest nations of the earth have created and hoarded in the course of ninety generations' (1835: 350). The idea of an obligation to disseminate the wealth of the language has deep roots in a heroic view of history itself; of the special calling of 'civilized' nations and their relevance to the task of history. Seeley, the Regius Professor of History at Cambridge at the end of the century, was able to summarize the century of prejudice in the manner of Macaulay and Carlyle, acclaiming the British Empire as 'similar to that of Rome, in which we hold the position not merely of a ruling but of an educating and civilizing race' (Williams, 1972: 170–1).

In *Oscar and Lucinda*, the teleology of history is firmly linked to the divine order of things. The titles of the chapters ('Ascension Day', 'After Whitsunday') give the direct sense of a coherent and ordered movement of history. Thus the church calendar becomes the metaphor for the ordered and *authorized* movement of historical time. The idea of the ordered progression of history towards a higher good found a particular foundation for nineteenth-century historians in the idea of a divine plan. In a lecture on the Puritan Revolution, Lord Acton stated: 'But we have no thread through the enormous intricacy and complexity of modern politics except the idea of progress towards more perfect and assured freedom, and the divine right of free men' (1906: 202).

The divine right of free men seems to derive from the divine ordering of the affairs of men. The link between teleology and theology is particularly evident in Carey's work and it is a link which his theme of chance is out to untie. It is put perhaps most explicitly by Acton in a lecture on 'Political thoughts on the Church' when he says: 'the wisdom of divine rule appears not in the perfection but in the improvement of the world . . . achieved liberty is the one ethical result that rests on the converging and combined conditions of advancing civilization' (Williams, 1972: 45). He concludes by invoking Leibniz' summation of this principle: 'History is the true demonstration of Religion.' Thus the teleological view of human progress seems inevitably allied in imperial history to the dogma that the civilized nations are the chief subject of history; 'The most precious Histories are those in which we read the successive stages of God's dispensations with man' (*ibid.*: 42). In response to this, the aims of post-colonial writing seem curiously conflictual: on the one hand the aim is to insert post-colonial experience into the programme of history; on the other to reject history because of its imperial narrativization of the past; but the problem here is that in history, as in other discursive formations, the post-colonial exists outside representation itself. The remedy is not 're-insertion' but 're-vision'; not the re-insertion of the marginalized into representation, but the appropriation of a method, the re-vision of 'history'. This is crucial to the political interpretation of post-colonial experience because it is an attempt to assume control of the processes of representation.

The view of historical movement with which *Oscar and Lucinda* (Carey, 1988) responds to the teleology of imperial history is a mirror image, so to speak, of Marx's dialectical view of history. Where Marx hinges the progression of history upon moments of synthesis rather than continuity, Carey proposes its completely erratic progression in moments of *pure chance*. Chance not only profoundly influences the progression of the story, but is *the* way in which the narrative progresses. Time after time Oscar's and Lucinda's history proceeds through moments of chance. The completely accidental death of Lucinda's father, when he falls off a horse (*Oscar and Lucinda*, p. 76),[1] makes Lucinda an heiress and thus begins a chain of events which will lead to her meeting with Oscar. Wardley-Fish, by accidentally knocking on Odd Bod's (Oscar's) door rather than West's (*OL*, p. 105) begins Oscar's obsession with gambling and the guilt which will send him to Australia. Lucinda's mother, by dying before she can change her will, gives Lucinda the means to fund Oscar; but most importantly, perhaps, the narrative itself, a story told by Oscar's grandchild, is occasioned by the chance encounter of Oscar and Lucinda: 'In order that I exist two gamblers must meet' (*OL*, p. 225). Moments of chance, which appear to be the only driving force of the allegorical movement of the novel, could be seen as *aporia* which at each point where they occur, deconstruct the assumptions of causality and continuity on which (imperial) history is established. The novel deconstructs history by demonstrating the extent to which the sequential movement of Oscar's history is rendered completely provisional.

The most sustained demonstration of chance in *Oscar and Lucinda* is gambling itself. 'Oscar had never seen such a passion for gambling. It was not confined to certain types or classes. It seemed to be the chief industry of the colony' (*OL*, p. 308), but Carey takes this cultural phenomenon and uses it to subvert inherited notions of social and historical order. Something considered to be a 'typical' Australian trait is used as the basis for a theory about social time itself, a 'counter-teleology' in the novel which comes to affect almost every aspect of human life. Most important initially is the connection between gambling and the divine will, perhaps the ultimate teleological discourse. On three important occasions Oscar paradoxically confirms what he takes to be divine guidance by an act of pure chance, the most important one being to throw the 'tor' over his shoulder to decide his future. He wishes he were a pig rather than face the consequences of his lot throwing – becoming an Anglican – (*OL*, p. 37), but he never doubts the certainty of divine direction. Faith itself becomes the ultimate gamble, as he says to Lucinda on board the ship to Australia: 'Our whole faith is a wager, Miss Leplastrier . . . we bet that there is a God. We bet our life on it' (*OL*, p. 261). If faith and life are a gamble then one of the greatest gambles is love, as Lucinda demonstrates when she bets her inheritance upon the success of Oscar's journey as a sign of the gamble of her whole life (*OL*, p. 388–9).

The idea of *telos* is essentially a claim for order in the movement of human affairs and is disrupted in various ways. Theophilus, the naturalist who encourages Oscar to classify his buttons, is convinced of the link between taxonomy and an ordered creation. Yet order is not simply disrupted by the novel; its moral claim is turned on its head, for in the person of the appalling Jeffris, order is actually seen to be a source of evil. Jeffris, who leads the party on its expedition in manic emulation of Major Mitchell, is both the embodiment of order, and the demonstration of the malicious blindness of the 'orderly' incursion of European society into Australia:

> he planned to go about this journey like a trigonometrist, knowing always, exactly, where he was in space. . . .
> They would carry axes and they would be razor sharp at all times, for there is nothing a surveyor despises more than a tree that obscures his trig point. (*OL*, p. 437–8)

Through Jeffris, the novel interpolates its narrative into the moral universe which Theophilus claims to know and to which imperial ideology claims privileged access. Entering it is to disrupt its polarity.

The novel is thus founded on a fundamental tension: events move forward according to the operation of *pure chance*, yet the narrative recording those events, as 'history', is represented as the purposeful movement of civilization into the wild. This is the contradiction allegorized by the journey of the glass church up the Bellinger River: this extraordinary and fine, but fundamentally accidental project, represents the apparently inexorable project of imperial history. Conceived as an act of love for Lucinda, Oscar's journey is 'captured' by the tyranny of imperial discourse in the person of Jeffris. Thus the trip is an immensely subtle allegory of the fundamentally empty and deluded narrative enacting and inscribing the empire's vision of progress.

A crucial feature of this expropriation of the past by imperial history is the link between the control of time and the control of space. Maps are central to the project of defining and controlling the world that Europeans have called 'discovery'. Language is itself a way of mapping the world and Theophilus demonstrates better than anyone the power of imperial discourse to order the world by naming it. However, it is the unmapped territories of human experience which present the greatest possibility to post-colonial experience. When Lucinda takes her dolly down to the back paddock in order to give her a head of hair which is much more controlled and controllable than her own, she manages to achieve the opposite of what she intends; that is, she catches a glimpse of the regions beyond order, 'a land where maps were not drawn' (*OL*, p. 81). Australia is a place which exists in the unmapped territory of the imagination. Its open possibility is its greatest attraction, but typically, to Jeffris, it is a wildness to be tamed. His 'great obsession in life was that he should be an explorer of unmapped territories' (*OL*, p. 169) and, we might say, to make the invisible 'visible'. The importance of Major Mitchell as Jeffris' model is that he was the scientist, the surveyor, the most technical of Australian explorers. In the record of Jeffris' achievement we find enacted a parable of imperial history itself.

> Mr Jeffris was content. He had not made a great exploration . . . but he had done sound work. . . . He had put his name to several largish creeks. He had set the heights of many mountains which had previously been wildly misdescribed. He had established a reputation for courage, having led his party through places inhabited by desperate blacks. His journals recorded that he had 'given better than he took' from the 'Spitting Tribe'. . . . He had also successfully defended the party from the murderous Kumbaingiri. He recorded all this in a neat and flowing hand which gave no indication of the peculiarities of his personality. His sketches of the countryside, the long ridges, mountains etc. were as good as anything in Mitchell's journals. (*OL*, p. 472)

The importance of naming, the alienation from place, the significance of the journal, indeed of writing itself in the control of history, the demonization of the indigenous inhabitants, the power over representation; all these features of imperial history are located in the journal of discovery. Jeffris' 'putting his name' to several landforms is the narcissism which is 'History's inability to 'tolerate otherness or leave it outside its economy of inclusion' (Young, 1990: 4). The essential role of violence is also revealed when he says, 'Churches are not carried by choirboys. Neither has the Empire been built by angels' (*OL*, p. 473). The extraordinary and fine idea of the glass church is hijacked by the rapacity and violence of Jeffris and his embodiment of history. This contradiction of truth and fiction is a characteristic of the nature of glass with which Oscar and Lucinda become obsessed.

Truth, fiction and the real

Perhaps more intransigent in debates about the ontological status of history is the question of whether it is truth or fiction. 'Truth' and 'reality' says Hans Kellner, 'are, of course, the primary authoritarian weapons of our time, an era characterised by nothing more than the debate over what is true of reality' (1987: 6). The problem is that they are tenaciously difficult to dispense with. Foucault, for instance, confirms the constructedness of these concepts time and again, but 'he will not dispense with them, but rather examines the way in which discourse creates reality as reality creates discourse. His own fictions, therefore, are true because they are based upon a certain reality; this reality is real, in part, because it has been figured by his fictions' (*ibid.*). What strikes us here is the fascinating intransigence of the dialectic of truth and fiction. The very act of piercing this dialectic to isolate the 'thesis' – reality – is one which invokes the fictive, because constructive, strategies of our discourse.

One solution has been to propose the idea that history is fiction, but this cliché only consolidates the inherent binarism of the distinction between the two. The binarism – history/fiction – is simply another way of expressing the binarism – truth/untruth – and hence, of course, that truth is untruth; but such a simple inversion is self-defeating. Both history and fiction are language games deployed in different contexts. History is a *method* rather than a truth – words create the history. The strategy of post-colonial writing is to collapse the binarism and deploy a method which does not do away with history but which emphasizes its provisionality. Carey's best-known entry into this truth/untruth conundrum occurs in his earlier *Illywhacker* in which the narrator, Herbert Badgery, claims to be a liar, leaving us with the problem of how to know whether a person who says he is a liar is telling us the truth. Lying is never simply opposed to truth, but is a sort of hybrid overlapping of different registers of narrative, a 'rhetoric'. In this mode, the 'grit of untruth' can be coated with 'creamy coats of credibility' to become 'a beautiful thing, a lustrous pearl it was impossible not to covet' (Carey, 1985: 60). It is both truth and untruth.

Oscar and Lucinda addresses the question of truth, reality and their interpretation at several levels. Much of the movement of the plot hinges upon the misinterpretation of what is 'true' or 'real'. The elaborate misunderstanding built up between Oscar and Lucinda in their oblique discussions about the glass church and its intended recipient is a clear example of the recalcitrant impenetrability of words. But Carey fixes upon a consummate material representation of this paradox of truth and fiction: glass. Glass is the substance which best represents the indeterminacy of existence, which focuses the problem of history itself. Glass stands for the contradictory and paradoxical transparency of life, the Promethean possibilities of being. It represents the unity of truth and illusion. It is a 'lovely contradictory thing . . . a thing in disguise, an actor, is not solid at all, but a liquid . . . in short, a joyous and paradoxical thing, as good a material as any to build a life from' (*OL*, p. 135).

Lucinda has taken her great gamble in life by purchasing a glass factory with her inheritance. Glass, and in particular the glass drops called Prince Rupert's drops, are the symbol of Lucinda herself and of Lucinda's and all people's desire to control their own history (*OL*, p. 131). The drop itself is unbreakable, steel-like in its capacity to withstand breakage, trauma attack, powerful in its resolution. But it has a weak spot; a spot so weak that cracking that spot can blow the whole thing apart. This weak spot in Lucinda is the great gamble, the gamble of love. The wager is her commitment to resolution and happiness, a wager focused in the glass church. That weak spot in her own teleological narrative blows the whole edifice of her life apart.

While Lucinda desires to create something extraordinary and fine in glass (*OL*, p. 361) and in the astonishing glass church seems to achieve it, the aborigines' song about glass, which they sing after the expedition has cut a bloody path through their midst, is salutary.

> Glass cuts.
> We never saw it before.
> Now it is here amongst us.
> It is sacred to the strangers.
> Glass cuts.
> Glass cuts kangaroo.
> Glass cuts bandicoot.
> Glass cuts the trees and grasses.
> Hurry on strangers.
> Hurry on the Kumbaingiri.
> Leave us, good spirits, go, go. (*OL*, p. 470)

Glass, the medium of something extraordinary and fine, is also its opposite. Glass becomes the representation of the paradox of colonial history, the paradox of the distinction between ideology and materiality, between rhetoric and practice. Above all, it can be out of place, which is the significance of the aboriginal song: 'It came up the river, its walls like ice emanating light, as fine and elegant as civilisation itself' (*OL*, p. 490). A luminous metonym of civilization and its effects: beautiful, dangerous, contradictory, ambivalent, a gamble of love that goes wrong.

If glass is the material symbol of the ambivalence of civilization in imperial history, a comparable motif in national history is invisibility. In *Illywhacker*, Goon Tse Ying teaches Herbert to disappear, a trick he learned at Lambing Flat, the site of a notorious gold-field massacre in which many Chinese were killed. He teaches Herbert because he is an orphan and it will make him safe, but also 'I do it to show you the terror of we Chinese at Lambing Flat. Because it is only possible to disappear by feeling terror' (Carey, 1985: 216). Herbert does indeed learn to disappear. Goon Tse Ying's ability is a 'magically real' ability, for what it demonstrates is not only the terror, but the wider invisibility of the Chinese and other groups in Australian history. His invisibility is met-onymic of the place of the marginalized in relation to the 'facts' of history. That this invisibility is a 'skill' prompted by terror is a disturbing revelation of the place of the 'unofficial' in national history. It is in Goon Tse Ying's ability to disappear that the ambivalence of truth and fiction in history becomes most clear.

The crucial ambivalence of post-colonial history lies in the fact that the boundaries of time and space become blurred. The importance of the link between time and space to settler cultures is the experience of spatial dislocation which disrupts the smooth trajectory of sequential history. Place becomes the traumatic site of cultural reconstruction which involves a conflict with many inherited assumptions, including a received sense of historical time. Often the most compelling way of accommodating this is to develop a contestatory national history, but the great epic movement of discovery and settlement precisely maps the trajectory of the meeting of the imperial and the national. What Paul Carter calls the epic theatre of imperial history (1987: xiv), the theatre of an inevitable movement towards the telos of civilization, becomes, at the same time, the authenticating narrative of nation. The birth of the nation emerges uncannily from the narrative of empire through the mediation of space, or, more specifically, through the narrative of discovery.

Perhaps even more conclusively than the specific differences of race, ethnicity, gender or nation, place unravels the universalist assumptions of history. Goon Tse Ying's ability to 'disappear' under the impetus of terror may be an archetype of the post-colonial relationship with 'place', for history desires above all to make the discovered place 'visible', a 'location'. That which occurs in the absent spaces of post-colonial reality, such as the plight of the Chinese in nineteenth-century Australia, hap-pens in a different way, in a different order and with a different valency than in the place inhabited by those who control the language. Funda-mentally, place itself is a 'location' in language. The place which exists outside the divine order of historical progress is in the strategic place to dismantle the centripetal illusions of imperial history. Carey's movement of discovery and settlement, the penetration of an incomprehensible wilderness, depicts a journey upriver as an allegory of the movement through place, bringing it into history.

The story of Oscar's glass church sailing up the Bellinger River is a *prophetic* vision of the past because it embodies, in its continuity, tele-ology, aspiration and purpose, the illusion of civilized progress, of 'development' as a continuous mode of being, moving into the post-colonial present. Yet most significantly, it is also the story of the capture of the resistant and transformative potential of the post-colonial by the continued impetus and authority of 'imperial' power. The church is something extraordinary and fine in concept; it is conceived in innocence as a rejection of the authority of the old order; it begins as the antithesis of mapping and exploration, proceeding into unmapped territory, not to impose order but to embody paradox, to offer praise to the lovely contradictory nature of experience; it is hijacked by the impetus of exploration, discovery and colonization in the person of the tyrannical Jeffris, becoming a reason for mapping, taken over by that authority to which it is antithetical; it proceeds into the future without regard to any past; it is the great gamble, but the inheritance is squandered. Like the civilizing mission, like progress, the fine idea collapses into a narrative of greed and robbery. Because the allegory depicts the allegorical nature of history itself, it goes beyond 'then' and 'now', projecting into the future its prophetic narrative of aspiration and disillusionment.

In their ambivalence and many-layered demonstration of post-colonial interchange, and because their history has an unavoidable beginning point in the 'moment' of colonization, settler colonies have an unusually strong investment in the teleological trajectory of imperial history. The growth of the colony is the very embodiment of the imperial dream of civilization. This is why Oscar's extraordinary journey up the Bellinger River is such an evocative narrative: because as an allegory of the historical movement of colonial civilization it is an allegory of the future of the settler colony as well as the past. It is in this capacity of the fictional text to reconnect time and place, to gaze cautiously at the movement of imperial history itself, that the prophetic vision of the past is most vividly realized.

Notes

1. Hereafter abbreviated to *OL*.

CHAPTER 10

Irony, allegory and empire

J. M. Coetzee's *Waiting for the Barbarians* and
In the Heart of the Country

However strong the post-colonial strategy of destabilizing history, it is a tendency shared by postmodern deconstructions of the linearity and teleology of historical method. It is perhaps not surprising that the conflation of post-colonialism and postmodernism has been so widespread in contemporary commentary. The postmodern project of deconstructing the master discourses of the European Enlightenment is much like the post-colonial task of dismantling the discursive effects of European imperialism. The post-structuralist sources of major colonial discourse theorists like Bhabha and Spivak have had the effect of erroneously linking all post-colonial analysis to postmodern theory. As suggested in Chapter 2, postmodernism and post-colonialism can both be seen to be discursive elaborations of postmodernity. This is because Enlightenment humanism (the target of postmodernism) and European imperialism (the target of post-colonial transformation) are both strategic, and interconnected, features of modernity, but this is very different from saying that post-colonialism and postmodernism are one and the same thing. They are very different elaborations of postmodernity, because only one – the post-colonial – challenges the essential Eurocentrism of modernity itself. While one replaces the human individual with the discursive notion of a subject, the other emphasizes the material context and worldliness of cultural texts. While one operates within Eurocentrism, the other undermines it. While one finds itself drawn into the unproductive possibilities of the play of the sign, the other emphasizes the political function of signification. While one emphasizes the existence of reality effects, the other emphasizes the urgent material consequences of those effects.

We need to address this conflation from the point of view of 'post-colonial futures' because the political nature of the transformations of colonial culture by post-colonial societies runs the risk of being lumped into the universalizing and Eurocentric discourse of postmodernism. One of the most curious examples of this occurs in Latin American criticism which often resists post-colonial explanations of the literature in favour of theses about Latin American postmodernism (see Colas, 1994). While texts can be read in terms of both discourses, we need to recognize the politically and culturally transformative dynamic of post-colonial writing. This is perhaps *the* distinguishing feature of the future which post-colonial discourse creates. Post-colonial analyses emphasize the 'worldliness' of the text, as Said puts it, as well as the worldliness of the critic. Worldliness asserts that literary texts arise from a particular place and a particular set of cultural conditions. The worldliness of J. M. Coetzee's writing is of considerable interest because it emerges from the very ambivalent site of the South African anti-apartheid white community.

The conflation of postmodernism and post-colonialism is proposed nowhere more elegantly than in Linda Hutcheon's 'Circling the down-spout of empire' (1991). Although there is, says Hutcheon, a clear emphasis on the political in post-colonial discourse, it can be seen as a version of postmodernism because of the trope of irony which both share. Hutcheon makes much of this use of irony which, she claims, is a discursive strategy of both post-colonialism and postmodernism. Since then, Hutcheon has produced a wide-ranging examination of the theory and politics of irony in *Irony's Edge* (1994) which avoids, in the main, her earlier assertions of this link. It is to this assertion that I want to return, because when we examine the function of irony, and examine its possible claims in relation to Coetzee's work, we discover certain distinctive aspects of the dynamic of post-colonial writing. Coetzee is an important focus for such an analysis since his work is read so consistently in postmodern terms.

My purpose in this chapter, therefore, is twofold: to examine the genealogy of this notion that irony is 'the trope for our times', the category under which all doubleness can be subsumed, and to see how Coetzee's *Waiting for the Barbarians* (1980) and *In the Heart of the Country* (1977), while appearing 'ironic', clarify the tendency of post-colonial writing to employ other counter-discursive tropes such as allegory. These two novels hinge on two of the recurrent issues in Coetzee's work – history and language – but both negotiate with particular urgency the territory in which ambivalence and allegory overlap. What is at stake here, ultimately, is an understanding of how post-colonial writing might articulate the political future of postmodernity. However, my specific task is to demonstrate that the tropological strategies of post-colonial writing, indeed many of the major political energies of post-colonial textuality, are directed not towards a simple opposition to the dominant discourse, but towards a transformation of that discourse through the strategy of interpolation. Coetzee's work is strategic in this examination because it so manifestly typifies that body of contemporary writing over which post-colonial and postmodern interpretations appear to be in contest.

What is not immediately obvious about Hutcheon's attraction to irony is that it has a venerable genealogy, extending as far back as Vico, reinterpreted through Kenneth Burke, Foucault and Hayden White. This theory of irony is based on what may be called the 'tropological structures' of discourse which Frye (1963, 1982) and White (1978) elaborate as the great innovation of Vico. Vico's theory is that human society evolves through various stages which may be represented by the function of language within it, namely the dominance of one of the four 'master tropes': metaphor, metonymy, synecdoche and irony. This conceptual evolution corresponds to different stages of social rule as a 'dialectic of the exchange between language and the reality it seeks to contain' (White, 1978: 209). Thus the primal or metaphoric stage is that in which words and objects share the same essence. The transition from this stage to the next, metonymic stage, in which words stand for objects, is analogous to the transition in society from the rule of gods to the rule of aristocracies. The transition from metonymic reductions to synecdochic constructions of whole from parts, genera from species, is analogous to the transition from aristocratic rule to democratic rule. The final transition from synecdochic construction to ironic statement is analogous to the transition from democracies ruled by law to the decadent societies whose members have no respect for that law. Irony becomes, in a sense, the ultimate trope of modernity, the trope in which the fragility of modernity's project of imperial regulation of human life is finally unmasked.

In his *A Grammar of Motives* (1945), Kenneth Burke suggests that the four master tropes deal in relationships that are experienced as inhering within or among phenomena, but which are in reality relationships existing between consciousness and a world of experience calling for some statement of its meaning: they are ways of talking about experience. Metaphor explicitly asserts a similarity in difference and implicitly a difference in similarity; meaning is provided in terms of equivalence or identity. As 'secondary forms' of metaphor, metonymy, which represents the whole by the part, is reductive, while synecdoche is representative. The ironic is the more difficult trope, being constituted as dialectical, but sanctioning the ambiguous, and even ambivalent, statement. Irony is 'the linguistic strategy underlying and sanctioning scepticism as an explanatory tactic, satire as a mode of emplotment, and either agnosticism or cynicism as a moral posture' (White, 1978: 73–4).

Such a linguistic strategy, I would argue, precisely represents those conditions in which the subject itself is constituted as constructed and passive in postmodernism. It is in the status accorded to subjectivity that post-colonial representations distinguish themselves from the 'ironic cynicism' of postmodern discourse. In this respect these two novels of Coetzee's are significant; written in the first person, they situate themselves at the most anxious point of contestation in this debate, the contest between 'Cartesian individualism' on the one hand, and subjectivity as a function of language, discourse or ideology on the other. What we detect in Coetzee's novels is that the subject, which is in most respects *subjected* to the dominant discourse, can act in resistance by making use of the fractures which open up within it. This, as we saw in Chapter 5, is the tactical mode of all post-colonial counter-discourse, and the fractures in discourse may be occupied and that discourse disrupted in various ways.

The fact that, in Coetzee and many other writers, the instrument very often chosen for this disruption is allegory, is an interesting comment on Frederic Jameson's contention that 'all third-world texts are necessarily . . . *national allegories*', because 'the story of the private individual destiny is always an allegory of the embattled structure of the public . . . culture and society' (Jameson, 1986: 67). Without commenting on the notoriety of the words 'necessarily' and 'national' in this statement (see Ahmad, 1986), we can see in Coetzee's allegory a use of the trope which addresses both the urgency of subjective agency and the public political predicaments in which this subject is either forced to act or not to act. The link between the 'private' subject and the 'public' domain of imperial discourse in these texts is also accomplished in metonymy, a trope which becomes particularly obvious in *Waiting for the Barbarians* in the material fate of bodies through activities such as torture, eating, healing or sexuality. However, the 'doubleness' of the magistrate's subjectivity seems manifestly ironic, so we need to determine whether, in Coetzee's novels, irony, the trope of postmodernity or some other figurative dynamic is at work.

The problem with the tropological model is that it can become endlessly protean, serving to describe (or replace) virtually any group of categories whatever. In his essay 'Foucault decoded' (1978: 230–60), White describes Foucault's *épistemes* (classical, modern and postmodern) in terms of the four tropes, as a description of the ways in which the discursive practices within them make the phenomenal world available to consciousness. The linking of the postmodern with the trope of irony within this 'archaeology' has become widespread, and it is precisely such a genealogy which allows critics such as Hutcheon to see irony as both the ultimate trope of modernity (the trope of the postmodern) and a trope conflating the postmodern and the post-colonial. In Vico's formulation, irony is the last stage of development, the stage of dissolution. This echoes Weber's view of the ambiguous nature of modernity in his classic study of the 'Protestant ethic' (1958); rationalization makes the world orderly and reliable, but it cannot make the world meaningful. Yet if irony is a stage of the dissolution of modernity, can it also be a trope of that which contests the major project of European modernity – imperialism itself? If post-colonial textuality exists in the 'stage' of this dissolution, is it as *agent* or *object*?

What this neat tropological structure fails to account for is that the cultures in which post-colonial literatures are written often traverse the immense distance between mother tongues which may be distinctly metaphoric in Vico's sense – in that they identify words and objects as sharing the same essence (White, 1978: 205) – and the 'demotic' English which extends in usage from the metonymic to the ironic. This throws into disarray the very basis of the tropological model: the assumption that there is an evolution of human consciousness which moves along the trajectory of these tropes.

Such an idea of evolution underlies the imperial rhetoric by which the 'barbarians' are constructed, and *Waiting for the Barbarians* shows the extent to which the existence of empire relies on its ability to construct its primitive others. If such an evolution between the metaphoric and the ironic is accomplished within the confines of that English text which issues from an oral culture, then our definition of evolution must undergo a radical revision. For to see the trope as the ground upon which events in the phenomenal world are related to language is to infer a seamlessness in human action which is reductive (metonymic in Burke's sense), universalizing and ethnocentric. In short, the tropological model applies a spurious historicist continuum to the categories of cultural difference. Even if we avoid the historical fallacy of the evolutionary model and see the tropes as representative of 'stages of social rule', what stage of social rule, we might ask, manifests itself in the complex *transcultural* (Pratt, 1992: 6) interchange of colonialism?

The ultimate problem with irony, in Kenneth Burke's formulation, is that it sees the possibility of all possibilities at once:

> Irony arises when one tries, by the interaction of terms upon one another, to produce a *development* which uses all the terms. Hence, from the standpoint of this total form (this 'perspective of perspectives'), none of the participating 'sub-perspectives' can be treated as either precisely right or precisely wrong. They are all voices, or personalities, or positions, integrally affecting one another. When the dialectic is properly formed, they are the number of characters needed to produce the total development. (1945: 512)

Such an explanation of the trope shows how problematic irony must become for any text involved in cultural or political contestation. For, as a vehicle of scepticism, cynicism and agnosticism, it does not lend itself to *transformation* (whatever Burke may mean by 'development'). The great attraction of irony for Hutcheon is that it is a trope which 'works from the power field but still contests it' (1994: 176). However, the doubleness of irony is that of the two-sided coin – the duality may contradict but it is still a kind of dialectical unity; the power field is unmoved. The way in which the power field may be disrupted, I would contend, is by the *appropriation* of dominant textual forms, the *interpolation* of dominant social, political and economic structures, the *counter-discursive* representation and rewriting of canonical modes (see Ashcroft, 1995). By transgressing the power field rather than attempting to stand outside it, the dominant discourse may undergo radical transformation *at the level of local practice*.

Waiting for the Barbarians is a case which may seem to meet all the requirements of irony, a novel in which J. M. Coetzee allegorizes the ambivalence of white resistance in South Africa, indeed allegorizes the dilemma of any dissenter in an oppressive regime. In this novel the Magistrate who tells the story is situated at the edge of the 'Empire' conducting the humdrum business of the outpost town in relative tranquility, until he is forced to face the harsh reality of the Empire's oppression in the person of Colonel Joll. This functionary of the 'Third Bureau', the secret police, arrives to extract, by torture, any information about the 'barbarians' that can be gathered from a motley collection of old men, women and children, who are 'captured' on a prisoner gathering foray. The fact that the whole enterprise is manifestly absurd, that there is no threat from the barbarians, a nomadic people who come to town from time to time to trade, that there were no 'border troubles' before the arrival of the 'Third Bureau' (*Waiting for the Barbarians*, p. 114),[1] does not deter Colonel Joll. For clearly the Colonel is in the business of creating the enemy, of delineating that opposition which *must* exist, in order that the Empire might define itself by its geographical and racial others. When it is intimated to Colonel Joll that the fishing people could not possibly help him in his enquiries, he replies, 'Prisoners are prisoners' (*WB*, p. 22).

On the face of it, the Magistrate's position is deeply 'ironic'. As a magistrate he is the representative and upholder of imperial law, yet his complacent and refined, self-indulgent but humane administration, his disdain for the gross excesses of Colonel Joll and the secret police, mean that his position is profoundly ambiguous. His face turned in two directions, he is both judge and judged, both law and transgressor, protector and enemy, imperial official and imperial outcast. He is, in fact, an embodiment of the profound and disabling ambivalence of imperial rule, of imperial discourse itself. As he realizes much later, he and Colonel Joll are two sides of the same coin:

> For I was not, as I liked to think, the indulgent pleasure-loving opposite of the cold rigid Colonel. I was the lie that Empire tells itself when times are easy, he the truth that Empire tells when harsh winds blow. Two sides of the imperial rule, no more, no less. (*WB*, p. 135)

Significantly, this perceptiveness is only possible after the Magistrate has rebelled, stepped outside the irony of empire. He is obsessed by a girl made lame and blind by Colonel Joll and left behind by her people. His obsession seems focused in his inability to completely fathom his motives in 'rescuing' her. This in turn is a result of her impaired vision – he cannot form a clear impression of her nor remember her face, since he himself does not appear to fully exist in her gaze. He sees to his horror that his erotic attentions are perhaps merely a different version of Colonel Joll's tortures, which are, in a perverse way, the ultimate intimacy. He is thus both rescuer and torturer.

The doubleness of the Magistrate in this novel can be seen to represent all the unresolvable irony of linked oppositions. As Burke says, 'true irony, humble irony, is based upon a sense of fundamental kinship with the enemy, as one *needs* him, is *indebted* to him, is not merely outside him as an observer but contains him within, being consubstantial with him' (1945: 514). The Magistrate, and, by implication, all subjects who contest the power of empire, are examples *par excellence* of this ironic mode.

However, the point at which the irony solidifies into opposition is the reality of the girl's pain. The urgent material effects of colonial discourse disturb the equanimity of the ironic. The Magistrate cannot understand his own motives in employing the girl, nor why he performs a nightly ritual of washing her damaged legs, but its function as an act of atonement for the damage caused by Colonel Joll is obvious, since he, the Magistrate, is himself implicated in, 'consubstantial with', the Empire. Yet his very desire to heal the girl is confirmation of his identity as the obverse side of imperial rule, a fact that implicates him in a kind of re-invention of the girl's body, an attempt to penetrate its inscrutable otherness. The Magistrate's care for the girl's body is the obverse of Colonel Joll's attempt to inscribe the Empire's will on the bodies of those subjects it needs in order to define itself. The pointlessness and absurdity of the Colonel's torture is balanced by the very logic of power, its need to inscribe itself on the bodies of its nominated 'barbarians'. Though the Magistrate's position in relation to the girl may be ironic, her pain represents an unequivocal 'reality' from which he cannot distance himself. It is only when he undertakes a hazardous journey to return her to her people that he manages to perform an act of expiation. The journey is one of 'return' in two ways because it takes him outside the moral vacuum of empire and 'returns' him to a position (grammatically) 'prior' to the irony of his function as magistrate.

Captured on his return for 'treacherously consorting with the enemy' he is able, from a position now outside it, to see the profound irony of empire: 'We are at peace here,' I say, 'we have no enemies.' There is silence. 'Unless I made a mistake,' I say. 'Unless we are the enemy' (*WB*, p. 77). The irony of the Magistrate's retort is no longer the irony of his position as magistrate, for he has now attained (or regained) the 'perspectival' view of metaphor. The Magistrate inhabits the ambivalence which represents the fatal fracture of imperial discourse. His statement sums up and dismantles the contradiction of empire and why it must construct itself in terms of its enemies, because it *is* its enemies. In this way, revealing and entering the fracture in the logic of empire, he frees himself: 'I am aware of the source of my elation: my alliance with the guardians of empire is over, I have set myself in opposition, the bond is broken, I am a free man' (*WB*, p. 78). An ambiguous freedom, perhaps, for he undergoes a physical and mental torture from this point, but it is a moral freedom, a 'truthfulness', which will unravel the Empire's control of history like a ball of string. For the outpost, and by extension the Empire, falls prey to its own xenophobia, life becomes apathetic, paranoid, until with the decimation of the expeditionary force in the desert, simply *from its failure to contact the barbarians*, the outpost virtually disintegrates.

The significant issue in this act of separation is the subject position of the Magistrate, for he is not colonized in the way the barbarians may be. We have no real idea of his ethnicity or background except that he is given his position by, and may be one of, the ruling class. Nevertheless, he is a subject of colonial discourse, as well as becoming *subjected* to it as consummately as the barbarians, but it is a subject position from which rebellion, the simple act of saying 'No!', is indeed possible. The Magistrate is metonymic of the settler culture itself, ambivalent, 'schizophrenic', both colonized and colonizing. He is not only a representation of the ambivalent subject but of the *positionality* of subjectivity within the discourse of empire, but the far-reaching revelation of his action is that resistance can emanate from just such a subject position. His resistance is not a function of his separation from power, but of his very ambivalence, which brings with it a capacity to expose the contradictions of the system. The first-person narrative of the novel makes the subtlety of this process much clearer, but the Magistrate seems to metonymize everything about South Africa's post-coloniality which arouses so much anxiety and hostility in critics, particularly in regard to Coetzee's writing. For he demonstrates that the dynamic of imperialism is fluid, discontinuous, transnational, and the subject positions it constructs are themselves in continual process. This is much more fluid and anxious than the 'doubleness' of irony, yet it is a fluidity which allegory can easily accommodate.

The point of fracture through which the Magistrate is able to disturb the logic of empire is the very point of its identity construction, its need to invent itself by inventing its others. The invention of the barbarians in this novel is a process which lies at the heart of five centuries of European domination of the globe, a process continually replicated in regimes such as the apartheid regime of South Africa. The category of the 'primitive' is, of course, crucial to justifying the civilizing mission of empire, and the construction of European fantasies of inhumanity in its prospective 'subjects' is extremely elaborate. The fact of Caliban's primitiveness must be established before the self-authenticating processes of 'nurturing' through language can take place. The fantastic and anomalous inventiveness of this process in European society is remarkable. John of Holywood's *Sphera Mundi* (1498), for instance, describes the natives of America as 'blue in colour and with square heads' (White, 1978: 186), and colonial accounts are replete with the *transgressive* singularity of indigeneity.[2]

The process of 'ostensive self-definition by negation' is extremely widespread and not limited to the colonial enterprise. Thus 'if we do not know what we think "civilisation" *is* we can always find an example of what it is not' (White, 1978: 152). This is the most fundamental strategy of Western epistemology – the establishment of boundaries. The most critical of these boundaries in the central project of modernity – Europe's self-creation – is the boundary between the civilized European and primitive other. In Coetzee's text we are introduced, through allegory, to the fragile illusoriness of its ontological project.

It is often a consequence of resistance that this process of othering is met with a simple reaction and the colonizer constituted as the 'barbarian'. This is not an unexpected response to such nightmare figures as Colonel Joll, but the novel dismantles the binary 'civilized/barbarian', by showing the construction of the barbarians as an elaborate and absurd fiction. The colonized subject can be both oppressor and oppressed, like the Magistrate himself, and it is not only the obvious example of settler colonies which bears this out. The process works transdiscursively, so to speak, with power working *through* the subject according to the way the subject is *positioned*. Thus the ambivalence of colonialism works across the political, gender, racial, geographical, and various other social discourses in which individuals are variously constituted.

The disintegration of the Empire is a process in which the Magistrate, the failed upholder of empire, is no longer ironic – his journey from complacent official, through torture, to degraded, dishevelled, disintegrating human remnant, becomes a synecdoche of empire. His degradation enacts the disintegration of that which in fact first gave him authority, that empire which he represented. His torture by the Third Bureau indicates the Empire tearing at itself, collapsing from within, not from the pressure of outside force. The failure to find the barbarians has been the failure to constitute self against other, the failure of imperial discourse to constitute the subjectivity of its subjects. The Magistrate's refusal to leave becomes catalytic in the process.

The magistrate is clear that this is the disintegration of imperial history. Indeed, it is the creation of history which stands as the Empire's greatest oppression:

> What has made it impossible for us to live in time like fish in water, like birds in air, like children? It is the fault of Empire! Empire has created the time of history. Empire has located its existence not in the smooth recurrent spinning time of the cycle of the seasons but in the jagged time of rise and fall, of beginning and end, of catastrophe. Empire dooms itself to live in history and plot against history. One thought alone preoccupies the submerged mind of Empire: how not to end, how not to die, how to prolong its era. (*WB*, p. 133)

By extension, of course, history is the most 'imperial' of discourses, and it is in his view of history that the Magistrate seems most ironic, for he has the 'ironic' view that comes from his knowledge, through his archaeological digs, of other empires which had existed in this place before. He is aware of the similarities of his position and the Colonel's, but also questions his own resistance; he continually asks whether things would be different under another regime, and he questions the value of any of their actions in the light of history. Nevertheless, the simple logic of the Magistrate's act of resistance cannot be countermanded. His is not a simple binary opposition; he does not 'become' a barbarian, for he realizes that history cannot be escaped. It is at this point, when the subject realizes the necessity of engaging the hegemonic, that the post-colonial is defined.

The moment appears in the novel when the Magistrate – now that the army has left the town in a shambles, the place half-deserted, its economic structure virtually destroyed – tries to write his journal. This is the point at which Coetzee rehearses that central question of all resistance literature: 'Why write?' When the Magistrate sits down to write 'a record of settlement to be left for posterity' (*WB*, p. 154), he finds that what he begins to write is not some clear autonomous history, not the annals of an imperial outpost 'or an account of how the people of that outpost spent their last year composing their souls as they waited for the barbarians' (*WB*, p. 154), but a description that is in large part determined by the genre in which he is writing.

> I think; 'I wanted to live outside history. I wanted to live outside the history that Empire imposes on its subjects, even its lost subjects. I never wished it for the barbarians that they should have the history of Empire laid upon them. How can I believe that is cause for shame?' (*WB*, p. 154)

The post-colonial writer finds that it is impossible to live outside narrativity, and therefore to live outside history; that it is impossible either to reject history or re-invent it. The attempt to do so merely results in the capture of the written word in some other kind of discourse. The act of writing itself is one which, to use Burke's term, requires a 'scene'. To this extent the act of writing cannot avoid the narrativity of history, nor should it. Its agency is interpenetrated with its 'scene' and 'purpose'. The problem with an alternative history can be seen when the Magistrate asks himself whether a 'barbarian history' would be any different from the Empire's. What might be called the 'post-colonial' option is to interpose, to interpolate history, to stay and fight as the Magistrate stayed, even to see the disintegration of empire. In fact, it is his decision to stay which causes most consternation to the military administration; they simply don't know what to do with him, and this is the secret of his survival. The alternative to staying, the Magistrate realizes, would be to join the exodus 'as one of those unobtrusive old folk who one day slip away from the line of march, settle down in the lee of a rock, and wait for the last great cold to begin creeping up their legs' (*WB*, p. 132). This kind of death might also be seen as metaphoric of the attempted exodus from history.

In a sense, Coetzee has already provided one kind of answer. A resistance history which does not simply reflect the Empire it resists is provided by allegory. The clearest example of this allegory is that which appears to be formed by the remnant message slips that the Magistrate has recovered from his archaeological site.

> 'It is the same with the rest of these slips.' I plunge my good hand into the chest and stir. 'They form an allegory. They can be read in many orders. Further, each single slip can be read in many ways. Together they can be read as a domestic journal, or they can be read as a plan of war, or they can be turned on their sides and read as a history of the last years of the Empire – the old Empire I mean. (*WB*, p. 112)

Allegory is not only a function of writing but of reading. Allegory opens up the resistance of reading and this is the function of the allegory of this novel itself. For in allegory a history is adumbrated in which the Empire is negated. Inasmuch as allegory enables the writer to operate oppositionally within the master narrative (to gain access to publishing and distribution, avoid censorship, be read by a widespread audience) it is very similar to Hutcheon's definition of one kind of irony:

> a mode of 'speech' (in any medium) that allows speakers to address and at the same time slyly confront an 'official' discourse: that is to work *within* a dominant tradition but also to challenge it – without being utterly co-opted by it. (1994: 1–2)

This would certainly seem to describe much post-colonial writing, but the difference between this ironic stance and post-colonial allegory is provided, I think, by the example of the Magistrate himself. For his tenacity in refusing to go away, and thus his ability to interpolate himself in some respects into its destiny, allows him to assume a degree of instrumentality in the disintegration of empire. Not only does he avoid being co-opted by the dominant tradition, he participates, albeit at the edges, in its change. It is not an unimportant fact that this agency can be seen as simple survival, for survival has been elaborated by Margaret Atwood (1972) as a particularly resolute form of settler culture discourse. There is little doubt that *survival* has been a cause for celebration in the post-colonial writer's enterprise in South Africa.

The question of history is an appropriate point at which to engage *In the Heart of the Country*, for the tension between sequentiality and imaginative narrative which is set up in this novel by the numbering of the paragraphs precisely replicates the tension set up in Western historiography. The compelling sequentiality of a numbering system is the sign of that time-consciousness developed within European society, a sign of modernity itself, a time-consciousness which becomes central to the discursive control of history and which has structured its relationship to space (Habermas, 1987a; Giddens, 1990). Yet everywhere in this novel, time and sequentiality are undermined by the corrigibility of memory, the apparent irruption of different narratives of the past leading to the same end (for instance, the different accounts of the father's death, different accounts of the daughter's rape); in short, a variable and chaotic teleology in which space rather than time becomes the ordering principle. History, the discourse of time and truth, is left floundering.

The arbitrariness of history is a function of the very dislocation, the displacement which characterizes this isolated and *unheimlich* farm. Like the situation of the magistrate in *Waiting for the Barbarians*, there is an irony of doubleness in the place of the farm at the very edge of civilization, the very edge of 'empire', one which reorders the link between time and space and disrupts the rules of the discourse of civilization. However, the irony is subsumed within a grim and distopian rewriting of Shakespeare's *The Tempest* which nevertheless opens the way for a distinctly unironic, transformative view of the post-colonial relation to time, language and history. This is a rewriting in which the focus is not Caliban, but an isolated, unappealing and eventually crazy Miranda who emerges, as she does in so many post-colonial readings and rewritings, as the metonym of the settler culture – displaced, marginal and finally alienated from both the language of civilization and the language of Caliban. In some respects Magda, this scarecrow Miranda figure, is as 'ironic' as the magistrate. However, whereas the subjectivity of the Magistrate confirms itself within the fractures of imperial discourse, by invoking the non-existence of the barbarian horde, Magda's capacity to represent a dimension of possibility comes from her very isolation at the crumbling rim of civilization.

The counter-discursive energy of this rewriting of *The Tempest* comes from Magda's inversion of the Miranda figure. 'Instead of being the womanly warmth at the heart of this house' she says, 'I have been a zero, a null, a vacuum towards which all collapses inward' (*In the Heart of the Country*, p. 2).[3] She keeps the hallway clock wound and corrected and fights against becoming 'one of the forgotten ones of history' (*IHC*, p. 3). Magda, the isolated, unloved daughter of a harsh and formidable Afrikaans farmer, a man who has desired a son and regards her as an irrelevance, becomes the sign of a culture that is stranded on the edge of the past and the future, separated from history and ultimately from conventional sanity. She is lost in the 'heart' of the country which, to her, is an emptiness, a vacuum as complete as herself, she is living 'at the heart of nowhere' (*IHC*, p. 4). As the voices she hears later in her decline reveal to her, 'The feeling of solitude is the longing for a place. That place is the centre of the world, the navel of the universe' (*IHC*, p. 135). It is the constant disruption of the link between time and space, the search for the place that can be constructed in a different language which becomes the characteristic of Magda's search for a new language.

Magda's relationship with her father is also an inversion of Miranda's and Prospero's affection, but it is still the relationship between settler colonial and imperial centre, transplanted with its patriarchal and political significance intact, but with its transformative potential triggered by the father's death. Magda kills him accidentally while discharging a shotgun through the bedroom window because he has coerced Klein-Anna, the wife of Hendrik the farm labourer, into his bed. She solicits Hendrik's help to bury him, thus putting herself under his power. Hendrik achieves the sexual union with the master's daughter which had eluded Caliban, but it is an unsatisfactory and pointless union and just as barren as the relationship between Prospero and Caliban because it is a simple exercise of power, an inversion of colonial dominance.

The real transformative dimension of the allegory occurs when Hendrik flees the farm, for now Magda can enter the full landscape of her isolation, and can cross the borders of civilization and sanity. Whereas Magda's situation is, from the beginning, far more radically exterior to imperial discourse than the Magistrate's in *Waiting for the Barbarians*, it is also, for that reason, more laden with possibility. This possibility circulates around the disruption of two fundamental elements of the imperial control of colonial space: the link between time and space, and the imperialism of language in its construction of the world.

The disruption of the link between time and space comes from a particular fracture in imperial discourse, caused by the very isolation that its pioneering ideology has imposed on the farm and its allegorical Prospero and Miranda. For this relationship between time and space, the chronographic and chronological ordering of space, is the very core of history, and in this monotonous dead heart of nature, history peters out, first because time can no longer order events, second, because it can no longer create place. For 'we are the castaways of history' (*IHC*, p. 135), says Magda, 'that is the origin of our feeling of solitude', and the feeling of solitude is the beginning of the desire for place.

> I for one do not wish to be at the centre of the world, I wish only to be at home. Much, much less than all would satisfy me: to begin with, a life unmediated by words: these stones, these bushes, this sky experienced and known without question; and a quiet return to the dust. (*IHC*, p. 135)

The desire to be at *home* is the desire to be in place – *heimlich* – which constitutes the very substance of settler colonial anxiety. However, 'a life unmediated by words' is an illusion, for all experience is the mediated in language. However, for the Colonial, the *sense* of an unmediated world occurs when language becomes transparent, when the ironies and catachreses of an inherited language are replaced.

Thus language is the key to place and Magda's excursion finally into what appears to be madness brought on by isolation is a journey into a language beyond the limits of the discourse which determines and distinguishes the sane from the insane. It is her personal isolation which engenders this:

my words are not words such as men use to men. Alone in my room
with my duties behind me and the lamp steadily burning, I creak into
rhythms that are my own, stumble over the rocks of words that I have
never heard on another tongue. (*IHC*, p. 8)

This reaches right to the heart of the tension between the private
experience and the public dilemma, of subjectivity and community. For
isolation is not just a personal experience, but a state of separation from
language through which a different kind of language, a different kind of
world, may come into being. Magda is further alienated from this
language when she hears the words 'you' and 'we two' which her father
uses to seduce Hendrik's wife. 'How can I speak to Hendrik as before'
she asks, 'when they corrupt my speech? How do I speak to them?'
(*IHC*, p. 35). This is not just the disruption of her personal relationships
caused by the predatory actions of her father, it is a disruption of the
whole experience of power and subjection which language brings with it
because it is used as an instrument of power.

The insufficiency of language becomes starkly clear when her father
is gone. In a passage which stands as a profound revelation of the place
of the inherited language, of Prospero's tongue, and its inadequacy in
enabling her to reach some kind of real contact with Hendrik, she says,

I cannot carry on with these idiot dialogues. The language that should
pass between myself and these people was subverted by my father
and cannot be recovered. What passes between us now is a parody. I
was born into a language of hierarchy, of distance and perspective. It
was my father-tongue. I do not say it is the language my heart wants
to speak, I feel too much the pathos of its distances, but it is all we
have. (*IHC*, p. 97)

This is what makes the colonized Hendrik so much more dangerous
than the illusory barbarians beyond the reach of empire; Magda is locked
into a language which can only say 'No!' to Hendrik's 'Yes!' – the
language of the Father. This passage is an inverted response to Caliban's
'You taught me how to speak and my only profit on't is I know how to
curse'. Magda, the epitome of the settler colonial caught at the interface
of empire and wilderness, of language and silence, of sanity and madness, of being and not being, must invent a language out of which a new
reality can emerge.

She must invent this language because the language of her father, the
colonial language, is out of place here even when describing, or perhaps
particularly when describing her most private feelings to Klein-Anna, in
an attempt to reach authentic intersubjective contact:

Do you know what I feel like Anna? Like a great emptiness, an
emptiness filled with a great absence, an absence which is a desire to
be filled, to be fulfilled. Yet I know that nothing will fill me, because it

is the first condition of life forever to desire, otherwise life would cease. (*IHC*, p. 114)

What Magda expresses here is the paradox of desire, the emptiness of the subject when faced with the power of language to create the world, yet its apparent powerlessness to create an acceptable reality. The desire to be filled is a metonym of the desire to *be*, and this desire can only be granted, ultimately, by language. Yet language has no valency in this place because it has no history.

> That is what she gets from me, colonial philosophy, words with no history behind them, homespun, when she wants stories. I can imagine a woman who would make this child happy, filling her with tales from a past that really happened. . . . But these words of mine come from nowhere and go nowhere, they have no past or future, they whistle across the flats in a desolate eternal present, feeding no one. (*IHC*, p. 115)

This one passage encapsulates perfectly the anxious and contested relationship between time, space and language which must be re-imagined by the settler colonial for it to have the power of the real. For it is not only re-imagined in language but in the stories which language inhabits and creates.

Significantly, once her father is gone, there is no structure of power, of order, no structure of language in which to keep the world in place, and so it gradually collapses; but where does a new language come from to take its place? Once she has stepped past the limits of sanity she is free to hear the 'universal Spanish' which is spoken by the people in the flying machines. Carting rocks from the *veldt*, she attempts to inscribe her 'place' with messages to these speakers, palpable signs of her attempt to communicate. However, Magda's frantic attempts to communicate are not simply the chaotic desperation of an individual entering madness, they are a reaffirmation of that discovery she made when hearing her father with Klein-Anna, Hendrik's wife. 'He believes that he and she can choose their words and make a private language, with an *I* and *you* and *here* and *now* of their own. But there can be no private language' (*IHC*, p. 35). So too, the language which she speaks through the rock words inscribed on the ground can only become language when their message is returned.

This, then, is the 'irony' of settler colonial ambivalence, this conscious-ness stranded between the rational order of Prospero's language and the 'mythic' history of Caliban's stories. Its difference from postmodern irony, the balancing of doubleness, the equivalence of all options, lies in the transformative direction of the counter-discourse. For, whereas Magda's descent into madness appears the option of despair, it is in fact a recognition that the construction of a world within the interstices of Prospero's power and Caliban's invaded space lies first in a giving of oneself to that space, and secondly in the construction of a language to bring 'place' into being. For language 'is the way we help give names to the nameless so it can be thought' (Lorde, 1993: 127), the way in which place, and thus intersubjectivity, comes into being, the way in which we enter the horizon of our possibility.

Coetzee's work is so significantly contextualized by his own theoretical sophistication and by the insistent debates within South Africa that it is necessary to consider these novels in the light of statements made by Coetzee about the relationship between fiction and history. These statements form a part of the text of the Magistrate's struggle with the Empire and Magda's struggle with a language beyond history, and are salient for that reason, particularly since they seem at variance with what I have been saying.

In his article on the problem of history in Coetzee's novels, David Attwell points out that in the South African debate about whether realism is the obligatory mode of literature's participation in social change, Coetzee's position is one which understands 'the difficulties of creating an epistemologically transformative fiction out of the resources of the more pedestrian forms of realism' (Attwell, 1990: 583). This is the basis of his defence of Alex La Guma. 'He argues that La Guma escapes the limitations of a mundane naturalism by the inclusion of gestures towards a revolutionary transformation of history' (*IHC*, p. 582). The fact that the novel might intervene in history to perform a transformative work underlies Coetzee's rejection of naturalism, since mere recognition 'does not necessarily lead to transformation: it simply confirms' (Coetzee, 1985: 45). The power of the literary text to transform seems to underlie the rivalry Coetzee sees between the novel and history. 'In times of intense ideological pressure like the present', he says,

> when the space in which the novel and history normally coexist like two cows on the same pasture, each minding its own business, is squeezed almost to nothing, the novel, it seems to me has only two options: supplementarity or rivalry. (Attwell, 1990: 586)

Coetzee's position is decidedly one of rivalry: 'a novel that operates in terms of its own procedures and issues in its own conclusions, not one that operates in terms of the procedures of history' (1988: 3).

Attwell provides a third alternative, that of complementarity, but I think there is a paradoxical conflict set up in Coetzee's position by the uncertain and contradictory relationship between transformation and rivalry. Although Coetzee is explicit about the fact that 'history is not reality; that history is a kind of discourse' (*ibid.*: 4), we can discover, in this argument, a conflict between the implicit assumption of history as a kind of transcendental signified, that texture of political imperatives which the novel might transform, and history as a corpus of constitutive writings, a discourse which is rivalled by the discourse of the novel. For if the novel might *transform* history, the polarizing notion of rivalry with it makes no sense: history is nothing less than the narratives which weave its intricate texture. The very idea of transformation makes fictional writing in some sense both supplementary and complementary to history, for it involves the novel in a narrative that might be *changed in a particular way*. However, it is not the supplementarity that Coetzee rejects, which provides the reader 'with vicarious first-hand experiences of living in a certain historical time ... and filling our experience with a certain density of observation' (Attwell, 1990: 586). It is not a complementarity which may provide a different perspective upon the same object (transcendental 'history'), but an engagement with, a resistance to, the authority of history. How, then, is this rival narrative to perform its transformative work? Surely by interpolating itself into that discourse which it contests. For the rival discourse cannot reject the other, since paradoxically it is history, the *idea* of history which gives the fictional narrative its historical power, *which gives it something to interpolate*. This process is one which could never be achieved by total rivalry nor by complementarity, for it is only the discourse of history that allows historical transformation to take place.

This does not necessarily reject Coetzee's underlying sense of 'rivalry' – of the distinction between the novel and history – rather it helps to show the process by which something that is not history can achieve historical transitivity. In Coetzee's, and many other novelists' cases, interpolation is achieved by allegory, as we have seen, and this is an intervention, rather than 'a different cow grazing on the same pasture', because history itself is 'allegorical'. The rivalry to which Coetzee lays claim is a stepping outside of the binarisms on which historical discourse, and the discourse of the realist political novel, are based. For the object of his writing is 'a novel that is prepared to work itself out outside the terms of class conflict, gender conflict or any of the other oppositions out of which history and the historical disciplines erect themselves' (1988: 3).

What Coetzee is saying is that these are the terms of the emplotment of history; they are the codes by which so much of the historical is written; but they are not history, they are narrativity itself. It is into narrativity, allegorical and transitive as it is, that the novel interpolates itself to perform its transformative work. The debates which rage around Coetzee's writing stem directly from its demonstration of the complexity of this process. However, unlike the balancing act of postmodern irony, Coetzee's use of allegory provides a ground for political transformation through its capacity to re-imagine the trajectory of change and the place of the ordinary subject within it.

Notes

1. Hereafter abbreviated to *WB*.

2. The caption of an engraving of 1505 describes the native in what Hanke calls 'fantastic' terms:

> They go naked, both men and women . . . They have no personal property, but all things are in common. They live together without a king and without a government, and everyone is his own master. They take for wives whom they first meet, and in all this they have no rule. . . . And they eat one another. . . . They live to be a hundred and fifty years old, and are seldom sick. (White, 1978: 187)

This description contains no less than five references to violations of taboos regarded as inviolable by Europeans of that age: nakedness, community of property, lawlessness, sexual promiscuity and cannibalism (*ibid.*). Conflated in the passage is that ambivalence which still informs the writing of *The Tempest* itself over a century later, an ambivalence born of the conflict between the principles of nature and nurture. For the natives are at the same time less than human, but participating in an ideal state of health, longevity and community.

3. Hereafter abbreviated to *IHC*.

References

Acton, John Emerich Edward Dalberg (1906) *Lectures on Modern History*. London: Macmillan.

Ahluwalia, Pal (1996) 'Founding father presidencies and the rise of authoritarianism – Kenya: a case study', *Africa Quarterly*, 36 (4): 45–72.

Ahluwalia, Pal, Ashcroft, Bill and Knight, Roger (1999) *White and Deadly: Sugar and Colonialism*. New York: Nova.

Ahmad, Aijaz (1986) 'Jameson's rhetoric of otherness and the "national allegory"', *Social Text*, 17: 3–5.

Albert, Bill and Graves, Adrian (eds) (1988) *The World Sugar Economy in War and Depression*. London: Routledge.

Appiah, Anthony Kwame (1992) *In My Father's House: Africa in the Philosophy of Culture*. London: Methuen.

Ariés, Phillipe (1962) *Centuries of Childhood*, trans. Robert Baldick. London: Jonathan Cape.

Arnold, Matthew (1869) *Culture and Anarchy*, ed. J. Dover Wilson. Cambridge: Cambridge University Press (1969).

Ashcroft, Bill (1995) 'Interpolation and post-colonial agency', *Factions and Frictions*, Special Issue of *New Literatures Review*, ed. Paul Sharrad *et al.*, 28/29 : 176–89.

Ashcroft, Bill (1997) 'A conversation with Edward Said', *New Literatures Review*, 32 (Winter): 3–22.

Ashcroft, Bill and Ahluwalia, Pal (1999) *Edward Said: The Paradox of Identity*. London: Routledge.

Attwell, David (1990) 'The problem of history in the fiction of J. M. Coetzee', *Poetics Today*, 11 (3) (Fall): 579–615.

Atwood, Margaret (1972) *Survival: A Thematic Guide to Canadian Literature*. Toronto: Anansi.

Baldick, Chris (1987) *The Social Mission of English Criticism 1848–1932*. Oxford: Clarendon Press.

Barber, C. L. (1964) *The Story of Language*. London: Pan Books.

Barrios de Chungara, Domatila (1978) *Let Me Speak!*, trans. Victoria Ortiz. Mexico City: Siglo 21.

Barthes, Roland (1957) *Mythologies*. London: Jonathan Cape (1972).

Barthes, Roland (1971) 'From work to text', reprinted in Rick Rylance (ed.), *Debating Texts*. Milton Keynes: Open University (1987), pp. 117–22.

Bataille, Georges (1956) Preface to *Madame Edwarda*, trans. Austryn Wainhouse. London: Marion Boyars (1989).

Bataille, Georges (1967) *The Accursed Share*, trans. Robert Hurley. New York: Zone (1988).

Bataille, Georges (1985) *Visions of Excess: Selected Writings 1927–1939*, trans. Allan Stoekl. Minneapolis: University of Minnesota Press.

Beale, Howard (1956) *Theodore Roosevelt and the Rise of America to World Power*. Baltimore: Johns Hopkins University Press.

Bhabha, Homi (1994) *The Location of Culture*. London: Routledge.

Bickerton, Derek (1973) 'On the nature of a Creole continuum', *Language*, 49: 3.

Blackburn, R. (1997) *The Making of New World Slavery: From the Baroque to the Modern, 1492–1800*. London: Verso.

Bloom, Harold (1988) *William Shakespeare's* The Tempest. New York: Chelsea House.

Bohr, Niels (1934) *Atomic Theory and the Description of Nature*. Cambridge: Cambridge University Press.

Bolt, Christine (1971) *Victorian Attitudes to Race*. London: Routledge.

Borrell, Brent, Sturgiss, Robert and Wong, Gordon (1987) *Global Effects of the US Sugar Policy* (Bureau of Agriculture Economic Discussion Paper 87.3). Canberra: AGPS.

Brathwaite, Edward Kamau (1971) *The Development of Creole Society in Jamaica 1770–1820*. Oxford: Clarendon Press.

Brooks, David (1990) *The Necessary Jungle: Literature and Excess*. Melbourne: McPhee Gribble.

Brydon, Diana (1984) 'Re-writing *The Tempest*', *World Literature Written in English*, 24 (2) (Autumn): 75–89.

Buck-Morss, Susan (1995) 'Envisioning capital: political economy on display', *Critical Inquiry*, 21 (Winter): 434–66.

Burke, Kenneth (1945) *A Grammar of Motives*. New York: Prentice Hall.

Burton, Richard Francis (1872) *First Footsteps in East Africa*, Introduction by Henry W. Nevinson. London: J. M. Dent (1910).

Cameron, John (1987) *World Sugar History Newsletter*, 11 (December). http://www.chass.utoronto.ca/epc/wshn/number11.html

Carey, Peter (1985) *Illywhacker*. London and Boston: Faber.

Carey, Peter (1988) *Oscar and Lucinda*. St Lucia: University of Queensland Press.

Carter, Paul (1987) *The Road to Botany Bay*. London: Faber.

Chakrabarty, Dipesh (1992) 'Postcoloniality and the artifice of history: who speaks for "Indian" pasts?', *Representations*, 32 (Winter): 1–26.

Cheyfitz, Eric (1991) 'Eloquent cannibals', in *The Poetics of Imperialism: Translation and Colonization from The Tempest to Tarzan*. Oxford and New York: Oxford University Press, pp. 142–72.

Christian, Barbara (1987) 'The race for theory', *Cultural Critique*, 6: 51–63.

Coetzee, J. M. (1977) *In the Heart of the Country*. London: Secker & Warburg.

Coetzee, J. M. (1980) *Waiting for the Barbarians*. Harmondsworth: Penguin Books.

Coetzee, J. M. (1985) 'Interview de J. M. Coetzee', interview with J. Sevry. Société des anglicistes de l'enseignement supérieur. Atelier Commonwealth, Colloque de Brest (9–11 May: 43–53). Cited in Attwell, 1990.

Coetzee, J. M. (1988) 'The novel today', *Upstream*, 6 (5): 2–5. Cited in Attwell, 1990.

Colas, Santiago (1994) *Postmodernity in Latin America: The Argentine Paradigm*. Durham and London: Duke University Press.

Colas, Santiago (1995) 'Of Creole symptoms, Cuban fantasies, and other Latin American postcolonial ideologies', *PMLA*, 110 (3): 382–96.

Conrad, Joseph (1902) *Heart of Darkness*, ed. Paul O'Prey. Harmondsworth: Penguin Books (1983).

Crawford, Robert (1992) *Devolving English Literature*. Oxford: Clarendon Press.

Dash, Michael (1974) 'Marvellous realism – the way out of Negritude', *Caribbean Studies*, 13 (4): 57–70.

de Certeau, Michel (1984) *The Practice of Everyday Life*. Berkeley: University of California Press.

Defoe, Daniel (1719) *Robinson Crusoe*, ed. Michael Shinagel. Norton Critical Editions. New York and London: Norton.

Derrida, Jacques (1967) *Speech and Phenomena and Other Essays on Husserl's Theory of Signs*, trans. David B. Allison. Evanston, IL: Northwestern Press (1973).

Dunn, Richard (1973), *The Rise of the Planter Class in the British West Indies*. London: Jonathan Cape.

Einstein, Albert (1920) 'Aether und Relativitätstheorie', trans. W. Perret and G Jeffrey, in *Side Lights on Relativity*. London: Methuen (1922).

Einstein, Albert (1936) 'On physical reality', *Franklin Institute Journal*, 221: 349ff.

Einstein, Albert and Infeld, Leopold (1971) *The Evolution of Physics*. Cambridge: Cambridge University Press.

Eisenberg, Peter L. (1974) *The Sugar Industry in Permambuco: Modernization Without Change*. Berkeley: University of California Press.

Eze, Emmanuel Chukwudi (1997) *Postcolonial African Philosophy*. Oxford: Blackwell.

Fairclough, Norman (1989) *Language and Power*. London and New York: Longman.

Fanon, Frantz (1952) *Black Skin, White Masks*, trans. Charles Lam Markham. London: MacGibbon & Kee (1968).

Ferro, Marc (1997) *Colonization: A Global History*. London and New York: Routledge.

Florio, John (1603) *The Essays of Montaigne*, trans. John Florio, Introduction George Sainstsbury. New York: AMS (1967).

Foucault, Michel (1969) 'What is an author?', trans. J. V. Harari, in J. V. Harari (ed.), *Textual Strategies: Perspectives in Post-Structuralist Criticism*. London: Methuen (1979).

Foucault, Michel (1971) 'The orders of discourse', *Social Science Information*, 10 (2): 7–30.

Foucault, Michel (1976) 'Lecture Two: 14 January 1976', reprinted in Colin Gordon (ed.), *Power/Knowledge: Selected Interviews and Other Writings*. New York: Pantheon (1980).

Foucault, Michel (1977a) 'The political function of the intellectual', *Radical Philosophy*, 17: 12–14. Also in Foucault, 1980.

Foucault, Michel (1977b) *Discipline and Punish*, trans. Alan Sheridan. London: Allen Lane.

Foucault, Michel (1978) *The History of Sexuality*, trans. R. Hurley. New York: Pantheon Books.

Foucault, Michel (1980) *Power/Knowledge: Selected Interviews and Other Writings*, ed. C. Gordon. Brighton: Harvester Press.

Froude, James Anthony (1886) *Oceana, or England and Her Colonies*. London: Longman.

Frye, Northrop (1963) 'New directions from old', in *Fables of Identity*. New York: Random House.

Frye, Northrop (1982) *The Great Code: the Bible and Literature*. London: Routledge & Kegan Paul.

Giddens, Anthony (1990) *The Consequences of Modernity*. Cambridge: Polity Press.

Glissant, Edouard (1989) *Caribbean Discourse: Selected Essays*, trans. Michael Dash. Charlottesville: University of Virginia Press.

Gosse, Edmund (1891) 'Letter to G. A. Armour, 31 January, 1891', reprinted in Paul Maxiner (ed.) *Robert Louis Stevenson: The Critical Heritage*. London: Routledge (1981).

Great Britain (1921) *The Teaching of English in England: Being the Report of the Departmental Committee Appointed by the President of the Board of Education to Inquire into the Position of English in the Educational System of England*. Committee chaired by Sir Henry Newbolt. London: HM Stationary Office.

Greenblatt, Stephen (1990) *Learning to Curse: Essays in Early Modern Culture*. New York and London: Routledge.

Grene, Marjorie (1974) *The Knower and the Known*. Berkeley: University of California Press.

Griffiths, Trevor (1983) '"This island's mine": Caliban and Colonialism', *The Yearbook of English Studies*, 13: 154–80.

Guillemin, Victor (1968) *The Story of Quantum Mechanics*. New York: Scribners.

Habermas, Jürgen (1981) 'Modernity versus postmodernity', *New German Critique*, 22: 3–14.

Habermas, Jürgen (1987a) 'Modernity's consciousness of time and its need for self-reassurance', in *The Philosophical Discourse of Modernity*. Cambridge: Polity Press.

Habermas, Jürgen (1987b) *The Philosophical Discourse of Modernity*. Cambridge: Polity Press.

Haggard, H. Rider (1887) *Allan Quartermain*. London: George Harrap (1931).

Harris, Wilson (1981) 'History fable and myth in the Carribean and the Guiana,' reprinted in Andrew Bundy (ed.), *Selected Essays of Wilson Harris* (London: Routledge, 1999).

Hegel, Georg Wilhelm Friedrich (1956) 'Introduction', in *The Philosophy of History*. New York: Dover Press.

Heidegger, Martin (1971) *Poetry, Language, Thought*, trans. Albert Hofstadter. New York: Harper and Row.

Heisenberg, Werner (1958) *Physics and Philosophy*. New York: Harper and Row.

Hobson, J. A. (1902) *Imperialism: A Study*. Ann Arbor: University of Michigan Press (1996).

Hoggart, Richard (1957) *The Uses of Literacy*. London: Chatto & Windus.

Holquist, Michael (1984) 'Introduction' to Mikhail Bakhtin, *Rabelais and His World*, trans. Helene Iswolsky. Bloomington: Indiana University Press.

Hulme, Peter (1986) *Colonial Encounters: Europe and the Native Caribbean 1492–1797*. London and New York: Routledge.

Hulme, Peter (1995) 'Including America', *Ariel*, 26(1): 117–23.

Hunter, Ian (1988) 'English in Australia', *Meanjin*, 47(4) (Summer): 723–44.

Hutcheon, Linda (1991) 'Circling the downspout of empire', in Ian Adam and Helen Tiffin (eds), *Past the Last Post: Theorizing Post-Colonialism and Post-Modernism*. New York and London: Harvester Wheatsheaf.

Hutcheon, Linda (1994) *Irony's Edge*. London: Routledge.

Illick, Joseph (1974) 'Child rearing in seventeenth century England and America', in Lloyd deMause (ed.), *The History of Childhood*. New York: Psychohistory Press.

Irele, Abeola (1995) 'Contemporary thought in French speaking Africa', in Albert

Mosley (ed.), *African Philosophy: Selected Readings*. Englewood Cliffs, NJ: Prentice Hall.

Jahn, Janheinz (1968) *A History of Neo-African Literature*. London: Faber.

Jameson, Frederic (1986) 'Third World literature in the era of multinational capitalism', *Social Text*, 15 (Fall): 65–88.

JanMohamed, Abdul R. (1983) *Manichean Aesthetics: The Politics of Literature in Colonial Africa*. Amherst: University of Massachusetts Press.

JanMohamed, Abdul R. (1985) 'The economy of Manichean allegory: the function of racial difference in colonialist literature', *Critical Inquiry*, 12 (1): 59–87.

Kamenka, Eugene (1984) 'Culture and Australian culture', *Australian Cultural History*, 3: 7–18.

Kellner, Hans (1987) 'Narrativity in history: poststructuralism and since', *History and Theory*, 26 (September): 1–29.

Kingsley, Charles (1908) *The Water Babies*. London: Dent (1949).

Kipling, Rudyard (1899) 'The white man's burden: the United States and the Philippine Islands', reprinted in *Rudyard Kipling's Verse: the Definitive Edition*. London: Hodder & Stoughton (1940), pp. 323–4.

Klor de Alva, Jorge (1992) 'Colonialism and postcolonialism as (Latin) American mirages', *Colonial Latin American Review* 1 (1–2): 3–23.

Kristeva, Julia (1982) *Powers of Horror: An Essay on Abjection*. New York: Columbia Press.

Kristeva, Julia (1983) 'Interview' *All Area*, 2 (Spring): 32–47.

Kuhn, Thomas S. (1967) *The Structure of Scientific Revolutions*. Chicago: University of Chicago Press.

Lacan, Jacques (1977) *Écrits*, trans. Alan Sheridan. London: Tavistock.

Lamming, George (1960) *The Pleasures of Exile*. Ann Arbor: University of Michigan Press (1992).

Larsen, Neil (1990) *Modernism and Hegemony: A Materialist Critique of Aesthetic Agencies*. Theory and History of Literature 71. Minneapolis: University of Minnesota Press.

Lawson, Henry (1903) 'A fragment of autobiography', in Brian Kiernan (ed.), *Henry Lawson*. Portable Australian Authors. St Lucia: Queensland University Press, pp. 3–65.

Leavis, F. R. and Thompson, Denys (1933) *Culture and Environment: The Training of Critical Awareness*. London: Chatto & Windus.

Leavis, Q. D. (1932) *Fiction and the Reading Public*. London: Chatto & Windus.

LeClair, Tom (1989) *The Art of Excess: Mastery in Contemporary American Fiction*. Chicago: University of Illinois Press.

Lévi-Strauss, Claude (1969) *Conversations with Claude Lévi-Strauss*, ed. G. Charbonnier, trans. John and Doreen Weightman. London: Jonathan Cape.

Lewis, W. Arthur (ed.) (1970) *Tropical Development 1880–1914: Studies in Economic Progress*. London: Allen & Unwin.

Locke, John (1693) *Some Thoughts Concerning Education*, ed. R. H. Quick. Cambridge: Cambridge University Press (1934).

Lorde, Audre (1981) 'The master's tools will never dismantle the master's house', reprinted in Cherrie Moraga and Gloria Anzaldúa (eds), *This Bridge Called My Back: Writings by Radical Women of Color*. Latham, New York: Kitchen Table Press (1983).

Lorde, Audre (1993) 'Poetry is not a luxury', cited in Adrienne Rich, *What Is Found There: Notebooks on Poetry and Politics*. London: Virago.

Low, Gail Ching-Liang (1995) *White Skins/Black Masks; Representation and Colonialism*. London and New York: Routledge.

Macaulay, Thomas Babington (1835) 'Minute of the 2nd of February 1835', in *Speeches / by Lord Macaulay, with His Minute on Indian Education*, selected with an Introduction and notes by G. M. Young. London: Oxford University Press (1935).

McClintock, Anne, Mufti, Aamir and Shohat, Ella (1997) *Dangerous Liaisons: Gender, Nation and Postcolonial Perspectives*. Minneapolis and London: University of Minnesota Press.

Macksey, Richard and Donato, Eugene (1970) *The Structuralist Controversy*. Baltimore and London: Johns Hopkins University Press.

Malouf, David (1978) *An Imaginary Life*. London: Picador.

Malouf, David (1985) *12 Edmonstone Street*. London: Chatto & Windus.

Malouf, David (1996) *Remembering Babylon*. London: Chatto & Windus.

Mannoni, Octave (1950) *Prospero and Caliban: The Psychology of Colonization*. Ann Arbor: University of Michigan Press (1990).

Marrouchi, Mustapha (1991) 'When others speak, or peripherality's interlocutors', *Dalhousie Review*, 280: 54–82.

Masolo, D. A. (1997) 'African philosophy and the postcolonial: some misleading abstractions about "Identity"', in Eze (ed.) (1997).

Mauss, Marcel (1954) *The Gift: Forms and Functions of Exchange in Archaic Societies*, trans. Ian Cunnison. London: Routledge & Kegan Paul (1969).

Mignolo, Walter (1993) 'Colonial and postcolonial discourse: cultural critique or academic colonialism?' *Latin America Research Review*, 38(3): 120–34.

Mintz, Sidney (1985) *Sweetness and Power: The Place of Sugar in Modern History*. New York: Viking Press.

Newbolt, Henry (1921) *The Teaching of English in England: Report of the Departmental Committee appointed by the President of the Board of Education to Inquire into the Position of English in the Educational System of England*. London: HM Stationery Office.

Ngugi, James (Ngugi wa Thiongo) (1964) *Weep Not, Child*. London: Heinemann.

Ngugi wa Thiongo (1972) *Homecoming: Essays on African and Caribbean Literature, Culture and Politics*. London: Heinemann.

Ngugi wa Thiongo (1981) *Decolonising the Mind: The Politics of Language in African Literature*. London: James Currey.

O'Gorman, Edmundo (1961) *The Invention of America: An Inquiry into the Nature of the New World and the Meaning of Its History*. Bloomington: Indiana University Press.

Parry, Benita (1987) 'Problems in current discourse theory', *Oxford Literary Review*, 9: 27–58.

Pierce, Peter (1999) *The Country of Lost Children: An Australian Anxiety*. Cambridge: Cambridge University Press.

Pratt, Mary Louise (1992) *Imperial Eyes: Travel Writing and Transculturation*. London and New York: Routledge.

Rabasa, José (1993) *Inventing A>M>E>R>I>C>A: Spanish Historiography and the Formation of Eurocentrism*. Norman and London: University of Oklahoma Press.

Rama, Angel (1982a) *La ciudad letrada*. Hanover, NH: del Norte.

Rama, Angel (1982b) *Transculturacion narrativa en America Latin*. Mexico City: Siglo 21 (cited in Larsen, 1990).

Renan, Ernest (1891) *The Future of Science*. London: Chapman and Hall.

Renan, Ernest (1896) *Caliban: A Philosophical Drama Continuing 'The Tempest' of William Shakespeare*, trans. Eleanor Grant Vickery. New York: AMS (1971).

Retamar, Roberto Fernández (1989) *Caliban and Other Essays*, trans. Edward Baker. Minneapolis: University of Minnesota Press.

Rhodes, Cecil (1900) *Cecil Rhodes: His Political Life and Speeches 1881–1900* (by VINDEX). London: George Bell & Sons.

Rousseau, Jean Jacques (1755) *A Discourse on Inequality*, trans. Maurice Cranston. London: Penguin Books (1988).

Rulfo, Juan (1955) *Pedro Pardamo*, trans. by Margaret Sayers Peden (New York: Grove, 1994).

Rulfo, Juan (1967) *The Burning Plain*, trans. with Introduction by George D. Schade. Austin and London: University of Texas Press.

Rushdie, Salman (1981) *Midnight's Children*. London: Jonathan Cape.

Said, Edward W. (1978) *Orientalism*. London: Routledge.

Said, Edward W. (1983) *The World, the Text, and the Critic*. London: Vintage Books.

Said, Edward W. (1986) *After the Last Sky: Palestinian Lives*. New York: Pantheon Books.

Said, Edward W. (1993) *Culture and Imperialism*. London: Chatto & Windus.

Said, Edward W. (1994) *Representations of the Intellectual*. New York: Pantheon Books.

Sarup, Madan (1992) *Jacques Lacan*. Brighton: Harvester Press.

Schrodinger, Erwin (1961) 'Image of matter', in Heisenberg *et al.*, 1961, pp. 50ff.

Seed, Patricia (1991) 'Colonial and postcolonial discourse', *Latin American Research Review*, 26(3): 181–200.

Senghor, Leopold (1966) 'Négritude: a humanism of the 20th century', trans. Clive Wake, *Optima* (March): 1–8.

Sheridan, Richard (1974) *Sugar and Slavery: An Economic History of the British West Indies*. Barbados: Caribbean University Press.

Shoesmith, Denis (ed.) (1977) *The Politics of Sugar: Studies of the Sugar Industry in the Philippines*, People Monograph No. 1. Canberra, Australia: Asian Bureau.

Singleton, Charles S. (trans.) (1975) Dante Alighieri, *The Divine Comedy – Paradiso*. Princeton, NJ: Princeton University Press.

Slemon, Stephen (1987) 'Monuments of empire: allegory/counter-discourse/ post-colonial writing', *Kunapipi*, (9) 3: 1–16.

Slemon, Stephen (1988), 'Post-colonial allegory and the transformation of history', *Journal of Commonwealth Literature*, 23:1: 157–68.

Smith, Adam (1776) *An Inquiry into the Nature and Causes of the Wealth of Nations*, ed. Edwin Cannan. New York: Modern Library (1994).

Smith, Paul (1982) 'The will to allegory in postmodernism', *Dalhousie Review*, 62(1): 105–22.

Spivak, Gayatri Chakravorty (1985) 'The Rani of Simur', in Francis Barker *et al.* (eds), *Europe and Its Others* 1. Proceedings of the Essex Conference on the Sociology of Literature July 1984. Colchester: University of Essex.

Spivak, Gayatri Chakravorty (1988) 'Can the subaltern speak?', in Cary Nelson and Lawrence Grossberg (eds), *Marxism and the Interpretation of Culture*. London: Macmillan, pp. 271–313.

Sprinker, Michael (ed.) (1992) *Edward Said: A Critical Reader*. Oxford: Blackwell.

Spurr, David (1994) *The Rhetoric of Empire: Colonial Discourse in Journalism, Travel Writing and Imperial Administration*. Durham and London: Duke University Press.

Taussig, Michael (1993) *Mimesis and Alterity: A Particular History of the Senses.* London: Routledge.

Taylor, T. Griffith (1919) 'Climatic cycles and evolution', *Geographical Review,* 8: 289–328.

Thomas, Clive Y. (1984) *Plantations, Peasants, and State: A Study of the Mode of Sugar Production in Guyana.* Los Angeles: Centre for Afro-American Studies.

Turner, Bryan S. (1990) *Theories of Modernity and Postmodernity.* Cambridge: Polity Press.

Vaai, Emma Kruse (1998) 'Producing the text of culture: The appropriation of English in contemporary Samoa'. Unpublished Ph.D. Thesis. School of English, University of New South Wales.

Vaughan, Alden T. and Vaughan, Virginia Mason (1991) *Shakespeare's Caliban: A Cultural History.* Cambridge: Cambridge University Press.

Verhelst, Thierry G. (1990) *No Life Without Roots: Culture and Development,* trans. Bob Cumming. London, Atlantic City, and New Jersey: Zed Books.

Vidal, Hernán (1993) 'The concept of colonial and postcolonial discourse: a perspective from literary criticism', *Latin American Research Review,* 28(3): 112–19.

Viswanathan, Gauri (1987) 'The beginnings of English literary study in British India', *Oxford Literary Review,* 9(1–2): 2–25.

Wallace, Jo-Ann (1994) 'De-scribing *The Water Babies*: the child in post-colonial theory', in Chris Tiffin and Alan Lawson (eds), *De-scribing Empire.* London: Routledge, pp. 171–84.

Wallerstein, Immanuel (1974a) 'The rise and future demise of the world capitalist system: concepts for comparative analysis', *Comparative Studies in Society and History,* 16(3): 387–415.

Wallerstein, Immanuel (1974b) *The Modern World System: Capitalist Agriculture and the Origin of the European World-Economy in the Sixteenth Century.* New York: Academic Press.

Walvin, James (1997) *Fruits of Empire: Exotic Produce and British Taste, 1660–1800.* New York: New York University Press.

Watts, Michael (1993) 'The geography of post-colonial Africa: space, place and development in Sub-Saharan Africa (1960–93)', *Singapore Journal of Tropical Geography,* 14 (2): 257–272.

Weber, Max (1958) *The Protestant Ethic and the Spirit of Capitalism.* London: Allen & Unwin.

Weiss, Allen S. (1991) *Aesthetics of Excess.* Albany: State University of New York.

White, Hayden (1978) *Tropics of Discourse.* Baltimore and London: Johns Hopkins University Press.

Williams, Eric (1972) *British Historians and the West Indies.* New York: Africana.

Williams, Raymond (1958) *Culture and Society 1780–1950.* Harmondsworth: Penguin Books.

Williams, Raymond (1965) *The Long Revolution.* Harmondsworth: Penguin Books.

Williams, Raymond (1989) 'Culture is ordinary', in *Resources of Hope: Culture, Democracy, Socialism.* London: Verso.

Young, Robert (1990) *White Mythologies: Writing, History and the West.* London and New York: Routledge.

Young, Robert (1995) *Colonial Desire: Hybridity in Theory, Culture and Race.* London: Routledge.

Zabus, Chantal (1985) 'A Calibanic tempest in Anglophone and Francophone New World writing', *Canadian Literature,* 104 (Spring): 35–50.

Index